FROM GUTENBERG TO GOOGLE

As technologies for electronic texts develop into ever more sophisticated engines for capturing different kinds of information, radical changes are underway in the way we write, transmit, and read texts. In this thought-provoking work, Peter Shillingsburg considers the potentials and pitfalls, the enhancements and distortions, the achievements and inadequacies of electronic editions of literary texts. In tracing historical changes in the processes of composition, revision, production, distribution, and reception, Shillingsburg reveals what is involved in the task of transferring texts from print to electronic media. He explores the potential, some yet untapped, for electronic representations of printed works in ways that will make the electronic representation both more accurate and more rich then was ever possible with printed forms. However, he also keeps in mind the possible loss of the book as material object and the negative consequences of technology.

PETER L. SHILLINGSBURG is Professor of English at De Montfort University.

FROM GUTENBERG
TO GOOGLE

Electronic Representations of Literary Texts

PETER L. SHILLINGSBURG

 CAMBRIDGE
UNIVERSITY PRESS

CAMBRIDGE UNIVERSITY PRESS
Cambridge, New York, Melbourne, Madrid, Cape Town, Singapore, São Paulo

Cambridge University Press
The Edinburgh Building, Cambridge CB2 2RU, UK

Published in the United States of America by Cambridge University Press, New York

www.cambridge.org
Information on this title: www.cambridge.org/9780521683470

First published 2006

Printed in the United Kingdom at the University Press, Cambridge

A catalogue record for this publication is available from the British Library

ISBN-13 978-0-521-86498-5 hardback
ISBN-10 0-521-86498-4 hardback

ISBN-13 978-0-521-68347-0 hardback
ISBN-10 0-521-68347-5 hardback

Contents

Introduction

Although this book focuses on the problems and potentials for electronic representations of the fundamental materials of document-based knowledge in literature, similar conditions obtain for representations of works in music, philosophy, history, the law, and religion. These fields find in paper documents the primary materials of their research and, as in all other fields, use documents as repositories of scholarly knowledge. It would please me if the principles emerging from this study were found applicable in these other fields as well.

The title, *From Gutenberg to Google*, came to me in Mainz, Germany, at the Gutenberg Museum. As I stood looking at copies of the first book printed from moveable type 500 years ago – its beauty, its endurance – I had a vision in the form of a question: where, in 500 years, would anyone stand to look at a museum display of the first electronic book and would the words "endurance" and "beauty" come to mind? The question may have a breath-taking answer, though I do not know what it is. Endurance and beauty were, perhaps, byproducts and not the primary goal of Gutenberg's enterprise. The future of electronic editing dawns as clearly bright to us now as the future of printing must have appeared in the first decades following 1452 to the scribes employed on the new medium of print. Other scribes employed in scriptoria continued to produce elegant manuscripts for over 100 years. No doubt the complex and tedious new technologies – casting type, composing texts using type-sorts with reversed letter images and representing an enormous investment of tin and lead, printing at large presses resembling the tools of oil and wine manufacturing, and involving so much labor before a single inked impression appeared on paper – must have seemed excessive to many scribes who could have copied any number of beautiful pages in half the time and at a fraction of the expense it took to set up a single page for print. But when the press began to be worked, hundreds of copies materialized in less time than it took to speak the text, let alone copy it.

So too, now, the vexations of electronic technology – involving interface design, the ease of error, the intricacies and mysteries of acronyms like XML[1] and TEI and its DTDs, to say nothing of the real fear of early obsolescence or hard disk crashes – are fearful costs in electronic environments seemingly more adaptable to short-lived "messaging" than as a medium for the preservation of enduring works of literary art. And yet, I believe with many others that the age of print has seen its peak and heyday, and will soon be surpassed, though not replaced, by electronic texts.

But why Gutenberg to Google instead of the equally euphonic and perhaps more expected Gutenberg to Gates? Gutenberg's invention revolutionized textuality by making available, to a wide public, books that previously had been the purview of only the wealthy or the monastic. What Gutenberg did to democratize books and other texts, the World Wide Web has done to democratize information. And Google has become the symbol for the gateway to information on the Web; information can be found by anyone. Furthermore, Google's resistance to the appearances of commercial intrusion in the user's search for information has given its pages an integrity and seriousness lacking in most search engines and information sites. Finally, Google's method of costing and financing its services through user-fees for its advertisers based on hits rather than on licenses or product sales suggests a way to structure the finances of electronic knowledge sites that is significantly different from the sale of books or subscriptions to databases.

Yet, web browsers, regardless of the sophistication of their prioritizing processes, have no scholarly refereeing system to vouch for the quality of information and disinformation accessed in a search. Web browsers are independent of concerted efforts to develop coherent bodies of knowledge, thus a search provides at least initially a disordered array of information sites where reliable information and accurate representations of foundation documents are undistinguished, and perhaps indistinguishable, from rumors and gossip. They depend on a notional "cream rises" process that is undermined by a counter "bread and circuses" notion. The boundaries are unprotected and unmarked. The problem of reliability is crucial to the effective implementation of a democratized world of scholarship and its documentary source materials.

---

[1] XML (Extended Markup Language), TEI (Text Encoding Initiative), DTD (Document Type Definition). As important as these matters are to anyone constructing an electronic edition, knowledge of them is neither assumed nor required at any point in this book.

This book addresses the proposition that the electronic representation of print literature to be undertaken in the twenty-first century will significantly alter what we understand textuality to be. A significant part of this book is devoted to what I call a script act theory of written language – a theory I discussed first in *Resisting Texts* (1997). Script act theory may be too fanciful a name for what I have attempted, and much of what I have used in formulating the theory is, of course, taken from the thinking of others. Script act theory represents an amalgamation and synthesis of previous insights and strategies for understanding written literary texts developed in separate, sometimes isolated, fields. Rather than identifying the one or two best or most complex or most simple or useful approaches to text, I attempt through script act theory to see how competing insights into the workings of written language can be arranged as a set of tools and options, each with some consequence for user-interaction with texts. I see the result of this effort as an overview of a variety of literary strategies rather than a comprehensive unified field theory of written communication.

The impulse to provide such an overview derived in part from a curiosity about literary theorists competing to provide new reading and critical strategies, in part from a distaste for the petty disputes among textual critics and scholarly editors about which way was wrong and which right for preparing new editions, and in part – and perhaps most importantly – from a desire to understand what might be needed or what might be possible in the electronic representation of print literature that was not possible on printed paper. Again it may be fanciful to think that such electronic representations might free print works from the artificial restraints imposed on textuality by the limitations of print. But such propositions must be raised before they can be tested.

The importance of script act theory, I believe, is that it provides a comprehensive basis for understanding what is happening when print texts are re-represented as electronic texts, particularly in ways that transcend the limitations of print or exploit capabilities unique to electronic media. If electronic representations of print literary texts achieve no more than a transfer of text from one medium to another with added ease in searching and indexing, such a comprehensive understanding of the nature of writing may not be needed. But if electronic representations actually alter the conditions of textuality, a fuller understanding of textual dynamics is necessary. As will become obvious during a reading of this book, I am concerned not only with texts and "their" textuality, but with writers and readers in a triangle of relations that together more properly constitute textuality. Thus, it follows that electronic representations of written texts have as much capacity to change the users as they have of changing the text. Computers have altered the way people interact with texts and the way they think about texts and thus have changed both textual uses and users.[2] But perhaps that is just a fuller acknowledgment of what was meant at first by the question: Does electronic representation of texts change the nature of textuality?

Electronic media appear to have freed readers and scholars – both literary and textual critics – from many of the restraints of print editions that kept books linear in spite of our efforts to make them radial and to provide random access. While many enthusiastic and some beautiful and some complex electronic projects have blazed trails into this territory,[3] there has been little effective development of a theory of electronic editing to support electronic editions, archives, or teaching tools. The conceptual structures developed in this book are understood interdisciplinarily under the label script act theory. This theory draws under one umbrella much that belongs to the traditions of bibliography, textual criticism, scholarly editing, linguistics (particularly pragmatics), literary theory, cognitive science, and modern technology.

It is very clear to nearly everyone that we are in the infancy of a textual revolution comparable to the one initiated by the invention of printing from moveable type in the fifteenth century, and our revolution is developing at a far more rapid pace. As yet we are but 15-20 years into an era whose counterpart introduced a 500-year reign. We have much to learn, and, though I have tried in a modest way to be futuristic, I have probably failed; for much of the thinking in this book is derived from other scholars, and technology already exists for much of what is described here. In a sense, the future is now.

This book begins with two chapters offering an overview of the coming dual task: first, of continuing the age-old process, undertaken by every generation, of collecting, maintaining, and transmitting the texts of its literary cultural heritage; and, second, of developing a sufficiently complex and sufficiently standard and stable way to do that in electronic form. As a means of understanding the complexity and the opportunities

---

[2] This idea, obvious though it now seems to me, was first suggested to me by Domenico Fiormonte.
[3] Rossetti, Blake, Beowulf, Piers Plowman, Emily Dickinson, Chaucer – to name a few cited in more detail later. But see also Lina Karlsson and Linda Malm's review of thirty-one electronic scholarly editions, "Revolution or Remediation?: A Study of Electronic Scholarly Editions on the Web," *HumanIT* 7.1 (2004), 1–46.

represented by that second task, I elaborate, in chapter three, a script act theory – an analysis of the condition of written works that distinguishes them from speech and identifies the elements required by the conditions of reading to be addressed in representing print works electronically. Chapter four outlines a conceptual space and shape for electronic editions, or as I prefer to call them, knowledge sites. These two chapters bear the mother lode of substance in this book: its theory and practice. In chapter five I provide a specific case for a type of textual information that is especially capable of electronic representation but that has been neglected in print re-presentations of older texts because in print it was too hard to handle and because that difficulty seemed greater than the benefits of trying. I look specifically to Victorian literature and to its rapidly fading iconic, material existence as a challenge to the new media for text preservation, editing, and (re)presentation. Chapter six surveys rather critically the litter of casualty electronic editions and the false bases and limited goals that informed so many early – that is, current – efforts; and it points hopefully to the best early, though still inadequate, efforts to provide electronic texts responsibly and with added scholarly value. This chapter returns to the problems of representing Victorian fiction, begun in chapter five. Chapter seven deals with the problems arising from the fact that script act theory is still not a unified field theory of textuality and that different scholars have different views of what constitutes a work and how the concept of the work relates to the surviving textual evidence of its existence. This chapter is in some ways a reprise of chapter two, but its approach to textual scholarship will, I think, seem different in the light cast on these issues in chapters three and four. Chapter eight constitutes a reality check on electronic enthusiasm. It maps out false hopes and unrealistic goals or demands for electronic editions – demands that should be resisted. Chapter nine addresses the distinction drawn between physical documents and the works of art represented by them and the disputes over whether it is the documentary text or the aesthetic text that is the primary object of representation in editorial projects. And finally, chapter ten, entitled "Ignorance in Literary Studies," provides a semi-philosophical analysis of the whole effort to devise a script act theory and electronic editions infrastructure – in short, a sort of disclaimer, perhaps a bit tongue in cheek.

From Gutenberg to Google is meant to stand alone, addressing thoughtful general readers as well as professional scholars and critics. It is not intended primarily for other textual scholars. A word about what I see as the enabling contexts for this book is in order, however; for readers cannot be expected to have read deeply in all the fields brought to bear on the subject. Indeed, I have not read all the relevant books, and I doubt anyone else has either. An important part of the immediate context of this book exists in other books I have written or edited and in some that I imagine writing and editing. Works by other scholars form greater and more important enabling contexts, knowledge of which might help the reader to assess my arguments for their intended effects.

This book could be seen as the third book of a trilogy that was not intended as such, but which seems to me to have happened accidentally. My *Scholarly Editing in the Computer Age* (1984, revised in 1986 and again in 1996) attempted to survey the prevailing notions about the nature of literary texts that propelled and guided scholarly editors. Its idea most relevant to the present work is that literary works are traditionally viewed from one of five rather different and mutually exclusive "orientations" which depend on how one posits authority for or ownership of the text. If the text belongs to the author, all others who affect the text must either do the author's bidding, fulfilling authorial wishes, or be considered inter-ferences. If, instead, one accepts that authors are not solitary geniuses but must enter social contracts with production and publishing personnel who may be seen as serving their own commercial interests and/or those of the book-buying public, one would be more likely to see the influences of such persons on the text as natural and necessary aspects of the work. If one eschews both of these views of ownership and sticks rather stubbornly to the literal fact that all that survives from authoring and production acts is the evidence of documents, one might be inclined to think of each surviving document as the repository of a version of the work regardless of the authority or agency that left its marks on the page. A person with a strong sense of the visual and material might go a step further and say that the nature of every text is to be embodied in a particular physical bibliographical form that influences every act of reading and that, hence, every copy of the work is unique, signifying its text in a way different from all other manifestations of the "same text." Finally, there are many persons for whom none of these considerations amounts to a hill of beans because for them the work is always an aesthetic potential – to be edited, adapted, abridged, translated, or morphed into whatever the appro-priating editor/reader thinks best. The history of editing, adapting, and staging of Shakespeare's plays – undertaken in most instances by persons who consider that they are being faithful in some sense to the author – attests to these attitudes.

In *Resisting Texts: Authority and Submission in Constructions of Meaning* (1997), the second book of the accidental trilogy, I attempted to survey the range of actions relating the composition, revision, production, dissemination, and reception of texts to see what effect such a survey would have on how scholarly editors and scholarly readers can or should desire scholarly editions to be produced. One of its major conclusions was that every attempt to edit a work, even when the aim of the edition was to restore earlier or more authorial or otherwise authentic readings, is not, in the end, an act of restoration but is instead a new creative act that merely adds to the accumulating stack of available editions.

The present book is aimed at a broader audience and attempts to survey the "communicative enterprise" in a broad way that might illuminate the range of activities and goals of authors and readers and shed the light of new research onto the means by which understandings are created. The basic impulse behind this new effort is the proposition that electronic media have altered the nature of textuality – a grandiose claim with, however, some truth. My hope is that my survey will free our reading methods from some of the habits developed under the constraints of print technology and, perhaps, enrich our interactions with written texts. For the most part, however, it seems to me that this book merely brings together what readers at one time or another have always known or desired.

What I am attempting in this book is also influenced by my interest in other projects that have not materialized but which I see as logical outcomes. One such would be a book of illustrative examples of the materials and approaches to texts that show the interpretive consequences of textual investigations into composition, revision, production, dissemination, and reception of literary texts. The present book incorporates my attempt to explore the theories and methods behind such efforts. It would be very pleasing to me to see other textual scholars focus more attention on presenting the interpretive consequences of their textual studies in literary critical essays and books.

Another such imagined project is an anthology of poetry for use in introduction to poetry courses. It would present each poem in multiple facsimiles of manuscript and printed historical forms and provide as supporting materials a range of the "things that went without saying" for most contemporary readers but which no longer go without saying with most students. The idea would be that students could use such information to help them to imagine the empowering meaning-generating "not saids." The experience that first led me to imagine this project was when two of my first-year students came to class one morning having read

John Milton's Sonnet XIX in which the line "Doth God exact day-labour, light denied," which to them seemed to suggest that the speaker could only work at night. When I mentioned that the sonnet is often titled "On His Blindness" these students felt a bit foolish – unnecessarily so, had they had an anthology of the sort imagined.

Far more important than such unrealized works are the scholarly books that have influenced my thinking and that represent the best work of textual criticism of recent times. Jerome McGann's *A Critique of Modern Textual Criticism* (1983) upset the scholarly apple cart which had plodded along for years serving, primarily, the authorial orientation to texts. Not only did McGann question in provocative ways the establishment views, he suggested the importance of the social condition of texts and brought the reader into prominence as a force to reckon with. Steven Mailloux's *Interpretive Conventions: The Reader in the Study of American Fiction* (Cornell University Press, 1982) had perhaps done a better job of positioning scholarly texts in relation to reader response criticism, but McGann, building on D. F. McKenzie's *The Sociology of Bibliography* (British Library, 1986), has been far more influential in bringing the social and iconic dimensions of textuality into the fore of both discussion and practice of textual criticism. McGann's *Black Riders* (1993) and *The Textual Condition* (1991), in particular, brought to our attention the interpretive importance of visual elements in literature. George Bornstein's *Material Modernism* (2001), Nicholas Frankel's *Oscar Wilde's Decorated Books* (2000), James McLaverty's *Pope, Print, and Meaning* (2001), and Robin Schulze's edition of the early works of Marianne Moore (2002), have extended our knowledge of how interpretive and editorial practice can respond to these new ideas. Without exactly ignoring McGann's ideas but building more directly on more traditional studies of composition and revision and on the genetic criticism of German and French schools of textual criticism, John Bryant's *The Fluid Text: A Theory of Revision and Editing for Book and Screen* (2002) provides a re-examination of the processes of authorial revision and the processes that readers try to use in dealing with revised texts. Bryant re-works and vitalizes for textual criticism and pedagogy a concept of compositional process that has been discussed extensively in textual circles in America since the early 1980s.[4] Bryant

---

[4] See for example Paul Eggert, "Text as Process" in *Editing in Australia*, Sydney: University of New South Wales Press, 1990; rept. in Phil Cohen, ed. *Devils and Angels*. Charlottesville: University Press of Virginia, 1991, pp. 124–33; his "Document or Process as the Site of Authority: Establishing Chronology of Revisions in Competing Typescripts of Lawrence's *The Boy in the Bush*," *Studies in Bibliography*, 44 (1991), 364–76; and Donald Reiman, "'Versioning': The Presentation of Multiple

proposes editions that enable a new way of reading that focuses on texts in motion as a fact of cultural change. His view of the ever-developing text that passes from its period of authorial intention and action onto the intentions and actions of an endless series of producers and users provides a method of reading that he applies not only to books but to cities, which he also sees as fluid texts, constantly being edited by benign and violent forces as buildings are raised and razed. He suggests that citizens can "read the city" as a developing text in which the narratives of the city at any one time are seen and understood in relation to the developing versions of the city and their own life narratives.

Equally important has been the body of thought against which much of the work mentioned in the foregoing paragraph was written; to wit, the work of R. B. McKerrow, W. W. Greg, Fredson Bowers, and G. Thomas Tanselle. These scholars and editors are frequently now dismissed in a lump, as if they were interchangeable representatives of a unified and discredited school, rather than what I believe them to be: highly individual critical thinkers with sinuous and flexible intellectual principles, malleable and adaptable to multiple textual situations. Tanselle is the only one of them who has lived and written his way through the paradigm shift affecting textual criticism in the last quarter of the twentieth century, with his annual contributions to *Studies in Bibliography* and two seminal books: the short and simple *The Rationale of Textual Criticism* and the massive collection of essays *Literature and Artifacts*. Greg's, Bowers's, and Tanselle's writings deserve a major reprise. Additionally, there is a sense in which this book is written against David C. Greetham's *Theories of the Text*, a brilliantly conceived and difficult exposé of the narrowness, biases, blind spots, partialities, and failures in the way modern scholarship and criticism handle textuality.

Two other traditions in textual criticism also inform, not always from the background, the development of this book: German historical-critical editing and French genetic criticism. The former takes a comprehensive and strict approach to historical documents to generate editions from which each relevant historical text can be constructed, eschewing most intervention on the part of the editor to improve the texts. A good introduction in English to the principles of historical-critical editing is *Contemporary German Editorial Theory* (edited by Gabler, Bornstein, and

Texts." *Romantic Texts and Contexts* (Columbia: University of Missouri Press, 1987), 167–80. Reiman seems to retreat from this position in his *The Study of Modern Manuscripts: Public, Confidential, and Private*. Baltimore: Johns Hopkins University Press, 1993).

Pierce). French genetic criticism has taken a very different approach, using manuscripts and other evidence of composition and revision to study the genetic processes as keys to interpretation. A good English introduction is found in *Genetic Criticism: Texts and Avant-Textes* (edited by Deppman, Ferrer, and Groden).

The portions of this book that attempt to discuss technological developments and their potentials are indebted in significant though general ways to the work of George Landow, John Lavangino, Willard McCarty, Jerome McGann, and John Unsworth. More specifically I depend on the work of Hans Gabler, Kevin Kiernan, Paul Eggert, Phill Berrie, Graham Barwell, Chris Tiffin, Susan Hockey, Dirk Van Hulle, Edward Vanhoutte, and Wesley Raabe. Perhaps the greatest influence on the final revisions of this book, particularly on the basic concepts of chapter four, has been the weekly interaction with Peter Robinson in the autumn of 2003. His knowledge of computing, his experience as an editor, his willingness to listen to strange ideas and to put his own spin on them, and his support for my electronic projects have shaped this book more than he knows. His essay, "Where We Are with Electronic Editions and Where We Want to Be,"[5] would have made a good chapter four for this book. I tried and failed to convince him to let me use it for that chapter.

In the fields of linguistics, speech acts, communication, and cognition I am an interested amateur, no doubt. But the relevance of these fields to the dynamics of written language and the tasks of maintaining, transmitting, and editing documents leaps out from the pages of scholarship in these fields. I owe special debts to Price Caldwell, John "Haj" Ross, Quentin Skinner, John Searle, Paul Hernadi, and Oliver Sacks for stimulating my ideas, opening doors, and in some cases giving me something to rebel against.

I am grateful to Peter Robinson, Dominico Fiormonte, Paul Eggert, Price Caldwell, Greg Hacksley, Barbara Bordalejo, Gavin Cole, Anne Shillingsburg, Linda Bree, Willard McCarty, and the anonymous readers for Cambridge University Press for making suggestions and raising objections that have led to revisions and, I hope, improvements. Not least, I thank my best critic, Miriam Shillingsburg.

[5] See *Jahrbuchs für Computerphilologie* 5 (2003), 126–46; also at http://computerphilologie. unimuenchen.de/jg03/robinson.html (accessed 23 November 2004).

CHAPTER I

Manuscript, book, and text in the twenty-first century

> ... the immutable condition of written statements: in writing down a message, one brings down an abstraction to the concrete, where it is an alien, damaged here and there through the intractability of the physical.
>
> Tanselle, *Rationale of Textual Criticism* (1989)

> ... the physical embodiment of text is not in itself the sign that text has been "damaged," or that we have entered a world of "intractable" materialities ... The textual condition's only immutable law is the law of change ... [that] declares that these histories will exhibit a ceaseless process of textual development and mutation ...
>
> McGann, *The Textual Condition* (1991)

In spite of a suspicion of widespread techno-enthusiasm, I have confidence and hope in the electronic textual revolution. My hopes are based in part on recent innovations in hardware and software, on the developing capabilities of and the improving appearance of electronic texts, and, more important, on the types of questions that are being asked about texts and about what to do with them.[1] Developments in editorial theory have put in question the whole purpose for editions and the concepts of how editions should take shape and function. Together these elements made real progress possible, I think.

It is easy to get lost or discouraged in the field of electronic texts. Every new whoop-tee-doo in these areas soon becomes last week's news in the face of even newer ones. We are tempted to wait out the turmoil, perhaps hoping to come in at the home stretch with the winners, like one who cheats in marathon races by joining for the last mile or two. The finish line, however, seems, like the horizon, to recede. The electronic future of

---

[1] An early version of this chapter was delivered as the key-note address for the inaugural meeting of the European Society for Textual Scholarship, at De Montfort University, November 2001, and published in the Proceedings, *Variants* I (2002), 19–32.

our profession needs to be mapped in a variety of ways, including constant monitoring of new hardware and software. Books are not the place to do that: newspapers, computer magazines, technical journals, and Internet publications have a better hope of being up to date. But fundamental conditions and principles of textuality are no less important in the electronic world than they were in the print world – even though the goals of editing may be radically different in the two.

Editing, whether for the ordinary production of commercial texts or for a scholarly project designed for specialists, creates new texts that (re)present the works of the past. So, in this century the editions produced will in a sense carry forward, as in the current of a river, the accumulation of texts from the beginning of recorded time to the very recent past. Archivists may preserve the actual, that is to say the physical, manuscripts and books, but editors undertake a miraculous process to reincarnate the texts from the past – or at least pretend to. The methods and forms for reincarnating works require special attention for what they imply. The focus of what follows will be on editing and on the question of exactly what editing does and what are the editor's responsibilities.

The central issues can be divided into three categories. The first fixes attention on the relations between physical objects called books, manuscripts, and the somewhat less universally agreed upon objects called texts. By *texts*, for example, some scholars mean physical objects, some mean a series of signs or symbols (the lexical text), and some mean conceptualizations only. From this first part arises an initial sense of the editor's responsibility. The second category consists of a brief meditation upon noise, designed to reinforce that sense of responsibility and turn attention to a neglected aspect of editing. The third category spotlights the responsibilities and opportunities of edition users, of critics, and of readers.

The problems and opportunities on which to attend first can be demonstrated by comparing three questions: What is a Manuscript? What is a Book? and What is a Text?

Academics all over the world have at least one thing in common – they will argue with a post. So it would be silly to suggest that the questions "What is a Manuscript?" and "What is a Book?" are rather cut and dried with fairly well established answers. The complexities of what constitutes a manuscript might surprise some of us. Distinctions between *holograph* and *scribal* pale in the glare of controversies over distinctions between *authentic* and *forged* and, let's not even mention, *reproductions*, whether scribal, photographic, or digital. And as for books, we could include scrolls, at one extreme, and boxes of loose-leaf pages that can be shuffled, at the other. And what happens when a collection of manuscripts is bound into a book or when a book that was blank gets written in by hand? Book manuscripts? or Manuscript books?

The related question of whether to consider physical texts as documents or as artifacts raises subsequent questions about whether the texts and their meanings were intended or whether texts signify without reference to the intentions of those who produced them. These interesting questions enter into the discussion in chapter three and can be set aside for now.

One hesitates to claim a general agreement that manuscripts and books have material existence, being made of paper and ink. Some exceptions to that formulation include Braille books that have no ink, and considerable space could be devoted to contemplating the question of whether digital books are material – that is, if we could avoid the question of whether they were books. We should try not to get sidetracked.

For the sake of argument, we might agree that most manuscripts and most books are material objects, which occupy space and have weight, such that no two books or manuscripts could occupy the same space at the same time. And we could conclude in most cases that a manuscript or book purporting to be a copy of another manuscript or book would not in fact be the same manuscript or book but would be a different one, there being two material objects each occupying a different space, though each purports to bear the same text.

If that sweeping generalization is allowed at least for contemplation's sake, we could also conclude when we speak of the manuscript and the book in the twenty-first century that we must either be talking about books and manuscripts created in previous times and surviving into our present century or that we are talking about manuscripts and books created for the first time in our century, either as new works or reproductions of older works.

The vision of the swollen river of time sweeping along into our century an accumulation of books and manuscripts and texts suggests that the topic, "Manuscript, book, and text in the twenty-first century," requires one to provide an analysis of the whole mass of forward-moving textuality – all that has ever been written, both archival and editorial – or provide some way of avoiding that task. So, I wish to set aside the archives of surviving material texts from previous centuries, acknowledging the enormous importance of libraries and other repositories of manuscripts and books already extant. It does not quite go without saying that the continued existence of these material archives, including the prolongation of life for deteriorating newspapers of the acid paper period, is of extreme importance. I also want to set aside any discussion of the creation of new manuscripts, books, and texts of works that had no previous existence in some other form – that is, newly created works. What remains is a big enough subject: editorial acts in the twenty-first century that reincarnate print works of the past.

I use the word "reincarnate" deliberately to refer to editorial acts that mine texts from one physical object, or more, surviving in an archive somewhere and "reincarnating" them in new physical or digital forms in the present; for it is a complex, nearly miraculous and certainly mysterious act with unintended consequences in every case. What the editorial act "acts upon" primarily is not a book or a manuscript but a text – in any case it is something that, although it exists in physical forms, is in some sense capable of existing in more than one form, and is, therefore, not itself physical but must be conceptual or symbolic. Its slippery nature makes it impossible to think simply of copying, transcribing, or transferring a text from one form to another as if it were a straightforward act.

An argument on behalf of that proposition might well begin with the question, "What is a Text?" This will lead to other questions about the implications of the forms, especially digital forms, for the reincarnation of past works.

Surely the twentieth century spilt more ink than any other over the question "What is a Text?" Just as it seems obvious to conclude that two manuscripts cannot occupy the same space at the same time, so we might just as easily conclude that a single text *can* occupy two or more spaces at the same time. That is to say, a text seems capable of being copied in such a way that most reasonable people would acknowledge the original and copied texts to be essentially identical. Hence, each copy is a text, each copy is a document, but where there would then be two different documents there would not be two different texts.

This way of speaking suggests that it would not be efficient or accurate to speak of manuscripts, books, and texts in one breath except in the same way that a veterinarian might speak of dogs, horses, and life in one breath: two being tangible and the other somewhat mysterious though irrefutable. Texts seem to be special because they seem to be iterable: that is, they (or at least some aspects of them) can be reproduced, copied, transmitted, articulated in a variety of mediums and have at least the chance of being considered unchanged in the process – the chance of being considered to be still the same text.

This is both true and false, as most textual scholars already know. But to the extent that it appears to be true, it gives many textual critics and most of the general public and many publishers the sense that in the twenty-first century the literary works we need from the past can be reproduced adequately in new books or in new digital forms.

But the process is not as simple as it might appear. Editorial acts involve various kinds of problems that interfere with the simplicity of "the accurate reproduction of identical texts." Scholars are already familiar with these problems, so I do no more than remind them. The most obvious problem is that errors might intrude, causing either non-sensical "words" or causing new words or punctuation to produce what appears to make sense but which is not accurate. Typos, whether producing nonsense (innocent errors) or adventitious readings (sophistications), have been the acknowledged bane of scribal, compositorial, and editorial existence for centuries. But it seems worth noting again that computers, spell-checkers, grammar-checkers, photo facsimiles, and photo digitizers have none of them put a stop to this problem. In some ways spell-checkers and global search and replace capabilities have introduced new avenues for the intrusion of error.

Not so obvious but on a similarly fundamental level, transcription always involves the decoding and re-encoding of symbols in a sign system with elements that are frequently invisible or at least transparent to the nonspecialist user of texts: type face, end-line-hyphenation, ligatures (not only æ and œ, but fi, ffl and ffi, ct, ft, etc.), line and page breaks (which in codex books makes it possible to arrange for facing texts). For many scribes, transcribers, and compositors such things simply disappear or appear from nowhere in the new copy and for most readers the presence, absence, or deployment of these features of text seems trivial. These problems, derived from transcriptions of printed texts, are multiplied for manuscripts in which decisions have to be made constantly about ambiguous forms and small marks that could be accents or insect droppings or flecks of ash or blood or ambiguously formed letters. Regardless of how trivial or insignificant any one reader might find these elements, two things remain true about them: that transcriptions either do or do not recognize and incorporate them and that some other reader will find them to be significant, such that a transcript that ignores them will be misleading.[2]

---

[2] Alan Renear argues somewhat differently for the same conclusion, mistakenly, in my view, assuming that critical editors have not fully considered the complexity of so-called "noncritical editing." But every scholarly editing project begins with so-called literal transcriptions, and everyone who has seriously undertaken critical editing is aware of the problematic nature of transcriptions. Some have throw up their hands in despair for lack of an adequate way to overcome

These small elements relating to the appearance of the signs that make up the text can be referred to generally as presentational elements, and they have a more obvious cousin in the proposition that a text's presentation, and therefore its reception, is deeply affected by the choice of paper, margin width, length of lines, distance between lines, style of binding, and presence or absence of a dustjacket. These presentation or design features constitute the "bibliographic codes" of a text to distinguish them from the more usually acknowledged aspects of text, letters, accents, and punctuation, that constitute the "lexical codes." By bibliographic codes it is usually meant that the appearance of a document – the type fonts, the formatting, the deployment of white space, the binding, and perhaps also the pricing and the distribution method – all affect a reader's sense of what kind of text is "contained" in the document. It is said that the bibliographic elements telegraph to readers the ways in which they should read the lexical text.

For example, if you visit a wealthy friend's home and find on the coffee table a luxuriously printed, gilt-edged, red leather book with silk ribbon place markers and pick it up to read in it the *Communist Manifesto* (I have not made this up) – one can hardly read such a book, in such a place, in the same way that one could have read its first edition hot off the press. Its meaning has been changed by its new print design and by the place where you have encountered it. Examples of the way the form of printing – the text as physical object – affects its perceived meanings constitutes the motif of George Bornstein's *Material Modernism*.[3]

An editor in the twenty-first century producing an electronic edition might be very tempted to insist that "the text" consists of those parts that can be reproduced and that the bibliographic codes had best just take care of themselves – as did the editors of most twentieth-century scholarly editions. Or they could hope that digitized images of the originals would go a long way toward representing the bibliographic codes. Does Byron's *Don Juan* in an anthology of British Literature or *Don Juan* glimmering out from a computer screen conjure "ways to take the text" that help us to understand the contexts of origination for the work? Is our *Don Juan*

the problems. And as Renear points out, the attempts to develop useful encoding for electronic representations of these features and ambiguities in texts are still not complete or standard. See his "Literal Transcription – Can the Text Ontologist Help?" in *New Media and the Humanities: Research and Applications*, ed. Domenico Fiormonte and Jonathan Usher (Oxford: Humanities Computing Unit, on behalf of Instituto Italiano di cultura per la Scozia e l'Irlanda del Nord, 2001), pp. 23–30.

[3] Cambridge University Press, 2002.

significantly different from Byron's? If so should something be done about it? and Can something be done about it?

The differences between bibliographic codes and lexical codes do not, however, encompass all the problems of twenty-first century editors. If one were to try to imagine the right or correct or most appropriate new garb for a new edition of the *Communist Manifesto*, what would it be? Would its cover be adorned more or less sparsely with images of labor? Would it be red? Would it be paperback or cloth? Surely not leather? The question I began with: "What is a Text?" has now I believe taken on some nuances. What was the text when first published? What has the text become in our time? For *whom* has the text become *what* in our time? It will depend in part on ourselves and in part on our publisher whether the new edition of the *Communist Manifesto* is intended to be a continuing propaganda tool, a tribute to a lamented past, a satire on an unlamented past, or what? (Should I pause and ask if I really wrote "intended to be"? Can the editor's or publisher's intention for each new edition be a matter of concern for scholarly editors? It may be of great concern to the editor and the publisher, though readers and purchasers and borrowers from libraries may not know what those intentions were – or, knowing them, might choose to ignore them.)

These ways of describing the differing effects that differences in editions have is parallel to the discussion in speech act theory, particularly in the writings of John Searle, regarding the iterability of "sentence" and the non-iterability of "utterance." Sentence amounts to the lexical text while utterance refers to speaker meaning as effected in a speech act by a speaker at a particular time and place to a particular audience. Utterance cannot be repeated because each repetition of its text would be a new utterance with different effects that depended on who spoke the words, when, where, and to whom. (This issue is taken up in detail in chapter three.)

Perhaps out of devotion to scholarship an editor might wish to believe that a new edition can be created, either as a book or as an electronic entity, that will go forth with the sweet kiss of neutral scholarship. Such a view tends to be naive at best and a deception at worst.[4] Look at the great weighty scholarly editions of the mid-twentieth century undertaken with the blessings of the Modern Language Association of America and the Center for Editions of American Authors and the financial backing of the

---

[4] However, see Alan Renear's exploration of the problems involved in the goal of the Women Writers Project at Brown University for neutral presentation that got "the whole text," "nothing but the text," and "without interpretation" ("Literal Transcription," 28–9).

National Endowment for the Humanities. They were conducted in the hope that, if done right, they would never have to be done again. It may be the case that they will never be done again, but it is not because they were done right. They were done in a conscientious way to fulfill a very clear notion of what a text is, but the results strike almost everyone now as quaint in their aspiration to fulfill the author's final intentions for a perfect clear-text work.[5] The editions are difficult to use if you are interested in the genesis of the work; for they were designed for a different purpose. The answers to the question "What is a Text?" or to that vexed question "Which is the text we should care about most?" seem to change from age to age. The sweet kiss of scholarship that produced those editions did, however, provide users with most of the information needed to criticize and even to compensate for the stances taken.

To summarize, we can say that the lexical part of a text, its sentence in Searle's terms, is iterable, though subject to error in iteration. As a script act, however, text is not iterable because script acts, like utterance in Searle's terms, are "agented acts" with specific historical and temporal contexts that constitute or indicate the things that go without saying in specific utterances and that point to or even determine the meaning of the words. A text is more than its linguistic components of letters, spaces, and punctuation, for it includes the bibliographic codes as well, and all the clues identifying its agents of being and its contexts of generation. A text seems to change and develop through history, even when neither the physical nor the linguistic text has changed, thus making it very difficult to know just exactly what parts of the work are being lost in the editing. I return to our friend with a copy of the *Communist Manifesto* to illustrate that. Suppose upon visiting his home you find on the coffee table the first edition, in more or less worn condition but still intact. Does that text function now as it did when first available in 1848?[6] Has its meaning taken on a difference because of events a few months later in France when the working man's revolt was put down or because of events in the

---

[5] A scholarly edition that puts all its editorial and historical apparatus at the back, keyed to page and line number in the text is said to be a "clear-text" edition because it does not interrupt the reader with note numbers or intrude with footnotes on the text page. This clarity of presentation suggests by its form – its body language – that the text has been "established" and the reader need not access the record of alternative forms except perhaps as a curiosity or to verify the editor's work. Editions with at least some apparatus on the text page seem to declare by their form that they are editions of the work, rather than the work itself.

[6] Actually, if it were the first edition, published in London in February 1848, it would be in German. The first English version translated by Helen MacFarland was published two years later in a volume along with George Julian Harney's *Red Republican* (London, 1850).

Soviet Union in the second decade and/or the last decade of the twentieth century? And does that text function in a peculiar way because of who your friend is and why that book is on his coffee table? And suppose it were a facsimile of the first edition, instead of the real thing. How would that affect your experience of the work? Or suppose your friend instead called you over to the computer and proudly displayed the ease of calling up the full text of *The Communist Manifesto*, with the ability to print it out at the push of a button.[7] Would that change your experience of the work? What would be the new aspects of the experience? Would they be advantageous or adventitious? What would be lost?

The most obvious conclusion is that the editor of any text has a very complex responsibility. Perhaps the most obvious is that the new text emerging as a result of editorial work should declare itself for what it is: a new iteration of some previous iteration as found in one previously existing physical object, or more. To do this, the new edition should state where its text was found; it should announce what exactly was done to the text in the editorial process; and it should say what differences exist between the source documents and the new document. It should say not only what lexical differences but also what bibliographic or visual or material differences have been introduced. To do that it should describe the physical objects that were the sources for the text. And of equal importance, the new text, in so far as its lexical text is to have been identical to that of the source text, should in fact be identical to it. In order to do that, there must be multiple proofreadings. And finally all of this work should be conducted in the editor's full realization that nothing he or she does is neutral. It all has a meaning. The color and shape and weight of the new edition say things about the function and value of the text contained. Deliberate decisions, not adventitious accidents, should govern in these matters.

Let me emphasize that I am *not* saying new texts must be identical to their source texts; that is, I am not saying that editors are supposed to bring forth new texts that fully represent the old texts that are being edited. On the contrary, I am declaring that new texts cannot be identical to old texts nor fully represent them and that an editor's responsibility is to be as self-aware as possible about the effects of editorial intervention

---

[7] I tried this by using the Google search engine, typing Communist Manifesto, and pressing the "I'm feeling lucky" button. I was taken directly to an English text, dated 1848 but claiming to represent the 1888 English edition with one textual exception. The same Internet site also contained a number of prefaces from various editions of the work. See www.anu.edu.au/polsci/marx/classics/manifesto.html.

and to be as explicit and articulate as possible about those effects, even before they cross some imagined lines between transcribing and editing or between editing and adapting. These are matters that do not take care of themselves. They are not matters that the computer or TEI mark-up or multi-frame screen presentations or any other electronic gizmo is going to handle for the editor. It will take conscious effort by the editor. Discriminating readers need to know which text they are using and what relation it bears to the history of alter-texts of the same work.

I have focused first on the difference that "bibliographical" differences make from edition to edition – and therefore, of course, to electronic representations of print literature. I've done so because for many people it is an unusual way to see the editorial enterprise, though it is easy to "see" once the issue is raised. But I return now to the difference it makes if the new editions do not transcribe the lexical text accurately or introduce deliberate changes designed to improve the work.

I was in Singapore at a conference on moving print texts into e-space. One of the speakers, who worked for Apple and who had worked for IBM and also for Adobe, was telling us about new products and new capabilities. He talked of electronic texts on screens that look and act like sheets of paper that can be folded and put in a pocket (I assume it could also be bound up into something resembling a book, but I do not know for sure). He also explained to us the rate at which the holding capacity of hard drives was developing. He predicted that within five or ten years (by 2007) further development of hard drives would cease to increase in byte capacity because they would already be capable of holding all the texts that had ever been or ever will be created. I have no reason to doubt that that will be true if it is not true already. But I did have one question: Who would vouch for the accuracy of the texts reproduced on these hard drives? I thought I had asked the unanswerable question. But he did not miss a beat. He said, "We all have to learn to put up with noise." In other words, he seemed to say, even though we cannot ensure the accuracy of our texts, the errors will register as noise which as readers we will filter out – somehow. Somehow a few errors will not matter.

My first reaction was to say "NO, I do not have to learn to put up with noise if that means putting up with inaccurate texts." But reflection suggests that it may be, on one level, a reasonable approach. I have often thought that the twentieth century will go down in history as the century of noise. We tolerated noise from vacuum cleaners, engines, jackhammers, exploding things, and the incessant hum of computers and printers and the high-pitched squeal of television monitors, and traffic; that is, we tolerated it until we grew deaf to the noise. I gather the purport of the Singapore conference speaker was to say that we would either learn to tolerate the verbal noise of inaccurate texts (if indeed we have not already), or in some other way, it would not matter if say only 99 percent of what we read was accurate. To give a sense of what 99 percent accuracy means, that is one error in every 100 letters, spaces, and punctuation marks on the page. In most books that is about one error for every line and a half. Now, I know that we have filters of all sorts to help us focus on what matters and exclude from our center of attention those things that are mere distractions. I lived across the street from railroad tracks at one time and learned to sleep through the noise of trains rumbling by at 2 a.m. When we heard phonograph recordings of music with attending scratches and scrapes of the needles moving over the vinyl platters, we tended to discount the little noises that marred the music. CDs have eliminated the noises, and some would say they did so at the cost of lost nuances. I am not good enough at listening to music to tell. But if that can serve as an analogy for texts with scratches and gaps and inadvertent fillips of one kind or another at the rate of one every line and a half, I believe I do read well enough to know that that will not do.

Another question is, however, "What are the chances that those errors will be in fact meaningless noises like little humps in the road, and how many of them will be misdirections like an arrow sign that has lost its top anchor and swung down so that it points in the opposite direction from the one intended?" Will we be fatally injured if the word was "celebrate", not "celibate"; "causal", not "casual"; "destruction", not "distraction", "tavern", not "cavern", or if the word "not" is occasionally left out?

I believe this question becomes one of importance because of the enthusiasm and hope and delight that often attends the new electronic revolution. Such feelings appear to mask the wrongheadedness represented by Michael Hart's plan in the early 1990s to put "100,000 vanilla texts" on the Internet by the year 2000 in the Project Gutenberg and the unbelievably strong support he has received from enthusiastic ersatz editors who have contributed to his project. Does anyone believe that a Project Gutenberg electronic text could be relied upon to be accurate? Do these productions state accurately what the source text was? Do they describe the bibliographic features of the source text? Did the "editors" pick as a source text one that has any sort of authority or historical importance? Did they indicate in any way how the editing or transcribing or scanning involved changed the text? I will not venture an answer to those questions because I have not investigated very many of the Project Gutenberg texts.

Those that I have investigated were unusable for my purposes, but that might not be the case every time. But, if some Project Gutenberg texts are reliable, how can we know which are which?

My only point at this time is that bringing a text from an old book or manuscript into the twenty-first century takes more than a computer – with or without a scanner or digital camera. It takes thoughtfulness about texts, an exercise of care and good judgment about methods, and an old-fashioned devotion to sight collation and proofreading that tends to dampen enthusiasm. In the absence of these onerous responsibilities, what will we have? Noisy texts, without any doubt. Misleading texts, very likely. Texts useless for scholarly purposes, of course. And texts that say much more about the editor than they say about any of the authors or publishers in that work's history. And, they say volumes about the readers who use them.

Turning finally to the quiet world of new textual scholarship for our new century, I suggest contemplation of the aesthetics of our enterprise. I choose the problematic word "aesthetics" in part to honor the bold use of it made by my colleague, a modernist and Yeats editor, David Holdeman in a paper titled "The Editor as Artist." His choice struck a chord with me that is worth plucking again.[8]

Aesthetics and beauty have not been fashionable words for use with science or scholarship, though I still remember the shock of recognition that I felt when reading in James Watson's *Double Helix* that he knew he had the right model for DNA because it was beautiful. Aesthetics has many definitions, but among them are the notions that what may seem to be multifarious may also be seen as unity, that the chaotic can have harmony, that the complex may have coherence, that the intricate can have pattern, that the disparate may have commonality. Out of the many, one: *e pluribus unum* – . We abandoned these notions when we recognized that the pursuit of Truth and Wholeness with capital letters represented a misguided combination of idealism and essentialism. In our flight from these positivist views, we may have stumbled into a different sort of falseness that leaves us timidly pointing to fragments or throwing up our hands in surrender to radical relativism. But in fact we know more than that, though we may not know all and may not be able to tell when or if we have truth.

We have come to know in textual critical circles that the well-wrought urn of literary art, the culmination of artistic effort, consists of many parts

---

[8] David Holdeman, "The Editor as Artist," Society for Textual Scholarship, New York, April 2001; revised, Annual Faculty Lecture, English Department, University of North Texas, November 2001.

and can be seen from many viewpoints and can be constructed and deconstructed and formalized and structured and interrogated and appropriated. The cultural discourse that has come to surround any work that has attracted literary attention and especially those works that have and continue to attract significant amounts of attention – the discourse surrounding these works, I say, has itself become very complex and has shown the work itself – any work – to be far more complex than any of us had dreamed. But attempts to see provisional or temporary relations and even harmonies in the complexity are not to be abandoned because perfection is not available to us.

Much of this complexity arises from the great job that librarians, collectors, and archivists have done to preserve the physical materials of textuality. There was a time when editors considered their job to be to sift through the surviving materials, much of it considered to be clippings from the workshop floor, in order not only to understand the history of textual transmission but to polish the end result for our aesthetic pleasure. The authenticity of the literary object, pored over by the keen eye of scholarship and presented in vouched-for pristine originality, as a beauty for contemplation and assimilation in the haute culture of academe – that was the goal of textual scholarship in an age in which the phrase "simple beauty" indicated high value.

I suggest that a new beauty is born out of and into the complexity of the textual condition as it is now generally understood. The textual condition can be seen in a variety of vectors of complexity: (1) that complexity which is created by our interest in the events and materials of genesis, revision, publication, re-publication, and dissemination of physical texts; (2) that complexity which is created by our interest in the cultural, social, biographical, psychological, and literary contexts of origination of a work – by which I mean the intellectual and emotional soup that went without saying for the author and original audiences and which they drew upon to generate meanings from the texts; (3) that matching complexity which is created by our own entrapment in the cultural, social, biographical, psychological, and literary contexts of our reception of works from the past, which for us exist only in the present; and (4) that complexity which is created by our disagreements about the discourses of criticism, which make some of us Marxists, others Feminists, others eco-critics, and others unreconstructed New Critics or Leavisites.

Out of many, one, but not a singularity or monolithic view – rather a general methodology of relational complexities: *that* can be the aesthetics of scholarly editing in the twenty-first century if we understand that the emerging oneness does not consist of simplification or elimination of the complexity but instead that it arises from our recognition of the textual condition understood whole. The word "whole" like the word "aesthetic" need not be misunderstood; it can mean that we try to see each of many understandings of a text in the context of a complex rather than a simple notion of the textual condition. The chaos that appears at first to be lists of variants or multiple texts or ethically compelling shifts in our political sensitivities is "a chaos" only because we have yet to grapple with the ways in which complexity can have coherence. If you are looking for simplicity, if you are looking for the easy way into the kingdom, I suggest you duck your head and go away sadly. If you want a challenge with a great pay-off, roll up your sleeves, buckle on your aprons, don your thinking caps and study the surviving materials.

Brave words, some will say. Where are we to find these materials upon which to exercise our enthusiastic labors? Scholarly editing in the last twenty-five centuries has suffered from a failure of the imagination and from a distrust of audiences. The challenge here is to develop, with the aid of the new medium of computers, sites of textual complexity from which the beauty of complex coherence shines: where text and counter-text, annotation and image, singularity and multiplicity of perspectives can serve readers upon whom nothing is lost. Let us leave to the simple-minded the creation of dumbed-down editions designed for the simple-minded; the world of knowledge, of scholarship, and of research demands editions that clarify without simplifying the textual condition.

CHAPTER 2

Complexity, endurance, accessibility, beauty, sophistication, and scholarship

With the sense of the splendour of our experience and of its awful brevity, gathering all we are into one desperate effort to see and touch, we shall hardly have time to make theories about the things we see and touch.

[. . .]

– we have an interval, and then our place knows us no more . . . our one chance is in expanding that interval, in getting as many pulsations as possible into the given time.

Walter Pater, *Studies in the History of the Renaissance* (1873)

The revolution in textual studies that tumbled down the gods of "definitive texts" and of "final authorial intentions"; that demoted the tyrants of textual control, of established texts and determinate readings; that scoffed at the idea of a unified field theory of textual studies – this textual revolution has erected in the place of tumbled gods the gods of multiplicity, comprehensiveness, and objectivity in new, attractive (mostly electronic) forms.[1] New gods are always arising to fill the vacuums left by fallen gods.

Where once all textual scholars agreed – Fredson Bowers and James Thorpe[2] told us on several occasions, perhaps more hopefully than accurately – that the goal of textual studies and the aim of scholarly editions was to establish the text of the author's final intentions and that

---

[1] This chapter is based on a paper delivered at the "Moving Text into E-Space" Conference, National University of Singapore, 31 July –2 August 2000.

[2] Thorpe wrote: "[T]he ideal of textual criticism is to present the text which the author intended." He admits, of course, that "this ideal is unattainable in any final and complete and detailed sense," *Principles of Textual Criticism* (San Marino: Huntington Library, 1972), 50. Bowers wrote: "The recovery of the initial purity of an author's text and of any revision (insofar as this is possible from the preserved documents), and the preservation of this purity despite the usual corrupting process of reprint transmission, is the aim of textual criticism," "Textual Criticism," in *The Aims and Methods of Scholarship in Modern Languages and Literatures*, ed. James Thorpe (New York: Modern Language Association, 1970), p. 30.

the new scholarly edition, the new edited text, would become the basis for all responsible literary interpretation and criticism; where once there was, or seemed to be, this unified view of the textual scholar's task, there now stands a general agreement that that is NOT the scholars' task. We are now told on several continents by Bodo Plachta and Siegfried Scheibe, by D. F. McKenzie and Jerome McGann that those old goals in textual studies were flawed by too narrow a view, too abstract an idea, and too idealistic a vision of the editorial task.[3] We are now told that the condition of textuality and the focus of scholarly textual interests lie in the artifacts of history, the surviving documentary texts. The new gods are the gods of diversity, multiplicity, process, and fluidity combined with a scrupulous observance of the limitations and integrity of surviving artifacts.

An analogy might clarify the issue. Where once we were told that a broken fragment of a statue was the kernel of a whole which should be reconstructed from the fragment and from such other surviving evidence as could be pieced together about the original whole, we are now told that if a fragment of a statue is discovered, it should be displayed in its fragmentariness which preserves the authenticity of the evidence as it now is.[4] Likewise, the manuscript or other document, which may bear signs of abuse and misuse both physical and editorial, is not to be (re)constructed into a conjectural whole of which it may once have been a part, because, the new argument declares, the demands of history and the integrity of evidence are obscured, effaced, or distorted by such attempted restorations.

To the extent that the new gods make positive statements about the value of the new methodologies and the new goals for the care, preservation, and uses of literary artifacts, they offer us ways to expand the brief interval of time vouchsafed to us in which to enjoy the beauty of thought, the excitement of investigation, and the satisfaction of living

---

[3] See McKenzie, *The Sociology of Bibliography* (London: British Library, 1986); Jerome J. McGann, *A Critique of Modern Textual Criticism* (Chicago: Chicago University Press, 1983), and *The Textual Condition* (Princeton: Princeton University Press, 1991); and Bodo Placta, "In Between the 'Royal Way' of Philology and 'Occult Science': Some Remarks About German Discussion on Text Constitution in the Last Ten Years," *TEXT* 12 (1999), 31–48; and Siegfried Scheibe, "Theoretical Problems of Authorization and Constitutions of Texts" 1990–91; trans. in Hans Walter Gabler, George Bornstein, and Gillian Borland Peirce, eds., *Contemporary German Editorial Theory* (Ann Arbor: University of Michigan Press, 1995), pp. 171–91.

[4] I am indebted for this idea to Paul Eggert, "The Golden Stain of Time," *Books and Bibliography: Essays in Commemoration of Don McKenzie*, ed. John Thomson (Wellington: Victoria University Press, 2002), pp. 116–28. See also Burghard Dedner's "Editing Fragments as Fragments," *TEXT* 16 (2004), 97–111.

fully in the moment of our philosophical, aesthetic, intellectual, and sensuous engagements with art and artifacts.

However, one must pay no attention whatsoever to nay sayings by new gods. One cannot expect an unbiased statement to emerge from the mouth of power and enthusiasm. The negative statements about old ways made by the prophets of the new gods of multiplicity and diversity are the ravings of mad enthusiasts and the railings of demagogues sweeping away the old indiscriminately to make room for the new.

When I was at the Gutenberg Museum in Mainz, Germany, in July of 2000, I watched an exhibit of typecasting, composition, imposition, and printing on a hand press illustrative of Gutenberg's own practices. I imagined myself in a world where the most sophisticated technology for the production of world class, enduring, and beautiful scripts and books was a quill or pen. Into that world steps a Gutenberg who is able to envision the whole array of mechanical elements of production that will enable a replacement procedure. It was impressed upon us, watching the exhibit, that Gutenberg was a businessman and inventor who saw his process as a moneymaking enterprise. A few minutes later I stood before the two volumes of Gutenberg's 42-line Bible on display in the museum. Oddly, the most impressive aspect of the books to me was the paper. It could have been made last week. There was no foxing, no yellowing – not even at the edges – no visible indication of brittleness or "antiquing." The thought uppermost in my mind was that progress in papermaking technology has brought us to the place where we can create cheaply, and in great quantities, a product that will not last. Of the 180 or so 42-line Bibles Gutenberg manufactured, about 45 still exist. It occurred to me that for most books, few if any copies now exist; in many cases less than 1 percent of copies survive 50 years. The first book printed from movable type, on the other hand, has at least a 25 percent survival rate after 500 years. The printed pages of the 42-line Bible have other remarkable qualities. The type-face itself is, to modern eyes, somewhat difficult to read, and the Vulgate Latin is not the lingua franca of scholarship or worship, but the beauty of the design is undeniable and the arrangement on the page of two columns, in a large but not too large type-size, with generous margins gives a sense of elegance and utility at the same time. And, I thought, how brilliant it was to choose as the first book printed from movable type, the book in the Western world whose content was the most likely to have endurance, importance, utility, and value.

Questions: Which was the first book created and distributed electronically? What are (or were) its qualities and characteristics? And, as mentioned before, will it be on display in a museum in 500 years' time? These are not "fair questions," but they triggered for me a train of thought that raised other questions that may be of interest.

Set aside for the moment any questions about whether Gutenberg was or was not the inventor of movable type, whether his first Bible was or wasn't actually printed with movable type, or whether there might have been some prototype books that have been suppressed that actually preceded the manufacture of the Gutenberg Bible. The points I wish to dwell on are indicated by words such as complexity, endurance, accessibility, beauty, sophistication, and scholarship. And of these, I will focus primarily on the last, scholarship, because in the general commercial printing world, it so frequently gets short shrift. But each of us has a special expertise and a special set of values for words and their display, distribution, and preservation. And we see the enterprise before us, the electronic book, to some extent through the lenses of our personal expertise and values – lenses which are not always well adapted to see the enterprise whole.

First, let us acknowledge that the electronic book is also a complex undertaking. This complexity is like a great web in which changes made in one area enable or require changes in others. The complexity includes all aspects of the electronic book, not just those in which you or I are expert. They include the mechanisms required (hardware, from CPUs [central processing units] to monitors and printers and every connector and wired or wireless gizmo that joins them locally and internationally), the materials required (electricity, light, and screens for text display – perhaps also paper if we print out texts), the software and basic coding (including character-sets, type fonts, the means for arranging, displaying, and transmitting or replicating texts and images, and the mark-up languages), the communication systems (both hardware and software for distribution and display), the expertise required for good formatting, attractive page design, elegant deployment of font faces and sizes and blank space to make electronic pages both readable and beautiful, and the expertise involved in selecting or creating texts that have value for their content and reliability in their every detail.

In short, I stand before the electronic text with an amazement equal to any generated by the Gutenberg revolution. Few have to be told why we are fascinated by the power, dexterity, speed, and elegance of electronic text phenomena. We all know firsthand the ways in which electronic texts outstrip and outperform printed books. Electronic texts are searchable, easily updated, easily distributed, easily analyzed in a hundred different ways, easily manipulable, easily converted into other iterations of themselves. Electronic books are fundamentally different from printed books, which have solidity, stability, and endurance. I have a special regard for electronic access, as a repository of scholarship in the form of journal articles, because of the many times I and my students discover that the articles we want to read in a print journal have been cut out by some previous student/vandal. Electronic articles can be "ripped out" without harm to the original. This is one of the magic elements of electronic texts, like the hats in Dr. Seuss's *The 500 Hats of Bartholomew Cubbins* (1940), a popular children's book about a boy who could not take his hat off before the king because each time he pulled his hat off another took its place.

But printed books also have advantages that electronic texts have not yet achieved: Since the invention of the codex, books are used with great ease in any place with sufficient light – from the library and the study to the bedroom and the porch swing, the park bench, and the beach. There is as yet no practical electronic text as thin as a sheet of paper. In what ways *should* the electronic book compete with the printed book? In what ways must it be better? In what ways must it be at least as good? In what ways is it okay for the electronic book to fail in competition with printed books? Does the fact that an electronic text is searchable compensate for the fact that we cannot guarantee its continued existence ten or twenty years from now? Does the fact that one can glean specific information from an electronic book faster than from a printed book, even one with an index, sufficiently compensate for the fact that few persons, if any, choose to read a 500-page book (perhaps not even a 20-page article) on a screen? These questions do not have definitive answers, and there are hundreds of related questions. They serve to drive the inventive amongst us to improve design and technology. But there remain other questions about the quality of the texts produced and distributed electronically.

The phrase "quality of the texts" is somewhat ambiguous. It might refer to the quality of the work: either the merits of the content or of the writing. Gutenberg, as suggested earlier, was brilliant in his choice of the Bible as the first exemplar of his invention, for it equated a book of great social and commercial value with his new production process. The fact that his process did justice to the quality of the work by providing world-class quality in production workmanship certainly has given strength to the legend of Gutenberg over the centuries. As students of texts, many of us seek to spend our lives working with texts of great value. We devote our time to adding value to the texts we work with. But it cannot escape notice that scholars of Aristotle, Goethe, Cervantes or Shakespeare never have to explain why they are interested in their texts or even tell you the first name of their author, whereas scholars of the works of Manilius, Paul de Kock, Thomas Love Peacock, or William Gilmore Simms have frequently to explain who these authors are and why one should be interested in their works before beginning to explain the specific scholarly problems upon which they are engaged.

Let us refrain for the moment from trying to distinguish the value of the substance of what is written in the text from the aesthetic value of the form or style of writing. Value of whatever sort is always a central scholarly interest because its opposite is a waste of time. One could diverge here into the dangers of dismissing as a waste of time things of whose importance we just happen to be ignorant, but suffice it to say that value and importance are relative to the questions being asked. The questions of cultural history and book history, for example, cannot be answered without regard to the ephemera of the periods being investigated. Likewise, although to me the minutiae of electrical engineering that made it possible for me to compose this page at a computer are of no personal interest, I acknowledge with gratitude the expertise which made my work easier. To the electrical engineers what I call minutiae is of central importance, and they do not care what I write while using the product of their careful ingenuity.

So, although it is a very interesting question, the value or importance of the work being converted to electronic form or created in electronic form is not the central concern here. Two other meanings for the phrase, quality of text, deserve more attention. The first has to do with a text's component details. In 500 plus years the printing industry has been afflicted from first to last with a bug that could not be eradicated: the typo. Stop to consider that a page of text with 25 lines of 10 words each has approximately 1,500 characters including spaces. That is 1,500 chances for something to go wrong on a single page – nearly 300,000 chances in a 200-page book. If some printers were able, through careful composition and even more careful proofreading and correction, to produce error-free books, each new edition was nevertheless a new opportunity to "screw up." In a distinction made by textual scholars for the errors of medieval scribes, unintended or unauthorized changes introduced in the normal course of copying a text could be called "innocent" or "sophisticated." An innocent change is a typo or scribal error that is immediately palpable as an error. A sophistication is not immediately palpable as error because it creates a new plausible reading, even though an erroneous one.

An example of both innocent and sophisticated changes occurs in *Vanity Fair*, Chapter 10, where Becky Sharp gives advice about "garden-beds to be dug." Several modern paperback editions (Everyman, Pan, and Penguin) rendered this as advice about "garden-beds to bed up." I have not yet found the physical source of this error, but it is not difficult to imagine that in some early edition the space between "be" and "dug" dropped out and the "d" of "dug" drifted over next to "be" so that the phrase appeared to say: "garden-beds to bed ug". That would be an innocent typo, obviously an error. But then an editor fixed it in the easiest of possible ways, by changing "ug" to "up" rather than by restoring the "d" to the right of the space – creating thus a sophistication, sensible but erroneous.

Electronic texts are just as susceptible to typos as penmanship and printing. Spell-check and grammar checks are capable of helping only the very ignorant to avoid only the most obvious of common errors. Anyone with linguistic sophistication knows that spell-checks call attention irritatingly to vocabulary missing from the electronic dictionary and encourage a false sense of security by ignoring misspellings that produce new words – spell checks may catch "innocent typos" but do nothing for sophistications, which of all typos are the most damaging.

Although the avoidance of typographical errors is a very important aspect of the quality of texts, it is not the main concern here, which is to focus on a quality of texts that is the special province of textual studies and scholarly editing. For a textual scholar the reliability of a text has little to do with whether the text has typos. It has everything to do with the history of the composition, revision, production and distribution of texts. Most of the texts with which literary scholars are concerned are texts that have recognized value of the sorts already mentioned. Such value almost always has resulted in the manufacture of a variety of printed editions and the creation and preservation in former times of multiple manuscript copies.

The existence of variant texts and their histories raise many questions, but I will consider three crucial elements of textual criticism: (1) What each text says (as opposed to what it said in some variant form); (2) The context in which each variant text was created (writer, audience, circumstances) – these are usually the things that "go without saying" in script acts because writer and target audience, at least initially, usually appeal to shared assumptions without making a fuss over it; and (3) Who created or revised or otherwise changed the text and why. Most users of printed texts and electronic texts act as if the text in hand is THE text, as if the context is sufficiently well known or does not matter, and as if any revisions that have been made in the text were proper and inevitable regardless of who made them. It is against these "as ifs" that textual criticism and editorial scholarship stand. Variant texts say different things; different contexts affect the meaning of texts even when the text does not change; and knowing who was responsible for each specific thing in a text affects how we understand it.

Textual scholars are supremely interested in variant forms because of what they reveal about the purposes and strategies of the texts' originators and about the manipulations by the texts' appropriators. Variant forms result from both intended and unintended actions both by persons who have legitimate authority over textual change and by those who do not.[5] The results of all textual variation are hidden in the texture of new texts. For any printed text you hold in your hand or any electronic text on your screen, you cannot know how or where or when the text has been changed or revised or corrupted or subverted or elided or augmented; nor can you tell by whom any of these changes were made – unless you compare all the surviving material witnesses or unless a textual analysis has been made and reported by someone else.

If the only changes referred to here were typos, we would not have an interesting topic for discussion nor a major problem to understand. It would in that case be a matter of quality control, merely a matter of making sure that the technology for scanning and the mechanics of transcribing texts produced accurate lexical renditions of their print and manuscript originals. But revised texts, designed by the reviser to be different from the source texts, can be quite dramatically different – as in the case of abridgments or systematic alterations to adjust the political or social cutting edge of a text. The verbs "correct" and "edit" are often used in very ambiguous ways to describe a variety of so-called improvements to texts by any number of persons, including the author and other persons involved in producing verbal works. Many people so involved believe that what they are doing is necessary and good. Many readers and some authors are grateful to correctors and editors for improving the text. But many well-intentioned ministrations to texts have unintended consequences, and many changes are readily acknowledged as falling outside the limits of what could be called corrections.

We use the word "revise" to mean the deliberate work of an author acting upon one motive, or more, to change or improve an existing text.

---

[5] That is to say, not all persons who introduce change into a text have the same or equal authority to do so. That is not to say that all users of texts, confronted with the evidence of who made the changes, would agree about the relative authority of those persons. Some would restrict authority to authors, others to those who financed the making of the book, etc.

The author may have had a change of mind or of purpose or sees a projected audience in a different light and so goes through a text of his or her own creation to change it and make it conform to some new or improved view of the work. Or the author with fresh eyes simply revises for improvement of style or expression. We use the word "censor" or the word "bowdlerize" most often to identify the work of some hostile agent intent upon suppressing some supposedly dangerous, unpleasant, or disagreeable aspect of a text. When I visited the Goethe Archive in Weimar I was shown the manuscripts of Goethe's "Venetian Epigrams" in both draft and fair copy. They were left unpublished at Goethe's death and eventually came into the possession of one of his most ardent supporters, the Princess Sophia, who donated a palace in which to house the Goethe Archive. However, she read the "Venetian Epigrams" in manuscript and decided that some of them were unacceptable because of their sexual frankness. Goethe wrote on both sides of most leaves; so, with the help of her handmaids, Sophia rubbed out the offending poems from both the draft and the fair copy, using a knife and a damp cloth or sponge to loosen the fibers of the paper and remove not only the ink but the layer of paper to which it adhered, but without damage to the acceptable poem overleaf. I had never before seen such effective or loving censorship. The losses are irrecoverable.[6] The publication of T. E. Lawrence's *The Mint* offers a much more hostile case, where at Lawrence's insistence the printed book leaves blanks and gaps to indicate the censor's work. But for most texts, the acts of censorship, like the acts of revision, are glossed over and disappear into the web of displayed text, leaving the reader in blissful ignorance that anything sinister or useful lies in the history of the text in hand.

The point I wish to emphasize here is, however, that texts are never simple texts; they are never "simply" text. Their origins, the history of their textual changes, and most importantly, the identity of the agents responsible for each change can and should affect how we read. We usually acknowledge these matters on a macro scale when we speak of a work as being "by the author." It is Shakespeare's or Chaucer's or Cervantes's work, and we read with that author's image in mind. We read either sympathetically, trying to reconstruct the author's meaning; or we read with indifference or even hostility to the author, trying to decode, demystify, or otherwise deconstruct the work. Either way, our

---

[6] Since writing that, I have heard that attempts to use ultraviolet light appear to be bearing results in recovering the obliterated poems.

perception of the identity of the author, as friend or foe, is central to what we think was meant or was hidden by the text. So, if our close reading of the text depends on words or even punctuation not supplied by the author – supplied instead by some other agent – our reaction to the text, whether sympathetic or hostile, will miss the mark because we have ignored the three elements that lie hidden behind every single polished text: What are the variant forms of the text? What contexts informed the origins of the text? And, Who is responsible for this precise form of the text?

Five hundred years of printed texts provided the world with very sophisticated, complex, and in some cases beautiful ways to deal with the textual scholar's concerns about texts. Many of the incunable books on display at the Gutenberg Museum in Mainz contain multiple texts: a main text occupying the center of the page and one secondary text, or more, wrapped around it, or trailing down a central column. Books with footnotes, endnotes, appendices, commentaries, and indexes attest to the ingenuity of printers and scholars to meld their concerns and provide multiple texts in a variety of ways that enabled the dialogic readings thought to be important. Readers of individual copies often also extend the dialog by adding their own commentaries in margins. In an odd way, marginalia may point to one of the ways in which printed books have always failed to fully satisfy: once the final formatting is decided and implemented the result is fixed and a different view of the materials, any view other than the one displayed best by the format adopted, is always rendered secondary. If an editor wished to rearrange the materials so that text and meta-text interacted in a different way, he or she would have to start at the beginning and create a new book.

Electronic editions appeared, at first, to provide a welcoming medium for housing the work of textual scholars: multiple texts that could be displayed and seen in more than one way. The verbal or lexical part of texts can be maintained cheaply and in small spaces and related texts can be displayed in close proximity. Electronic archives make possible this proximity even of unique material exemplars held separately in archives scattered to the four corners of the earth. Specialized programs for comparing texts have been developed, and hypertext links for variant texts can be created. The list of programs and products that electronic texts have achieved already is mind-boggling and impressive.

There has yet to be created, however, an environment or interface for text handling and display that integrates the capabilities needed for a comprehensive electronic scholarly edition/archive. And when such a framework or suite of programs is developed, will it and can it stand as the standard for textual scholarship? The hindrances to the development of such software are perhaps diminishing, but the complexity of the problem should not be, though it often is, underestimated. Textual scholars want to display text, and textual difference, and textual process, and textual origin, and textual context; they want to provide the visual as well as the lexical dimensions of textual works. They want links to textual, historical, social, and critical commentaries. They want to enable historically rich or thick reading experiences and at the same time to enable modern appropriations of text. They want to show dynamic texts, multiple in time and place as well as form. They want video and audio. And they want reader-friendly navigation that will allow all these displays and links at different levels of user sophistication. They want, in short, a comprehensive, electronic text-handling environment for archiving and displaying communicative acts in forms accessible for study and teaching. That's all – just that.

And they want to do all this, not just because they thought it would be neat to do it. They want to do it because they know that it makes a difference in how one interprets a text if we know who wrote what to whom, when, and in what place. A simple old example will demonstrate one part of this problem – the importance of punctuation. The ambiguity of

Woman without her man is helpless.

can be resolved variously without changing the order of the words:

Woman, without her man, is helpless.
Woman! Without her, man is helpless.

Punctuation determines who is helpless, or so it seems. But let us say that the second instance, "Woman! Without her, man is helpless," is spoken by a man who has just accomplished a task that has been thought to require a woman's touch. The words and even the punctuation would be the same but the ironic meaning entirely different. Or if a woman were to say the first sentence, "Woman, without her man, is helpless," in a voice of triumph – perhaps followed by the expression "Ha!" – having just completed a task thought to require a man's expertise or strength, the effect would be ironic and opposite, though the words and punctuation were the same.

There are many books in which these dynamics of text operate. One example is *A Woman's Friendship* by the Australian writer Ada Cambridge, published in *The Age* newspaper in the 1890s in Melbourne. When the novel was first published, it was apparently read by most as a straight account of a woman's place in society and her "normal" needs, frustrations, and helplessness. But when it was re-published for the first time in 100 years in 1989 in the Australian Colonial Texts Series, it was accompanied by commentary on the times, on the newspaper in which the novel was first published, and by biographical material on Ada Cambridge, all of which make it almost impossible, in the context of late twentieth-century feminism, to read that edition of the work in any other than an ironic light and, hence, a protest against 1890s social norms about "a woman's place." Similar new readings have raised our awareness of books like Kate Chopin's *The Awakening* in ways that must have been suppressed by most of the book's first readers. In both cases it is difficult for modern readers to avoid feeling that their rejection of readings by the original audiences puts them closer to the thinking of the authors.

So, it is because textual scholarship is devoted to the discovery, preservation, and display, not just of physical (or electronic) lexical texts but also of the whole communicative enterprise (who said what, to whom, where, and in what context), that it is desirable to find a truly complex, enduring, accessible, beautiful, and sophisticated electronic (representational) repository for textual scholarship.

Some examples will show how coming to know a text in its communicative complexity can work and give an idea of the range of electronic wizardry that is wanted for building a scholarly edition/archive that has suitable pedagogical as well as preservative dimensions.

William Makepeace Thackeray's 1848 novel *Vanity Fair* was begun in manuscript and had advanced in manuscript to Chapter 5 by March 1846. Although at that time there may have been a plan to accompany the text with full-page steel-engraved illustrations on heavy stock paper, as was the custom, it had no small illustrations integrated and imbedded in the text as it does now. Further, it had been rejected by as many as five publishers. In May 1846, the publishing firm of Bradbury and Evans accepted the work and had the first five chapters set in type for the beginning of a large serial publication, each installment to contain exactly thirty-two pages. But the fourth chapter ended on page 28 and the fifth chapter carried through to page 34. That may have been the reason the publisher postponed publication. The first installment did not appear until eight months later, in January 1847. In the meantime the Bradbury and Evans printery ordered all new metal type from a foundry that provided not only fresh type but also a new typeface.[7] Thackeray started a new manuscript by copying, revising, and from time to time cutting and pasting sections of the May 1846 proofs (which of course have the old typeface font) into his manuscript. He wrote a new Chapter 5, and he added illustrations, which he himself drew and which were from time to time imbedded in the text so that they took up space normally occupied by type. In this way he created a first installment of five chapters that ended on page 32. The old Chapter 5 was completely rewritten to become Chapter 6, the first chapter of the second installment. From January 1847 to July 1848, *Vanity Fair* installments appeared regularly without a hitch.

Among the things that happened to the text in this process is that Thackeray's rhetorical punctuation found in the manuscript was converted by the compositors into syntactical punctuation in the typeset forms. In rhetorical punctuation, a comma is a short pause, a semicolon is a slightly longer pause, a colon an even longer pause and a period is a full stop. The use of rhetorical punctuation is determined by how the writer wants the cadence of the sentences to sound when read aloud. Syntactical punctuation, on the other hand, is dictated by whether a clause is dependent or independent or whether a phrase is restrictive or non-restrictive, and by other rules of grammar, dictated by syntactic units rather than by oral cadence – though of course there is frequent overlap between the two systems. Thackeray's sense of the sound of his words, witnessed by the manuscript punctuation, disappeared into the compositor's sense of the syntactical structure of the sentences. Consequently there are thousands of punctuation changes between the manuscript and published edition. Furthermore, there are occasional revisions, my favorite example being a change in an early description of Becky Sharp. The manuscript says that "Ill-natured persons say that her birth preceded the lawful celebration of her excellent parents' marriage." This indication that Becky is a natural-born bastard is deleted and replaced by the comment: "And it was curious to note how as time passed this young lady's ancestors advanced in rank and splendour" – a comment referring to Becky's ability to change the narrative of her past.

A new edition of *Vanity Fair* was created in 1853, one that was cheap and had no illustrations. Its text was revised to remove all references to

---

[7] The full details of the publisher's purchase of new type and the production of the installments of *Vanity Fair* are given in chapter five of my *Pegasus in Harness: Victorian Publishing and William M. Thackeray* (Charlottesville: University Press of Virginia, 1992).

the illustrations, the punctuation was further revised by compositors, and a few passages were excised. There are other complexities to this story, but this is sufficient to suggest that the text of the novel is not simply a text and that no copy one happens to be reading is THE text of *Vanity Fair*. There were five different editions of *Vanity Fair* published in Thackeray's lifetime. The first edition alone was printed six times, among which there are over 350 textual variants. Computers can collate the electronic files representing each of these editions and compare them to produce lists of variants, and other programs display the differences in a historical collation so that they can be studied, and other programs can display any of the texts of an archive while allowing "on the fly" textual comparisons to "be on call" as a reader wants to find out what other renditions of a certain passage might be, and that will alert a reader, if such is wanted, that a variant exists for a certain passage. Unfortunately, so far, these are independent, stand-alone programs. Integration into a single standard package is still to come. And most were designed with editors, not readers, as their target users.

But those programs will not accommodate my second example, which I draw from the work of Jerome McGann on the Rossetti Archive. Dante Gabriel Rossetti was a poet and a painter. He wrote poems that stand in various relationships to his paintings and to paintings by others. They are accompaniments, or illustrations, or simple references to each other. So, the program needed must not only be able to deal with textual complexity but with the interaction of text and illustrations. Unlike the line drawings in *Vanity Fair*, the art in the Rossetti Archive includes oil paintings. The program needs to have some system for controlling color so as not to misrepresent the works. How can a user at any given monitor know if the colors are authentic? And should there be ways for the program to display the relations between paintings and studies for the paintings or for displaying x-ray or infrared photographs of the paintings to reveal earlier versions or the processes of painting? And what about the size of the paintings? Thackeray's illustrations for *Vanity Fair* were drawn for a book and so, though the print-page on the electronic screen may be different from the original, the relation of the size of the illustration to the print will be analogous. But with Rossetti, the size of the paintings relative to each other and to print can be "visualized" only by a statement about dimensions. Does that matter? How can it be dealt with for scholarly study or pedagogical purposes?

Finally, let us look briefly at the history of Bram Stoker's *Dracula*. The manuscript itself does not survive, but Stoker's manuscript notes for the novel do. There were seven editions published in his lifetime, one of which may have been abridged by Stoker himself. He seems not to have had any personal influence on adaptations for stage or screen. However, it is stage and film adaptations and the history of copyright infringements and the futile efforts by Stoker's widow to prevent or control unauthorized stage adaptations that tell the major Dracula story. From Stoker's death to the present, the proliferation of print editions, abridgments, adaptations for comics, stage, and film tell the story of the cultural impact of Dracula. Furthermore, the history of reviews and critical studies of this one story drives much of the psychological and sociological study of vampire phenomena. And of these, the adaptations, particularly in film, much more than Stoker's own text, constitute the materials for the study of *Dracula*, which seems to have ceased to be Bram Stoker's property in more ways than most novels escape from their authors. We shall want a program that will allow the display of dramatic adaptations and video of the motion pictures.

As librarians, archivists, scholars, and students gather the materials relative to any given text and write their textual histories, the results should have a place in a standard but hugely flexible text-handling and formatting system so that subsequent students will not have to start over each time and so that refinements, corrections, and augmentations to the history of each textual communicative act can grow over the years and adapt to new concerns and interests.

A basic challenge to developers of electronic text-handling engines is that they work towards integration of programs capable of handling all the elements of script-acts and the scholarship that attends them, and that editors of electronic editions keep ever in mind complexity, endurance, accessibility, beauty, sophistication, and scholarship.

CHAPTER 3

Script act theory

There is no discourse so obscure, no tale so odd or remark so incoherent that it cannot be given a meaning.

Paul Valéry

Complexity is not a crime, but carry it to the point of murkiness and nothing is plain. A complexity moreover, that has been committed to darkness, instead of granting itself the pestilence that it is, moves all about as if to bewilder with the dismal fallacy that insistence is the measure of achievement and that all truth must be dark.

Marianne Moore[1]

It is the function of scholarship to clarify, not simplify.

James B. Meriwether[2]

In order for developers of new electronic representations of print literature, be they computer technicians or textual scholars, to know what to do and what to create, there needs to be a fuller, more nuanced understanding of the nature of script acts. By script acts I do not mean just those acts involved in writing or creating scripts; I mean every sort of act conducted in relation to written and printed texts, including every act of reproduction and every act of reading. I hope this mapping of an inclusive view of acts relative to scripts contributes a provocative initial approach both to script acts and to electronic access and text representations to which other scholars will contribute ideas and practice. One implication of the mapping attempted here is that no single copy

---

[1] Marianne Moore's warning as quoted by Emmy Veronica Sanders as quoted by Robin Schulze in *Becoming Marianne Moore: The Early Poems, 1907–1924*, ed. Robin Schulze (Berkeley: UCLA Press, 2002), p. 385.

[2] A form of this phrase was repeated to me at least annually by Meriwether in my years as his student at the University of South Carolina.

represents a work in the same way that any other copy represents it. Perhaps this book will encourage readings conducted in relation to specific versions of a work – readings that see each script act as an event in a continuing, perhaps not entirely comprehensible, chronology and geography of actual and possible script acts.

"Script acts" identifies my overarching subject: how constructions of texts and constructions of understandings from texts in individual acts of writing and reading "happen" (or don't). Much has been made of the idea that not all writing, and especially not all literary writing, is communicative. The object of such observations seems often to be to undermine the notion that literary writers intend readers to understand the writing in certain ways and that success in reading could or should be measured by fulfillment of such intentions. Undermining that notion gives reading a freer reign than is allowed by the idea of "getting" the meanings put in writing by authors. There are very good reasons to subvert that idea. To believe that readers should be bound by what writers meant in their writing presupposes that such is possible. Not everyone believes it is. Some facts work against it. The fact that writers as humans have thoughts, intentions, and meanings in their minds or heads or consciousness and that our only access to such private acts is through their writing is one reason to doubt that the act of reading can be bound by what writers meant. The gap between thought and script is too great. The fact that written words are restricted to the marks on a page which will have to be decoded and to which specific meanings need to be assigned indicates that, regardless of a writer's desire to be understood in a certain way, such a hope or desire stands a very good chance of failing. And the fact that readers come to the written word with their own private thoughts, intentions, and skills, leads inevitably to the conclusion that meanings are constructed in terms the reader controls or is influenced by.

There are, of course, counter facts, perhaps the least disputed and most important being that language develops according to social conventions that enable reliability in it uses for social well-being. Perhaps that should be put the other way round: reliability in language use for social well-being reinforces certain ways in which language develops. Conventionality in language use compensates for the gaps and leaps indicated in the first three facts. But whether literary writing is "meant to be" communicative or not seems a less interesting and fruitful distinction than the observation that writers and readers handle language and produce understandings and undertake signifying actions under conditions that can be described and specified. It can be shown that such conditions affect one's decisions about how to articulate thoughts and the ways in which one understands during reading. Because the conditions of writing and reading can be specified, we can begin to see how and why "misunderstandings" are as possible as understandings, we can see how writers try to compensate for the inevitable loss of control that takes place over writing from the moment it leaves the writer's hand, and, for our purposes most importantly, we can begin to see how the creators of electronic representations of writing can represent both the texts and the conditions of writing, such that the "misunderstandings of writing," or should one say the attempts at understanding, can take place within a framework of sophistication about how communication is attempted in writing and reading.

There are other ways to understand the problem of the gaps and slippages between writer and reader, writing and reading. One example comes from linguistics. The extent to which language is "hard wired" biologically into the neuron capacities of the brain, though a debated topic, is one indication of possible, if not probable, success in communication by way of language. That is to say, if – as is more and more widely accepted among neurologists and linguists who study language acquisition, particularly in children – if language capacity and the principles of language development and use have a biological base shared by all humans, then it follows that, at some level, language is likely to work successfully. This idea entails the notions, also upheld by both neurologists and linguists that the capacity to think precedes the capacity to put thoughts into words – that the ability to perceive, to categorize, to generalize, to imagine, and to conceive abstract thoughts existed before a language of expression with its semantic and syntactic rules and conventions was developed.[3] But this biological view of language is complicated by the even more widely held view that language has been socially and culturally developed beyond the biological rudimentary capacities. For, though those biological capacities continue to be operant in each individual who thinks and then chooses how best to articulate thought, they may now be augmented by capacities to use language in ways that have developed differently in different cultures, among

---

[3] The linguist Derek Bickerton writes: "The theory argued here has claimed that many of the prerequisites for human language were laid down in the course of mammalian evolution, and that the most critical of those prerequisites – for even things like vocal tract development were necessary, but in no sense sufficient, requirements – was the capacity to construct quite elaborate mental representations of the external world in terms of concepts rather than precepts. In other words, something recognizable as thought (though clearly far more primitive than developed human thought) necessarily preceded the earliest forms of anything recognizable as language." *Roots of Language* (Ann Arbor: Karoma Publishers, 1981), pp. 294–5.

members of different communities of discourse within cultures, and differently among different individuals within communities of discourse. Thus, a shared base level of potential understanding of language might be subverted by a higher level of capacity that is unevenly available to users of the language.

It should be noted that many students of language and the mind/brain have held that thought is conducted *in* language, not prior to language, and have consequently concluded that spoken and written expression is a physical instantiation of unmediated thought. Some have even argued that thought or meaning does not exist apart from expressions in words, either elaborated silently or spoken or written. Yet, much recent experimental work in linguistics and brain mapping suggest that it is more likely that thinking thoughts and articulating thoughts are two processes, though often merged and mingled.[4] It is possible to think and then be at a loss for words, or to think, then articulate in words, then judge the articulation critically in thought, and then choose alternative articulations. All of these activities can precede speaking and writing or can be conducted aloud or in written drafts before a "final version" emerges. It would follow from that scenario that some articulations – whether imagined, spoken, or written – would be inadequate to the task of representing the thoughts fully or accurately and require revision in order to do so. Unfortunately at the same time that a speaker/writer recognized that the assayed articulation was inadequate and required revision, a second process could simultaneously begin whereby the speaker/writer had a new thought that entered the revision process, such that the revision was not merely a better articulation of the original thought but incorporated the new thought as well – or instead, completely subverted the original thought. And of course the finally revised revision might also be an inadequate representation of the writer's thoughts, meanings, or intentions for the text. Readers seem intuitively to know that texts can fail in that way because they frequently explain their inability to understand a text by assuming that it failed to articulate clearly that which is to be understood – either by reason of a typo, an omitted word or phrase, or a botched revision or otherwise botched transmission of text.

So, what we have as a result of these ways of viewing the process of writing, is a text (1) written in a language for which humans may have a

---

[4] A readable introductory presentation of such thinking is Ray Jackendoff, *Patterns in the Mind: Language and Human Nature* (New York: Harvester / Wheatsheaf, 1993). See also works cited by Calvin and Bickerton.

biological lower threshold of probable success in understanding, but
which (2) departs from and extends that biological common denominator
by cultural conventions and individual experiences which may not be
shared between writer and reader, and which (3) might or might not
represent accurately or fully the thoughts that impelled the writing of the
text, so that the reader's uptake of the text (4) is likely to be a partial
understanding and partial misunderstanding of the writer's thoughts but
which (5) stands a good chance of being a coherent readerly experience
independent and possibly different from the writer's experience.

If the full extent of a reader's desire in reading is fulfilled by condition
5 (the satisfactory experience of reading and constructing a full or adequate understanding of the text), then no further action is required. In
that case, texts untethered from their origins and pleasantly or efficiently
made available to readers will suffice. But if condition 4 proves bother-
some to the reader who, by some means, would like to know if the
reader's understanding corresponds with the writer's thoughts, meanings,
or intentions for the text, something more than a raw or simple or
innocent text may be required. In order to know what addition or
additions might be helpful, one must try to understand how writers
move from thoughts to meanings to articulations to intentions-to-
articulate-writing to the actions of writing and rewriting, and finally to
release of the writing to readers – usually through the mediation of a
publication process that compounds these interactions between mental
workings and material products. And then one would also want to
understand the effects on writing exerted by the conditions of writing –
the relations between writer and time, space, education, skill, experience
of life and of previous forms of expression, tendency to experiment or to
imitate, and so on. It has been the business of biographers, historians,
linguists, neurologists, psychologists, and literary critics of every stripe,
including historical critics and formalists, Marxists and feminists, structuralists and post-structuralists, etc., to try to determine the relevant
factors bearing on the interpretation of texts. Some of these thinkers,
analysts, and scholars have been interested in texts out of a desire to
know what writers were doing in producing them; others have been more
interested in texts as the loci for the activities of readers. Scholarly editors
and the creators of electronic representations of texts and knowledge sites
must be interested in both, if they are to exploit the full capacities of
electronic media to represent texts.

It is important to stress that this book is not about the myriad intricate
rules for meaning-making of the sort that have been so fruitfully pursued

by students of speech acts, syntax, semantics, social linguists, and pragmatics. Much of what they have investigated and explained about how speech works can be applied to literary texts. It is not entirely fruitless to talk about a novel in terms of what the author or writer "is saying" (though it might be more accurate to refer to what the readers' image of the putative author is saying) in the text. And when a character in a novel speaks, readers can easily imagine that the voice of the character is at another remove for it is a voice being voiced by the putative author. Reader response criticism has focused a great deal of attention on the relation between voices and the roles of speakers, whether as authors, writers, narrators, or characters and whether addressing other characters, implied readers, or real readers, and so forth. Whether readers are reading real authors or constructing author functions to help them respond to the text does not actually change the conditions of script acts, which is what I want to address. Script act theory focuses somewhat differently from speech act theory for reasons that will emerge in the discussion.

In this discussion I have not tried to avoid the notion that writing is communicative, for though I know that "communication of something specific" may not have been the "intent" of the writer of a literary text, I can see that the intent not to be communicative is a thing that can be communicated. I am also not overly concerned with the fact that even if something specific was intended to be communicated, many readers fail to "get it." These are simply facts about writing and reading, not successes, failures, or requirements of writing and reading. The interesting thing is not that texts "convey" many things that were not "intended" but that the conditions under which writing is produced and under which reading is conducted are similar and are processed by writers and readers similarly, even though what is understood at the end of the process may be very different for author and reader. The truth is that no one actually knows if they are different – or not. The point, if there is just one, is to understand the conditions of writing and reading in order to see the full range of factors and elements that are relevant to an electronic representation of print literature and the reasons for doing so in the context of a knowledge site.

Script act theory begins with the question: if speech – conversation, and face to face negotiations from ordering dinner from a menu to organizing space tourism – is tied to time, place, speaker, and hearer in ways that specify meaning, why is writing and how is writing different? Script act theory derives from an analogy to speech act theory, a field of study that began with analysis of how communication happens in oral exchanges – not just speaking but hearing and, perhaps, understanding.[5] Speech act theorists have also, of course, been very interested in written communication and have argued about the effects of considering speech as the primary form and writing as a derivative or secondary manifestation of speech – rather than considering them as equal or even separate acts and systems. In fact, I find it important to distinguish between speech/hearing and writing/reading as being activities that are more different than similar, though intuitively many see them as two forms of one kind of action, skill or behavior. The neurophysiologist, William H. Calvin, for example, in *Conversations with Neil's Brain: The Neural Nature of Thought and Language*, writes as if writing were a form – probably an artificial form – of speech: "written speech lacks many of the redundant clues present in real speech." Writing, he seems to think, is just a less real sort of thing than speech is: "When I'm talking, my voice rises and falls, my facial expressions change, I wave my hands and shrug my shoulders. That's additional information. When you're reading, the written word is all you've got."[6] Similarly, the linguist, Ray Jackendoff, writing about how the mental processes for converting auditory patterns into phonological structures take place in different parts of the brain, turns to analogous but different processes for processing writing, and also manages to make writing seem like a form of speaking: "Alphabetic written language is basically an encoding of phonological structure – one learns to 'sound out words' . . . "[7] Jackendoff immediately finds himself in trouble with this analogy, adding first, "though of course the encoding is not perfect, and English spelling is especially notorious for its idiosyncrasy" and then tacking on a footnote explaining that "Nonalphabetic writing systems such as Chinese characters also require a [mental] conversion process whose input is the visual system, but the output of the process is possibly syntactic instead of phonological structure." The qualifications seem to me to nullify the value of the original assertion of writing as a form of sounding; the qualifications seem more fruitful as separate observations about separate functions conducted in different parts of the brain. The act of writing, however, from the first inscriptions of the first writers – now lost in history – to the present, has

[5] A brief but convenient introduction is Barry Smith, "Towards a History of Speech Act Theory," in A. Burkhardt, ed., *Speech Acts, Meanings and Intentions* (Berlin/New York: De Gruyter, 1990); but see also J. L. Austin's *How to Do Things with Words* (Oxford: Clarendon, 1962), and works listed by Quentin Skinner, Paul Hernadi, and John Searle.

[6] William H. Calvin, *Conversations With Neil's Brain: The Neural Nature of Thought and Language* (Reading, Mass.: Addison-Wesley, 1994), p. 235.

[7] Ray Jackendoff, *Patterns in the Mind: Language and Human Nature* (New York: Harvester/Wheatsheaf, 1993), p. 44.

provided relative permanence to texts that "speak" in times and in places where the text originator could not be. Yet, it seems profoundly different from speech to me, in ways that will be detailed. And writing is only the first part of any script act transaction; reading and understanding is an equal though not exactly opposite partner. And that says nothing about production processes.

Perhaps the most obvious thing to say about writing, in contrast to speech, is that it has no intonation or tones at all, no facial expressions or gestures except explicitly verbalized ones, no rhythms, accents, or musical indications of piano or forte, adagio or andante. An astonishing counter analog to the loss of these aspects of speech in writing is found in the description of a form of aphasia in which all these extra-verbal elements are retained but the words themselves are lost. Dr. Oliver Sacks describes the difficulty of recognizing the loss of vocabulary in sufferers of this aphasia because victims seem to be able to understand what is said to them in ordinary language just as if they retained an understanding of words. He describes the phenomenon as follows:

> Thus to demonstrate their aphasia, one had to go to extraordinary lengths, as a neurologist, to speak and behave un-naturally, to remove all the extra-verbal cues – tone of voice, intonation, suggestive emphasis or inflection, as well as all visual cues (one's expressions, one's gestures, one's entire, largely unconscious, personal repertoire and posture): one had to remove all of this (which might involve total concealment of one's person, and total depersonalization of one's voice, even to using a computerized voice synthesizer) in order to reduce speech to pure words, speech totally devoid of what Frege called 'tone-colour' (*Klangenfarben*) or 'evocation'. With the most sensitive patients, it was only with such a grossly artificial, mechanical speech – somewhat like that of the computers in *Star Trek* – that one could be wholly sure of their aphasia.[8]

One might say, instead, "grossly artificial, mechanical speech ... somewhat like that of the *written word*" – which of course could not be used because the aphasia manifests itself as a loss of understanding of words as spoken. But the retention and perhaps even heightened sensitivity to the extra-verbal elements of speech, Sacks observes, means that one "cannot lie to an aphasiac. He cannot grasp your words, and so cannot be deceived by them; but what he grasps he grasps with infallible precision, namely the *expression* that goes with the words, the total, spontaneous,

---

[8] Oliver Sacks, "The President's Speech" in his *The Man Who Mistook His Wife for a Hat* (London: Picador, 1985), pp. 76–7.

involuntary expressiveness which can never be simulated or faked, as words alone can, all too easily" (78).

What is especially astonishing about the episode Dr. Sacks describes is that in the same ward with aphasiacs, those who had lost the ability to recognize words but retained sensitivity to expression, was a woman who suffered from tonal agnosia, that is, one whose vocabulary, syntax, and semantics were intact but who had lost all sensitivity to extra-verbal cues and, hence, had no ability to detect anger, joy, sadness, or any other aspect of emotion or feeling apart from the words themselves. She heard words as one might read them on a page if one read, without expression or emotion or understanding, only the words indicated by spelling and pauses indicated by punctuation. The occasion described by Sacks was of the ward's collective viewing of "The President's Speech," which in the sensitive aphasiacs who did not understand the words produced laughter because they all knew he was lying; and in the woman with tonal agnosia, who had vocabulary but no sensitivity, produced confusion because what the president was saying lacked logical coherence; and in the nurses and doctors, who had both words and sensitivity, produced the "proper," intended effect of being coherent and maybe even convincing. In the context of the aphasia ward, however, Dr. Sacks concluded "the normals – aided, doubtless, by our wish to be fooled, were indeed well and truly fooled ('*Populus vult decipi, ergo decipiatur*'). And so cunningly was deceptive word-use combined with deceptive tone, that only the brain-damaged remained intact, undeceived" (80).

I believe this analogy has value to identify what is missing from written words. And yet highly skilled and conventionalized readers ably and transparently supply the speech-like parts missing from writing – to the extent that for most of us the act of supplying non-verbal elements to written texts in the act of reading is virtually unconscious. If this is so, then it is worth examining how the script act of reading operates and how writers, knowing the paucity of the written words by comparison with the spoken, compensate by making explicit the missing cues or fail to compensate because, somehow, the cues are expected to go without saying, ahem, I mean, without writing.

It may be an accident of history that made English writing a phonetic system – representing the sounds of speech – rather than a pictographic one – representing images as is at least partially the case in Chinese or Hieroglyphics or American Sign Language for the hearing impaired. In strictly phonetic alphabetic languages we have an intuitive sense that the sounds of speech are recorded in and represented by our written texts, whereas pictographs suggest a parallel but different form of communication and understanding that frequently bypasses the sounds of words. Contrary to intuitive sense, written English, as a visual semiotic or sign system, probably has as much or more in common with pictographic writing systems than it has in common with the sounds of speech. Like non-phonetic or partially non-phonetic scripts, and unlike speech, when a written text is copied, it "speaks" multiply and simultaneously. Time and place of script generation cease to be the demarcating boundaries they are to speech generation – though they remain a palpable element of every script reception, as they are to listening. The advent of radio and television and of voice recordings which make possible the one-way extension of oral speech across distance and time has, of course, parallels to the conventions of writing and printing, as does the invention of the telephone and tele-conference communication that allow "real time" two-way communica-tion between individuals and small groups in separate locations. These similarities are important, particularly in any exploration of how com-munication fails. My subject is primarily writing and printing, and I draw on oral forms only for analogies and contrasts. Hence, script acts, not speech acts, are my focus.

Script act theory, as developed in this book, adopts two rather unconventional premises about reading and writing. The first is a concept of written works that entails three ideas: first, that a literary work is only partially represented in each of its physical manifestations (texts/books); second, that at any point in a work, even a very long one, readers can take in or handle more than one version of a work at a time; and third, that acknowledging the partiality of any one representation of the work along with an attempt to deal with more than one version at a time can change and enhance the way we understand written texts. Paradoxically, the primary effect of this concept is to sharpen one's awareness of any given text as a witness to specific scripting acts in the past, undertaken in what becomes each time a new script act in the present.

The second concept central to script act theory is that reading any work, especially works longer than a few lines, never takes place as a whole but is rather like taking a canoe ride down a long river at night with a flashlight. The focus of interest is always at the point of light, the purpose is to read or float along with a sharp eye, perhaps connecting what is currently under our limited gaze with our memories of what has gone before and our anticipations and guesses about what is to come ahead. I borrow this image from Joyce Cary's notion of the comedy of life. Unlike life itself, however, written texts can be read again, and one points a focus of light as in the first reading but with some memory of what is to come ahead. The point of this analogy is that script act theory does not try to deal with understandings of whole books but rather with the processes, both temporal and spatial, involved in specific acts of writing and reading one word, phrase, sentence, paragraph, or scene at a time. Of course that focus has a context that includes a sense of the work as a whole and a sense of history and a sense of the present, etc. But focusing on specific acts is complex enough as a place to start.

Script act theory, as I use it, is meant to serve as the underpinning for conceptualizing an architectural or "infrastructural" design for electronic scholarly editions (in chapter four). To oversimplify somewhat, readers generally pick up a copy of a book – *Anna Karenina*, *The Marble Faun*, or *A Time to Kill* – and read as if the copy in hand fully, or at least adequately, represented the work, frequently without regard even to acts of translation, let alone of repackaging and marketing. Script act theory emphasizes the idea that each copy of a work is the local focus of three distinct types of scripting actions, each in some measure occluded from the others: authoring, producing, and reading. Each copy of a text is both spoor and spur: the traces left by authoring and production and the impetus to understand those traces in some coherent or otherwise satisfactory way by reading.[9] By itself, this concept can change the way anyone reads any book – just by raising awareness of the specificity of the act of reading, in this place and time, this particular copy of a work that is elsewhere represented by many other (variant) copies which stand as witness to a multitude of other scripting acts, each similar, but also each uniquely different. For a study of literary works for which the genesis, production, and reception of the work become relevant aspects, script act theory provides a theoretical framework for representing the work as a series of related historical events, each leaving its record in manuscripts, proofs, books, revisions, reprintings, and translations.

CONVENTIONS: SAID/NOT SAID; MEANT/UNDERSTOOD

The conventions of writing that make possible communication to audiences absent from the script originator are not simple. Literate persons

---

[9] It is, perhaps, impossible to use the word "trace" without invoking Jacques Derrida's use of it in a somewhat different sense: the unintended evidences of suppressed or underlying bias or tendency. The idea of spur/spoor involves the suggestion that writing itself, as a document, in its entirety amounts to no more than markings indicating the passage of a sentient being and that from these spoors left behind, the significance of that passage can be deduced and reconstructed. Trace in Derrida's sense's then is one subtle element of spoor.

have spent significant portions of their childhood and youth acquiring skills in reading and writing, and as adults they continue to learn new aspects of their language and its written forms. Values, experiences, and personal verbal skills vary widely amongst individuals; and, over time, so do the values, experiences, and skills of whole groups of people. Frames of reference fade and change; unchanged texts take on new looks and support new meanings with the changes in the looks and surroundings of those who read. And even within one language such as English, these conventions are not permanent, not universal, and not foolproof. Signs and signing systems develop in their uses and thus in their meanings. Language itself changes in its conventions and thus in its meanings. A young lady, for example, explaining to her papa in nineteenth-century England that her young man had been "making love to her" would in the twentieth have had to say he had declared his desire to "court her" in order to convey the same meaning – if indeed she mentioned it at all. In addition to the ravages of time, one need note also that copied texts are always different lexically, visually, and materially from their originals and that such differences have their effects on meaning and understanding.

These rather obvious observations about written texts have interpretive consequences that are repeatedly documented in literary analysis and, thus, seem to demonstrate beyond dispute that written texts function in ways speech never does. Perhaps the most radical approach to these observations is known as "deconstruction." It is said that deconstruction is not a method of reading and that therefore there is no such thing as a deconstructionist or a deconstructive criticism.[10] Rather deconstruction is what is constantly happening in the acts of writing and reading. Put in that way it is impossible to argue with it, for it is presented as a given condition of textuality – a condition in which determinate meaning is constantly slipping away, undermined by the fact that meaning seems to happen and then disappear in the relationships between things that differ and which are constantly deferring and unstable. Be that as it may, it is convenient to speak of it as a methodology or at least as a way of describing textuality. Recognizing that deconstruction just happens, or asserting that it does, seems to entail that one emphasize certain aspects of

[10] Peggy Kamuf, "Preface," *A Derrida Reader: Between the Blinds* New York: Columbia University Press, 1991. Though Jacques Derrida seems to have invented the word as a critical term and shaped its original concept, it has swept through literary criticism in theory and practice in many forms. My use of the term is not meant to elucidate Derrida's or anyone else's use of it or argue its finer points, but rather to acknowledge a debt and to point out a similarity that might help clarify my own somewhat different notion of writing and reading.

writing that many readers find counterintuitive. Deconstructive analyses
of texts seem to show how they have been constructed, what it is that
made their construction what it was, and thus to show how the ideologies, assumptions, and unconscious aspects of text construction expose a
text's inclusions and gaps, successes and failures. These failures are not
necessarily due to an author's lack of skill with language; they may result
simply from the slipperiness of language, a condition no one can fully
control. To give it its due as a methodology with integrity, deconstruction
further acknowledges that its own attempts to analyze text construction
deal always only with re-constructions – it is after all the words read *off*
the page, not the words still *on* the page that are being analyzed – and that
the object of inspection, through the act of inspection, tends to recede
into the distance. Although radical deconstructists assume that all texts
fail, that all writing is a continual failure, this "fact" does not, therefore,
vitiate meaning, though it frequently "reveals" meanings that were very
likely not "intended" to be understood or simply were not understood at
the point of origin. Because deconstruction does not aim solely or even
primarily at "author meaning" or what Frank Kermode once called
"voluntary meaning," it has seemed to some readers to be a hostile
approach to texts. Hostility to texts is not, however, endemic to deconstruction, though in the hands of a hostile critic deconstruction is a
powerful tool. For my purposes in this work, deconstruction serves both
as a revealing analytical tool to examine how written communication
works (or doesn't) and as a partial and inadequate tool revealing what has
yet to be accounted for in script acts.

   Deconstruction is compatible with, or even essentially identical to, my
concerns in that it finds meaning in the difference between what was said
and what was not said, between what might have been meant and what
might become the meaning. But unlike my concerns, deconstruction
focuses primarily on the ways social pressures, the slipperiness of language
itself, and a writer's unconscious assumptions subvert or extend or even
contradict the ostensible surface meaning of what is written. Deconstruction is also parallel to, if not identical to, my concerns in that it
begins with assumptions of its own about the author. Though decon-
structionists usually begin by disavowing the "author's authority" over
the text, they always begin by assuming something about the author or
the writer, such as that the writer was blind to certain aspects of the
writing which the deconstructionist is in a position to explore. I
acknowledge that possibility, but my assumptions about authors begin
with the notion that writers are frequently very aware of and are master

manipulators of that which they do *not* say, as well as what they do. I assume that all adept and most inept users of language say and write explicitly things whose indirect and unspoken "meaning" is "intended" to be "understood" in direct relation to something that is pointedly not said or not written because those silent/absent elements of the language "go without saying" with the expected audience.

In sum, then, two elements are common to deconstruction and script act theory: that meaning derives from differences between what is said and not said and that criticism begins with assumptions (unprovable assumptions, one should add) about the writers. The author may be dead as the conceptual authority over meaning, but this exaggerated death has not removed the author from interpretive acts. The author continues to be important in two forms (at least): readers as social beings continue to reach into the author's grave in search of "real" meanings and readers replace the "real" author with an author function of their own making. In the first case, readers may fail at an impossible task, and in the second they may fail to construct a publicly convincing replacement. The real author may be inaccessible as the validator of "intentions" – even when still alive – but this does not vitiate the function of the author's real intentions in writing – they were there and they made a difference. And readers sophisticated enough to know that their reading is being conducted under the eye of a substitute, self-made author function may nevertheless want that construction to resemble as much as possible the real thing. It is not uncommon for lay and professional readers alike to treat written texts as if the absent author were speaking from the page. That can be done naively or with sophistication. Probably most readers can attest to a sense in which it appears that authors speak in or through written texts, and it is not my aim to disabuse them of this view which remains an element of readers' experiences regardless of the number of times it is demonstrated that written texts function in other ways, some of which are antithetical to this commonsense view.

Nor is it my intention to provide deep and new analyses in each and every aspect of script action or even to provide a survey of existing scholarship in each area of expertise. Instead, I hope to draw together in an introductory way the web of signifying elements involved in script acts and, thus, to provide an expanded overview of the complexity and diversity of the scripted communicative enterprise. I will explore how individual acts of reading successfully take up or focus upon one aspect or more of script acts even as they fail to take up or consider others. Most readers are already familiar with both the terminology and the concepts, if for no other reason than that they have been studying and using them since first learning to read. But most developments in literacy are designed to increase the reader's or writer's skills in using language and thus decrease the need to focus specifically on the methods one is employing, thus making reading a transparent activity; the aim here, contrarily, is to focus more attention on the systems and conventions that skilled users of the language usually see through or use automatically or transparently in their pursuit of literate meanings and effects. And the purpose for doing that is to articulate the functions of script acts that can be accommodated in electronic representations of print literature.

TIME, PLACE, AND MATERIALITY

Few new special terms will be required to explore how "writing" as an action verb and "writing" as a noun – both as skillful doing and as physical product – relate to the concepts of time, place, and materiality. To see writing in terms of time, place, and matter will involve not only the temporal setting of the scripting act but the physical endurance of its signs through time, and the repeated and varied acts of its reception at different times, in different places, and in different physical forms. Nor will it be new territory for most readers to contemplate a variety of contexts in which each act of writing or of reading takes place. It may be unusual to some readers, but not difficult, to comprehend a broadening of the idea of contexts to include not only the historical, economic, political, geographical, and biographical moment of each script act – whether of authoring, producing, or reading – but also to include the text's own documentary contexts developed through its generative history of drafts and editions traced through composition, revision, production and re-production, dissemination, and reception. The written work is thus seen as one or another documentary text in relation to the history of its other forms as found in manuscript drafts and alternative printed versions and in relation to the written responses of readers. This generative context is sometimes fruitfully seen as a series of discrete snapshots of the work, each version having integrity of some sort – related to such things as altered intentions dictated by a change of mind or by a changed audience or market – and sometimes it is seen more fruitfully as a fluidity, developing from fitful beginnings toward a finished goal that itself evolves in the process of continuous composition.

In addition to contingent historical, personal, and textual contexts – which only begin the process of mapping the elements that affect the significance (functional meanings) of written texts – every form of writing, and especially every literary form, has generic and thematic contexts that impinge on both the writing and the reading. Intertextuality may be a fresh term for some readers, but even without that name for it, most readers are well experienced in seeing how any given text invokes previous texts through formal structures, allusions, responses, or anxieties. Intertextuality refers to a continuing literary conversation in which new novels, poems, and plays are written and read in the light of previous literary works. It also refers to ways literary works affect and are affected by those to come. It notes how any given text seems to change its significance as new texts comment on or react to its forms, themes, style, or arguments in ways that were not relevant at the time the text was scripted or generated.

Reception acts (readings) that engage with the social, generic, thematic, and historical contexts of a text's generation or of subsequent textual re-materializations of a literary work inevitably add another type of contextualization: that of the reading experience itself, individualized to the particular reader. Thus, while on one level reading is a simple and second-nature activity for literate persons, on another level it can be a very complex matter with rich cultural, historical, and intellectual dimensions far exceeding the focus of attention that may have motivated the work's generation, publication, or re-publication.

Many aspects of textuality are hotly contested, not the least being the commonsense view that texts should mean what authors meant them to mean rather than what some clever or hostile or mischievous or incompetent or unsocialized reader makes of them. Regardless of one's stand with regard to authorial intention, two things seem fairly clear. The first is that no matter how radical one's objection is to the concept of intention as a controlling element of textual interpretation, some aspect of intention by some agent of intention is inescapable in any reading act. Texts do not themselves have either intention or meaning; they are inanimate physical phenomena. If they have purpose it is that which is invested in them by authors or attributed to them by readers. The second is that certainty in identifying and describing intention, even when it is the intention of the reader or commenter on the text, can never be achieved or conveyed completely or conclusively. Even for readers who reach sympathetically across the gulf dividing them from authors, there is no escaping the fact of the "death of the author" that curtails communication. Nor can one ignore the ways in which the meanings of written texts tend to expand beyond the putative "intentions" of their origins or originators. But these observations fall short of demonstrating an autonomy for texts; for these caveats seem balanced somehow by the fact that even the most obdurately hostile opponent of "intentionality as an element of interpretation" employs some posited construct of textual agency. Authors may have lost control over meaning in spite of their best efforts, or they may have willingly abdicated control. Either way, readers knowingly or blindly participate in a negotiation over authority in script acts, finding or inventing concepts of authorship and intention, which they then ignore or flout or seek to embrace. The fact that readers can flout the intentions of writers, either by indifference or by malice aforethought, does not indicate that the script was without intended meanings. The fact that friendly readers seek to identify what those intentions were does not indicate that they can succeed in their quest.

One should pause momentarily, here, to remark that scholarly editors of the so-called "intentionalist school" draw a finer line even than this about authorial intentions. Though they are widely accused of falling afoul of the "intentional fallacy," the charge is fuzzy and probably false. The intentional fallacy involves valuing a work as the author intended it to be valued, or judging its success as the author intended, or believing that the text succeeds in meaning whatever the author "had in mind." Scholarly editors have always avoided these fuzzy, illusive concepts of intention, leaving readers to determine or reject them as they will. But when the physical evidence of manuscripts, drafts, proofs, or print points to the high likelihood that what looks like an 'e' on the page was intended as an 'i' or that the omission of an article was inadvertent, or that an abbreviation was used when the idea was for the word to be spelled out in print, scholarly editors have good grounds for fulfilling the author's intention for what the text should be. Even attempts to "transcribe only what was actually written" involve critical decisions about what the marks on the page were "intended to be." Further, when the author's clearly executed work in manuscript is changed by an intermediary editor or compositor, scholarly editors frequently have clear choices that can be made between the author's words or those of some other agent of textual change. And scholarly editors who reject the thought of divining the author's intentions, choosing instead to be faithful to a document, have by that choice frequently committed themselves to a set of readings that mixes the work of authors and other agents of textual change. Thus, the choice not to choose already entails an interpretive act. At that level of intention, no editorial act escapes being implicated. But this is an aside to the matter at hand.

It is worth noting that many critics, responding to the death of the author, have altered their way of speaking, without essentially altering the way they behave, by substituting "the intention of the text" and "the meaning of text" for the phrases "author intention" and "author meaning." Other similar locutions include "sentence meaning" and "utterance meaning" – used in opposition to "utterer meaning" – preferred probably because the former locutions seem to leave aside the human intention as the agent of meaning. And so, I repeat the contention that texts have neither intention nor meaning. Only people have them. Authors had them; compositors and readers have them; texts, however, are inert until acted upon by sentient agents. To posit a disembodied intention or meaning inhering in a text independent of human agency is a mere obfuscation.[11] Of course, the conventions or "rules" of reading tend to prevent readers from making any meaning they like from a given text, but imagination and ineptitude combine on occasion to produce some amazingly unconvincing reading results.

Written texts, at the basic level of documents, consist of molecules (usually paper and ink) in configurations conforming to a semiotic or sign system (often an alphabet) arranged according to some rules of deployment (a grammar). They do not, therefore, consist of words, sentences and paragraphs – which are terms for what humans understand from the arrangement of inked signs in a document. Authors arrange the signs in conventional patterns that conform to the rules for making words, sentences, and paragraphs. Publishers and their assistants – editors, compositors, printers, and so on – copy, regularize, beautify, and multiply what the author has done, creating many new objects consisting of molecules of paper and ink. They can do so because they are familiar with the rules and conventions of composition and transmission of texts.[12] Readers then receive these material objects and, seeing recognizable

[11] Web-crawlers and pattern recognition machines that seem to "read" texts and categorize content according to the "meaning of the text" or to index or otherwise parse texts on behalf of readers might be thought of as an exception – reading for meaning without human agency. But the "machine" has to be taught by a human agent how to react to the text and can only react in programmed ways to patterns already foreseen. Ambiguous, ironic, indirect or mendacious or facetious texts would very likely be misread in ways humans might be expected to avoid. However that might be, the subject of my comments relates to the way humans read things that were written by humans for human consumption. Agency at both ends seems an unavoidable element affecting understanding of texts.

[12] It is possible, of course, for a person with no knowledge of a language to copy onto a blank page what is seen on a written page, with no knowledge of the significance of any of the marks. Such a person might even produce an accurate copy – as a human photocopy machine – indeed, for very low prices, typesetting and data input services are frequently provided by such persons. Skill in copying, not understanding, is the key.

patterns, construct meanings by appealing to the rules and conventions they have learned and which they hold in common with authors and publishers. Put in that way, it would seem that communication of meaning, encoded by the author, distributed by the publisher, and taken up by the reader is a straightforward process with a high level of predictability – though susceptible to scribal and typographical error in copying.

That it is not a straightforward process is evident to anyone who has ever misunderstood a text and later come to a realization that a mis-understanding had taken place. The scary thing is that we do not know how many of our understandings are misunderstandings that have yet to be revealed as such. And worse, when we develop a new understanding that reveals an old one to have been a misunderstanding, we really have no sure-fire way of knowing that the new one is not also a misunderstanding.

The arguments have raged from Plato's time to our own about how written texts work. Plato, noting that authors are frequently inarticulate when asked what their writing meant, concluded that authors wrote more from inspiration than from full knowledge of what they were doing.[13] It would, then, seem a waste to inquire what the author meant and whether the work had been misunderstood, though perhaps it would still be worth pursuing the meanings by which, unconscious though he may have been, the author was inspired. Plato further noted that once written, a text was vulnerable to being read and interpreted by inappropriate as well as unintended readers, who might from the text take knowledge to which they were not entitled or who might put constructions of meaning upon the texts that were not "put there" by the writer or would construe meanings that would not be seen there by the appropriate – or, we might say, properly conventionalized – audience.[14] Hence, Plato did not believe

---

[13] In *Phaedrus* 244–5 poetry is described as a result of a mad or divine frenzy and in *Ion* the poet is gently pressed to admit that his knowledge of anything is limited, perhaps amounting to less than that of other men. At 275 Plato has Socrates say of written words: "they seem to talk to you as though they were intelligent, but if you ask them anything about what they say, from desire to be instructed, they go on telling you just the same thing for ever." But as with all Plato's remarks on art and poetry, there is room for debate or to suspect that his message is inconsistent.

[14] In *Republic* Plato has Socrates imagine an educational system for young people in which they would be told only true narratives, thus eliminating 'misapprehensions' and the false from their field of knowledge. However, the conversation turns then to certain kinds of stories about which he says: "I think that even if these stories are true, they oughtn't to be told so casually to young people and people who lack discrimination ... " (trans. Waterfield; Oxford: Oxford University Press, 1993, 378a). The hinge, then, is not truth and falsity. The key words here are not the prohibition of certain kinds of stories but the casualness of telling them to young people and people who lack discrimination. It was, in the end, lost on Socrates or Plato that the good

authors had special knowledge of their own works and favored control of texts by the elite.

Plato identifies two out of a variety of difficulties – difficulties that have led people to the idea that texts are indeterminate or autonomous or so multi-valant that they are impossible to "mis"understand, since every interpretation is necessarily a misunderstanding and therefore as good as anything that might be called an understanding. Plato didn't go there. He preferred, as others have, to keep writing and written texts within an elite interpretive community of the like-minded who would know the "proper" way to read. Plato is dear to us, but dearer still is truth.

In twentieth-century academic circles, particularly in university departments of philosophy and literature, thinking about how writings work (or don't) was a mixed bag of intellectual arguments and turf battles. As we look back upon those times, I have a strong sense that we now misunderstand their arguments by oversimplifying the thinking of those days, but in simple terms, the insight that written texts are better understood when they are "read in context of historical events" played itself out in pursuits that dominated philology in the first third of the

philosophers who were making these recommendations for a more perfect community were themselves the product of education that included all sorts of stories and poetry. So, again, when Plato later returns to a specific discussion of the role of poetry he claims that "this whole genre of poetry deforms its audience's minds, unless they have the antidote, which is recognition of what this kind of poetry is actually like" (595b). Well, of course, anyone with the recognition that poetry was poetry or fiction was fiction is already forearmed not to be misled by realistic representations of falseness or of bad morality. The premise upon which Plato's proscription of poetry is founded is that people generally lack discrimination and do not recognize fiction and poetry for being the types or genres that they are. It would follow that such people will only be misled.

Having held poetry up to a number of inappropriate standards and found it not only wanting in rational intelligence, in usefulness, and in true information, but excessive in its emotions or sentimentality and tendency to mislead, Socrates then poses as a hypothetical the chance that apologists for poetry might successfully mount an argument on behalf of poetry, showing that despite these failings and bad effects, it might be beneficial (607d–e). Glaucon agrees that that would be a very good outcome because, in fact, he enjoys poetry and appears to hate the idea of seeing it banished – as apparently does Socrates also. They imagine an audience, enjoying a tragedy while on guard and "worried about the possible effects, on one's own inner political system, of listening to it and should tread cautiously; and they should let our arguments guide their attitude towards poetry" (608b). Socrates includes poetry in a list of items with potential to corrupt but which are things desirable in themselves, "prestige, wealth, political power, or even poetry" each of which can interfere with one's "applying oneself to morality and whatever else goodness involves" (608b).

In short, Plato's clearly artificial and hypothetical Republic, based for the sake of argument on a purely rational assessment of what it is to be human and good, is designed from beginning to end for young, inexperienced, unregulated masses of people who lack a variety of intellectual gifts in order to prevent them from falling into error, crime, or uselessness. And yet, ostensibly at the same time, the principles Plato is developing are to identify the best traits of the leaders of society.

Western enlightenment education has repudiated these hot-house forcing techniques based on censorship on the grounds that no strength of mind can be developed in the absence of resistance.

century. The insight that written texts are better understood if one knows who the author was played itself out in the pursuit of biography and psychological criticism of the mid-century. New Criticism and Practical Criticism, beginning as early as the 1920s, both rebelled against these tendencies, focusing attention on the text and away from history and author. Demonized in Wimsatt and Beardsley's essay, "The Intentional Fallacy," as a sentimental and illogical appeal to authorial intention as a validator of meaning – the label "intentional fallacy" became an effective buzz-word with which to denigrate the work of literary historians and biographers. Similar impulses against historicism developed in the field of linguistics, stemming from the early work of C. S. Peirce and Ferdinand de Saussure, emphasizing the arbitrary nature of language; likewise philosophical trends, stemming from Nietzsche and the later thought of Wittgenstein and the sociological theories of Claude Lévi-Strauss, focused more on the structural relations of things rather then what they essentially were or had been. These ideas influenced Michel Foucault, Roland Barthes, and Jacques Derrida in their strong statements about the death of the author, the birth of the reader, the endless deferral of meaning, and the autonomy of texts. But both Derrida and Foucault, who are most frequently aligned with interpretive strategies emphasizing the freedom of the reader, have made clear statements to the effect that texts can be misunderstood, that texts are determinate in that they cannot be made to mean just anything, and that, though the boundaries of that determination may be slippery and broad, they are not absent or invisible. A rereading of Wimsatt and Beardsley also shows that, though they were bent on demonstrating that intention was inaccessible, they were committed to the notion that texts had determinate meanings.

Umberto Eco, author of the influential *The Open Work*,[15] has complained that readers have been too quick to emphasize the "open" part and not enough constrained by the "work" part of his agenda. His way of insisting that the reader is restricted in what the text can be made to mean, developed clearly in *The Limits of Interpretation*,[16] focuses on the way text itself limits possible readings and exposes misreadings. His is a lexical and syntactic approach to the limits of semantics. My arguments are not in favor of or against the so-called freedom of readers to make texts mean whatever they want. I begin with the fact that readers often

---

[15] *The Open Work* (Cambridge: Harvard University Press, 1989) was first published as *Opera aperta* in 1962.
[16] *The Limits of Interpretation* (Bloomington: Indiana University Press, 1990).

make whatever they want out of some texts. And yet I note that many readers prefer to make meanings that they hope correspond to what the author meant by the text. I observe that no one can stop the former or reassure the latter. I do not mount an argument about which way one should lean or pull or push in the argument between those who hold for reader freedoms, those who prefer authorial or even socially intended meanings. I am not sure where I stand with regard to those who hold that the specific words, word order, and punctuation alone provide limits to possible meanings that can be extracted from them or constructed upon them. That view seems to have common sense, but it also lacks a full sense of the complexity of acts constructing meaning. Instead of arguing for a "proper" or "necessary" way of reading, I ask, how do readers construct meanings from texts? The answer I find very convincing, and that underlies the thinking and recommendations of this book, is that the process of understanding begins with the words of the text in hand, whether fully authentic or not, which serve at the moment of reading as the lexical and visual evidence of textuality that a reader uses to construct a meaning. It is important to add that the construction of meaning is a complicated process that begins with the reader appealing to his or her experience of how the text words have been used, relying perhaps on a dictionary to suggest a larger range of ways those words have been used, and then adding to that the experience and skill of syntax and semantics that have been developed in and for the reader through a life of reading to that point, and that these activities are conducted within a supposed or imagined or otherwise supplied sememic molecule that delimits, determines, or enables specific meaning constructions by triangulating the putative speaker, tone, situation, time, place, and intended audience(s) in order to determine the meaning most satisfactory to that reader's purposes. These elements are, I contend, at work whether the reader is feeling very free to make up scenarios to justify radical (mis)readings or is trying to reconstruct author meaning, or otherwise historical meanings.

Perhaps the clearest thinking and least recognized twentieth-century apologist for this broad but determinate, slippery but bounded concept of the meaning of texts was E.D. Hirsch, Jr., most notably in *Validity in Interpretation*.[17] Writing in the late 1960s, Hirsch addressed, reviewed, and refuted arguments raised on behalf of abandoning history, biography, and authorial intention as interpretive aids. He analyzed and demolished arguments in favor of the autonomy of texts. Hirsch was committed to

---

[17] *Validity in Interpretation* (New Haven: Yale University Press, 1967).

the notion that the reader's job, particularly the reader in the university who was paid to be an authority on his subject, was to ferret out author meaning, perhaps, in the end, only by demonstrating which interpretations of the text could not have been authorial. He decried any hopes of actually proving which ones were authorial. In the end, he says, there is no positive proof of authorial meaning, though there may be proof that an interpretation was not authorial. Hirsch was forsaken by American literary academics in the mad rush of the 1970s and 80s to embrace post-structural theories. He was cast further into shadow by some of his own later writings that seemed ethno-centric,[18] but his early work was actually more intelligent and philosophical and more fruitful as an analysis of interpretive strategies than the work of many critics who have fallen, it seems to me, into reliance upon what might be called the Unintentional Fallacy or the Fallacy of Unintentionality. Hirsch cut the interpretive pie more finely than many of his successors, noting that writing embeds not only meanings of which the writer is conscious but many of which the writer is unconscious. He distinguished these meanings from adventitious, clever, and untethered meanings that can be demonstrated to be misunderstandings.

Some of Hirsch's arguments will be opened again in this book, but not from the point of view he apparently held – that there were author meanings that it is our duty to understand and elucidate. Instead, in this book, I will try to ferret out the working principles of script acts, particularly those parts of a script act that are omitted because "they go without saying" and the consequences of the assumptions and behaviors of readers positing functional (fictional) unsaid or unwritten parts in order to make sense of script acts.

This may be the appropriate place to acknowledge the age-old distinction between expository and literary functions in writing. In simple terms, it is said that expository writing, avoiding the frills, decorations, and indirections available to the language, is used in attempts, more or less straightforward, to write what one means with a clarity designed to make the author's meaning accessible to the reader. Writers of instruction manuals, contracts, and court opinions, for example, typically strive for this kind of simple clarity – often falling sadly or disastrously short, but designing the writing really to have determinate meaning. Literary writing, in equally simple terms, is said to be on purpose ambiguous, compact, indirect, provocative, lush or cryptic, and figurative, and, therefore,

---

[18] E. D. Hirsch, *Cultural Literacy* (Boston: Houghton Mifflin, 1987).

open to multiple interpretations rather than having determinate meanings. As useful and thought provoking as it is, I find such a distinction also highly disingenuous, for it tends to absolve the critic of literary texts from any responsibility to justify interpretation as the completion of or fulfillment of complex communicative acts. The resulting freedom to toy with texts is purchased by sleight of hand rather than by clear or open analysis. In particular it suggests that literary authors either have no message "to convey" or that, if they did, it does not matter. It takes as a given that literary authors are more interested in the rich fecundity of language than in its ability to provide determinate effects. It may even suggest that all writers of literary texts accept and exploit the notion that what they are writing must be "intended" to be open and somehow autonomous. I would not say that was never so; but I would say that expository writing has at its disposal all the tools of literary language and that literary writing is frequently intended by its authors to have expository effects; the genres are not mutually exclusive. It is worth exploring the methodology and the concepts of text that enable successful written communication of determinate effects between authors and readers, without ignoring the limits on that success imposed by the conditions of writing. Another way to say this is that serious writing in both expository and literary modes can be both communicative and involve the beauty, elegance, complexity or richness provided by figurative and literal tropes. So, too, can artistic provocations, jokes, half-truths, lies, encodings, encryptions, double-sayings, innuendos, obfuscations, and puzzles be used in serious communicative writings. And in all these cases, whether simple and clear or ambiguous and indirect, there is not only a potential for both understanding and partial understanding but also for misunderstanding.

MORE ON MATERIAL TEXTS

The visual aspect of writing is frequently ignored by readers in the belief that what counts is the words and word order. Perhaps in languages that use pictographs rather than phonetic alphabets, greater attention is paid to the appearance of written language, but in poetic forms in English, eye-rimes and concrete poetry (where the shape of the poem itself is iconic, as in Herbert's "Easter Wings") usually exhaust the attention readers and perhaps writers and publishers are willing to pay to the visual qualities of writing. There are spectacular exceptions – in fact every exception is spectacular because they are rare occurrences. (Whitman's

Leaves of Grass and Peter Carey's *The True History of the Kelly Gang* spring to mind.) It remains the case, however, that most books are treated by both writer and publisher as a linguistic text in a saleable commodity designed separately and, with luck, not inappropriately. Writers lavish attention on the right choice of words and tropes and sentence structures, while editors focus attention on grammar and spelling and punctuation, and style, often actually consulting with writers to see that meaning was not altered in the editing. But then both writer and editor turn the text over to book designers and compositors, frequently checking the results only to see that the lexical text – spelling, punctuation, and word order – was not altered in the production process. Type font and size, arrangement on the page, spacing and margins, quality of paper, and book covers and jackets are frequently left to the production process and at best seem collateral aesthetic issues, not part of the text as a conveyer of meaning. Speech is sometimes thought also to lack the visual character, but quite frequently listeners are acutely aware that speech is accompanied by facial expressions or body language that qualify and point the literal "text." In neither the case of speech nor of writing is the whole effect achieved by the words and word order; both forms find ways to "accent" the words to influence uptake. Often readers register the bibliographic or iconic aspects of texts without being aware that they have done so. Readers are used to seeing children's books telegraphed as children's books by their covers and type designs and illustrations, textbooks by glossy paper, romances by lurid soft covers, and poetry by thin hard boards and, of course, lineation appropriate to verse. Each genre or type of writing takes expected forms so that when violations occur – as so often happened with Modernist writings in limited editions, the "gap-full" lineation of beat poets, or the artful lineation of concrete poets – the visual aspects of the writing call special attention to themselves, ceasing to be the "transparent objects" of lexical texts. That many readers and publishers continue to think of the visual aspects of texts to be purely decorative or otherwise meaningless is clear from the fact that anthologies of poetry almost always reduce all of their content to a single type font and a standardized format, rubbing out the body language of poetry's original forms.

The body language of writing is sometimes appropriate and happy, as it was in the green covers Walt Whitman chose for *Leaves of Grass*, or they can be disastrous or disgusting as they were for Gary Myers' "For Now and Always," a poem commemorating a visit to Auschwitz and with a poignant reference to ashes, printed in *The New Yorker* where inches away was a small cartoon drawing, perhaps intended as a space filler, of a brush and dustpan.[19] The perhaps innocent "intention" of the magazine layout and production crew can have little to do with the way readers have responded to this juxtaposition of the sublime and the offensively ludicrous. One should note that no claim is here being made that the author's intention or the magazine editor's intention or the production crew's intention was to comment ironically, sardonically, or irreverently on the text of the poem or on the meaning of the poem; instead the example shows that a concept of intention plays a role in the readerly uptake of the poem in relation to a non-lexical but visual aspect of it. I imagine that the question "Who did this – and why?" leaps to the mind of every reader who noticed the dustpan, even though there may be no answer.

The relevance to my concerns of these propositions and some additional ones summarized below, is that they indicate an analysis of scripted communicative events that informs the overarching investigation of the difference between print and electronic texts as they are illuminated by our knowledge of the creation, distribution, and consumption of texts in various forms. Electronic "books" mean what they mean, to some degree, because we perceive that they are not print books. Print books have, by virtue of the existence of electronic books, become not just books but print books. Can you imagine the day when Emily Dickinson's poem "There is no Frigate like a Book" will have an annotation for the last word that says "Book = Print book; Dickinson was unaware of electronic books"?

MEANING GENERATION: THE WRITTEN, THE UNWRITTEN,
THE UNDERSTOOD

A major proposition of script act theory is that the meanings of texts are generated from a posited difference between what a text says and the relevant alternatives that it does not say. One example of that proposition is that my subject here is *not* a technical history of mechanical developments in text production from the age of Gutenberg to the age of Google. By contrast, though it is also true, it would not be relevant or helpful to say my work is *not* the tale of a global hunt for a white whale. The difference is that the first "un-said" is a relevant alternative but the latter is not. (I can see now some reader taking that declaration as a challenge to see the parallels and contrasts between the pursuits of this work and

---

[19] I provide a fuller discussion of this poem in *Resisting Texts* (Ann Arbor: University of Michigan Press, 1997), pp. 156–9.

Ahab's obsession with Moby Dick. With a little effort, anything can be shown to be connected to everything else, as in chaos theory a butterfly's movements in Brazil somehow affect the weather in Chicago.) Not only my title, but the whole text will be understood, in part, in relation to the work's "failure" to be a history of the mechanics of print and of electronic technologies because that history serves as one important but unspoken background to the text provided here.

Another demonstration of this proposition about meaning generation lies in the fact that, for example, the word "out" in various contexts derives its meaning from a variety of different relevant alternatives. In short, it does not mean what it means by virtue of being the word "out" but by not being a certain select other word. If one looks up "out" in a dictionary, it will not help determine the meaning of the sentence, "He is out." It will only identify the conventional range of meanings that the word has been used to convey. If I could arrange for the sentence "He is out" at this point to be printed near the foot of a right-hand page so that readers could not easily glance ahead, I could ask readers to indicate what they think the meaning of "out" in that sentence is by filling in the most relevant alternative statement which determines the specific meaning in this case. The unwritten alternative is: "He is _____." At this point the bottom of the page would be reached, and I would wager that 90 percent of readers would guess "in" to be the unsaid relevant alternative to "out" to fill in the blank: "He is out" means what it means because the speaker did not say, "He is in." Or perhaps they will have taken the even more conventional route of declaring the alternative to be "He is NOT out." The important thing would not be that they would be wrong – it would be that they thought they could guess without seeing clues to what the "relevant other" might be.

Most people in this sense-making world try sympathetically to leap to the speaker's or writer's meaning as soon as possible and, in the absence of pointers or clues, have a tendency to go for the most familiar or most conventional meaning as the likely one. Slow speakers, in particular, are used to having other people finish their sentences for them – frequently with great accuracy but often also inappropriately. Ten percent of readers, I would guess, will say, instead and with perfect justice, well, it depends on who says it, where it is said, the circumstances under which it is said, and the person to whom it is said. When the baseball umpire says "He is out," we understand "out" to mean what it means because the umpire did not say "He is safe." He would never have said "He is in," though presumably by "out" he could mean "no longer IN play." No one would actually use "in" as a functional alternative for "out" in this situation. But when the doctor's receptionist says "He is out" we understand "out" to be an alternative to "in" – "out" means "not in the office" – which would be a ridiculous proposition in baseball, unless it referred to a substitute who was being taken "out" to make room for another player being put "in" – but then it would be a coach and not an umpire speaking. Just so, the anesthesiologist says "He is out" as opposed to "He is still conscious," which would be a similar but not exactly the same meaning used by a fight announcer in reference to a defeated boxer, the other being declared winner by KO. Given the right context, "He is out" could mean he is gay or that he is retired, or he is irrelevant. The text "He is out" untethered from any context at all is meaningless; it is no longer part of a communicative event and has no determinate or determinable meaning.

Untethered text can be made to mean anything, but first it must be put into a posited functional/fictional context that will determine that meaning. My concern in this book is not with untethered texts, which can be teased and tortured at will, but with tethered texts: texts tied to their sources and contexts but seen as developing through time and through reiterations such that each publication and re-publication is tied or re-tied to new sources and contexts. My examples here, I admit, all posit a spoken, not a written, text. Speech is very hard to "untether" from its place and time. Written text is easy to untether, and in our haste to make sense of written texts, we often fail to realize how quickly and easily we make up the enabling notions of time and place that determine the meanings we believe are inherent in the text but which in fact are supplied by us as we read.

A corollary to the idea that texts mean what they mean in opposition to relevant unsaid alternatives is that readers and listeners have to supply these unsaid and unwritten alternatives, and they have to judge the relevance of alternatives in order to select those that apply. That is to say, readers and listeners must draw on their historical knowledge, on their own experience, on their observations of the circumstances, or on their imaginations to supply and select the relevant meaning-generating counter text. Note that the untethered, out of context, condition of texts does not "actually" apply even to poems or jokes, though often enough critics who invoke the "death of the author" pretend that it means the poem is virtually authorless. The fact is that for the poem to work – and this applies to jokes as well – a functional context has to be assumed so that expectations can be raised, thus making violations of expectations possible. How many of us have read a poem or heard a joke concerning which we had not a clue and therefore could not understand. And how many of us have laughed aloud at a joke for which we constructed an unintended – or worse, an inappropriate – functional context and thus missed the point that was being made? Or otherwise made fools of ourselves?

For example, when an Australian friend explained to me that on a previous visit to Canberra he had a flat in Campbell and walked to work at ADFA – I, an American, could see that someone in a hurry and caught with a flat tire in Campbell could easily walk to ADFA, no worries. But, it soon developed that he walked every day and lived in the flat. Written texts are frequently subjected to this kind of adventitious interpretation as when Juliet's plaintive "Romeo, wherefore art thou" is understood to be a request for information, or when confusions arise from Yeats's "Lapis Lazuli": "They know that Hamlet and Lear are gay/Gaiety transfiguring all that dread."

Two propositions arise from these examples: First, that reader/listener-supplied relevant unsaid alternatives against which the written words are understood may not be the same as those employed by the writer/speaker and, second, that successful misunderstanding, at least initially, feels exactly like understanding. It follows that sometimes the mis-understanding may persist – in fact may never be detected. That possibility is addressed in chapter ten titled "Ignorance in Literary Studies." Closely related is the fact that the potential disjunction between what a *writer* may have thought were the relevant alternatives to what is written and what the *reader* posits as an alternative will always leave the reader not knowing if the plausible posited alternative was a historically significant one. If it was not, reader meaning and writer meaning are unlikely to coincide. If it was, the reader cannot know that for sure. This potential disjunction has informed many hermeneutical strategies in which "intended meanings" have been set aside as unimportant or irrelevant, perhaps because they seem unachievable. Certainly there seems to be no point in pretending that one has in fact determined what the intended meaning is. It is not just that disjunctions between writer meaning and reader meaning can occur. It is that even when they do not occur, the reader cannot know for sure that reader meaning actually coincides with writer meaning.

Hence, why bother with "intended meaning" as a desired goal in reading? Perhaps the desire for such coincidence is misplaced. However, in "expository" situations, people who sign contracts or treaties assume that by affixing a signature to a document, they are attesting to a mutually agreed upon and coinciding meaning as well as to a fixed set of written words. They would object to any party to the agreement deciding either that meaning was to be determined by readers at a later date or that the meaning of the document would change over time. In "literary" situations, I contend, determinacy of meaning is not irrelevant, though dexterity in the use of language, both by the writer and by the reader, may be greater than with most expository writing. For example, a literary text "meant" as a provocation with open-ended consequences is in fact "meant to be an open-ended provocation" rather than "meant to have a closed meaning." A reader's recognition of that intention will have an effect on the reaction to the text just as will failure to recognize it.

But a more immediate case can be made for attempting to match reader meaning to author meaning in literary works. The key word here is "attempting." The case does not prove that coincidence of meaning can be achieved, but it does demonstrate that the attempt to achieve coincidence of author and reader conditions for meaning produces results significantly different from the results of not bothering to make the attempt. This difference, I will argue, does not merely add to a pile of possible interpretations of text but occupies a special place in the history of reading and writing. Just as discipline of method is required to try to understand how understanding itself works, so discipline is required to distinguish those meanings for the text that were likely to have been intended from those that were not intended. The effort is wasted upon a lost cause only if it is undertaken without regard to the intricacies and uncertainties of script acts. The point of this exercise, in this book, is to demonstrate the sort of information that could be added to an electronic knowledge site to enable readers to identify and use the information needed to construct "the things that went without saying" in the text but that helped either the writer or original readers to know what the text was meant to mean.

An illuminating example can be found in W. M. Thackeray's *Vanity Fair* (1847–8) at the end of the installment in which the Battle of Waterloo takes place. The final two sentences in the first printed version, appear as:

No more firing was heard at Brussels – the pursuit rolled miles away. The darkness came down on the field and city, and Amelia was praying for George, who was lying on his face, dead, with a bullet in his heart.[20]

---

[20] Last paragraph of Chapter 22.

There is enough going on in this sentence (city and field; George dead; Amelia praying, the battle and the war fading in the distance) so that many readers might overlook the question of what is meant by "The darkness came down." Perhaps its most obvious meaning is "not still day," "evening has come" "not still sunshine." But some readers might say that, in addition to the coming of night, the darkness sent a symbolic or metaphoric shadow over Amelia as the war sent its darkness over Europe. But this cosmic meaning might be the product of the fertile imagination of the reader. Was it an intended meaning? Some hermeneutical strategies would claim that it does not matter. If the sentence had begun "Darkness came down," removing the initial article (Darkness, not The darkness), a reader might feel a bit more justified in thinking that the cosmic meaning was not just a product of readerly cunning but was rather a recognition of thought embedded in the text. And, in fact, readers of the revised edition of 1853 did read "Darkness came down." Although the capital letter may be fortuitous because the word now starts the sentence, we now know more than that the sentence originally said "The darkness" or that it later said "Darkness." We now know that an agent of the text, a speaker or writer or originator of text – probably Thackeray – changed it from "The darkness" to "Darkness." It is no longer possible to say of "Darkness came down" that it might have been an accident of style that put that word first with a capital letter; we now know that it was a deliberate act of NOT saying "The darkness." The reader no longer feels very creative in seeing not only that darkness has indeed descended on the land and night has come but that dark days for Amelia make personal what is dark for all Europe. Instead the reader senses a successful recognition of authorial meaning. We construct not only a meaning for the text but a meaning for the change in the text.

In short, in this case, it appears more interpretively fruitful to ask "what does the change from 'The darkness' to 'Darkness' mean" than to ask what either of the texts in isolation might mean. In particular it seems useful to see that "Darkness came down" means what it means because it is different from "The darkness came down." History has preserved for us in this case an alternative that we know existed as a relevant one for the writer. From this point of view, it seems silly to ask which variant reading is "the correct" one, as if we should prefer to read the correct one and not see the "incorrect one." Even if we could know that Thackeray considered the earlier reading ("The darkness") to be an error, it turns out that we gain confidence about interpreting the revised (or corrected) reading by seeing it over against the crossed out reading. Aside from the change itself, there seems to be no reason to consider either variant form as an error.

The passage from *Vanity Fair* is productive in other ways bearing on the proposition that texts mean what they mean in relation to that which they do *not* say. But rather than pointing to the way a written text means what it means by contrast to an alternative that would change the statement substantively – as is the case when the umpire says "he is safe" instead of "he is out" – these examples point to rhetorical differences where essentially the same thing is being said but the rhetorical effect is radically different. Two months before he wrote the sentence about Amelia "praying for George, who was lying on his face, dead, with a bullet in his heart," Thackeray received from his mother a complaint that Amelia was selfish. Thackeray responded explaining to his evangelical mother that he had wanted to

make a set of people living without God in the world (only that is a cant phrase) greedy pompous mean perfectly self-satisfied for the most part and at ease about their superior virtue. Dobbin & poor Briggs are the only 2 people with real humility as yet. Amelia's is to come, when her scoundrel of a husband is well dead with a ball in his odious bowels ... [21]

We now know what original readers of the novel did not know for a fact: that the published locution "lying on his face, dead, with a bullet in his heart" meant what it meant at least in part by virtue of its not saying "well dead with a ball in his odious bowels." The instrument of death is the same (a bullet) and the effect is the same (George is dead) but the flat, neutral tones of the published text contrast more sharply with what we know about George's character and how we feel about him as a man and husband than does the rhetorically hyped phrases "well dead" and "ball in his odious bowels." The writer, we know, has felt strong emotions about George and his death, as indicated in the letter to his mother – or at least we know he wanted his mother to think so. But the author has refused to indulge these feelings in the book, allowing the reader instead to supply his or her own feelings.

There is more. Several months after the novel was completed, Thackeray received a letter from a Miss Smith inviting him to dine; he declined on the grounds that he never dined out on that day "because it is the Hannawussary of the death of me dear friend Captain George

---

[21] 2 July 1847. *Letters* II, ed. Gordon N. Ray (Cambridge, Mass.: Harvard University Press, 1946), p. 309.

Osborne of the –th regiment." In the margins he drew marching soldiers, Napoleon on horseback ("Bony runnin away like anythink"), and a soldier lying on his face labeled "Capting Hosbin, ded a bullick through his Art." The comic drawing and Cockney accent provide a burlesque alternative that the novel did not – deliberately did not – use, and against which we can now further understand the deliberate rhetorical effect of the text that was printed in the novel: not righteously indignant and not facetiously trivial.

Another proposition fundamental to script act theory is that written texts or script acts create part of their meaning through the forms, both structural and physical, that they take. Forms in the sense of genre, were taken at one time (by formalists and structuralists) to be as important as the words or sentences themselves; and it is simple to demonstrate that the same texts used in a love letter might be seen as something entirely different if used on a note left on a refrigerator or on a billboard or in a poem. It is not my intent in this book to revisit formalist concerns except to note that they remain a very important aspect of sense-making and that they can be seen in the context of this study as deriving their "meanings" by "not being" a selected relevant alternative conventional genre or structure.

Likewise, the physical form of a work determines important aspects of its meaning and effect. Sometimes called the "bibliographical code," this aspect of script acts is frequently out of the writer/author's control and may convey nuances of meaning that were unintended. The importance of a text's "body language" has been frequently demonstrated, particularly in the scholarship by D. F. McKenzie and J. J. McGann. One easy example presented by McGann relates to George Gordon Lord Byron's famous poem *Don Juan*. Originally published in an expensive and beautiful edition by John Murray, the respectable London publisher nevertheless declined to display his publisher's imprint on the title page. The book in that form seems to have had the effect, among the relatively few wealthy enough to buy it, of commanding respect as an art object, comic and satiric and barbed, but on the whole a significant contribution to British poetry. Almost immediately a number of piratical printings became available in small, cheap, hurried editions that seemed to have the effect, among the relatively many readers who could easily afford the pirated editions, of titillating their sense of forbidden fruit, of reading a slightly salacious, racy, almost underground poem. The text of both types of editions was substantially the same, though the higher incidence of typos in the pirated editions may in fact have added to the sense of surreptitiousness to those versions. But the bibliographic signals of Murray's edition were very different from those of the pirated books. In each case, readers seem to have derived part of their understanding of the poem from the fact that they encountered it in a form that was NOT something else. And as we look back on that phenomenon, we understand the poem in part now from the fact that we see the two different kinds of physical forms the poem took.[22]

KNOWLEDGE, UNCERTAINTY, AND IGNORANCE

While none of these indications of "not sayings" or differences can justify a claim that we can know which interpretations reflect intended meanings, they do narrow the range of interpretations that can be claimed as historical and intended as opposed to modern or adventitious. It would appear that all interpretations, historical and modern, are generated from posited contrasts between the given texts and selected "not sayings" – and this is done even when the "not said" is assumed or created from whole cloth without regard to the historical conditions of the moment of inscription or to surviving extra-textual clues about the intentions or wishes of the speaker/writer. The readings of the passage from *Vanity Fair* illustrate, however, the fruitfulness of reading written texts in relation to recorded historical alternatives surviving in variant printed versions of the text as well as in "unselected" documents, such as drafts or letters.

Furthermore, noting the ways in which script acts are embodied and disseminated historically helps us to account for the misunderstandings, new understandings, and appropriations that mark the history of text reception and re-inscription.

The traditional "nonsense" sentence: "The square root of butter is yellow" demonstrates how any readers' imagination supplies interesting contexts against which texts "untethered" from originating contexts are understood. I first heard this sentence in a philosophy cum linguistics class as an example of a syntactically viable sentence that conveyed no coherent meaning. I should stress that in the context in which I heard this sentence it "meant" nonsense – nonsense is what it was supposed to convey. Its meaning for the class was supposed to be "a grammatically normal locution without sensible meaning." The claim that it was

[22] Jerome McGann, "The Gutenberg Variations," *TEXT* 14 (2002), 6. McGann notes that the discrepant reactions were described by a contemporary reviewer of the original editions in *The Quarterly Review*; see Hugh J. Luke, "The Publishing of Byron's *Don Juan*," *PMLA* 80 (June 1965), 199–209.

nonsense challenged me, however, to come up with a context in which the sentence would not only convey a clear idea but seem clever and apropos. Recalling a childhood experience with margarine, I imagined a scientist in the food production department of a large corporation like Kraft or Proctor and Gamble during the shortages and rationing of World War II. Butter was in short supply; margarine was white like lard, unsightly and not doing well in the market. Dyes that would give margarine the right buttery color were organic and reduced the shelf life of the product. (Incidentally I have no idea if there is any truth to these imaginings. Suffice that, to persons as ignorant of the real history of margarine as I am, they are plausible.) The scientist in my imagination came up with the idea of putting a measured amount of red dye in a plastic ampoule attached visibly to the inside of the margarine's clear-plastic package. Purchasers would press on and break the ampoule and then massage the margarine until the color pervaded the lard-like margarine, turning the product a creamy, buttery yellow. When he had demonstrated the strategy to his development team my imagined scientist concluded, with satisfaction: "See, the square root of butter is yellow." Perhaps that is an over-elaborate narrative structure. Most people are sufficiently adept "sense makers" to have arrived at that or a similar meaning with less effort. We are so good at supplying meaning-generating contexts that we do it without realizing it.

Whenever a reader confronts a text, the process of "understanding it" or interpreting it involves positing a relevant context that is usually not contained in the text but is inferable from it or attributable to it. If the reader is historically competent, there is a good chance that the "relevant unsaid" for the reader may be the same or very similar to what was deliberately left unsaid by the originator of the text. The fact that readers cannot know for sure that coincidence of writer and reader meaning has occurred does not detract significantly from the fact that for most texts in most practical situations and some aesthetic ones, readers strive to read sympathetically to obtain intended meanings, and they frequently act on the result of their efforts as if they had succeeded. They will talk about what Plato said or Dickens meant or about the effects achieved in Shakespeare's play or Frost's poetry as if they knew what those writers had achieved. Readers who lack historical competence may yet display quite a high competence in sense-making of an imaginative sort. A student has been known to respond to "Oh, Attic shape" in Keats's "Ode on a Grecian Urn" by exclaiming "oh, yes, my grandma has a really cool vase in her attic, too." See Jerome McGann's attempt to generate sympathy for such students.[23] The historically competent reader might object that Attic is capitalized and refers to a location in Greece, but the student has demonstrated skill in sense-making by employing an imagined "not saying" – Grandma's attic and vase – by which to "understand" Keats's Attic shape. Though we might – probably do – place a premium on historically competent readings over adventitious interpretations, it is worth pondering why that should be. In fact interpretive strategies that prefer "imagined" rather than "intended" meanings merely place priority on "interesting" or "clever" readings. The New Critics of the last century put the premium on "coherent readings" rather than intended ones, using history only as one resource from which to draw potential coherences. It does not always follow, however, that imagined readings are more interesting or more coherent then supposedly historically intended ones.

For example, it is very likely that most competent readers of Emily Dickinson's poems would find more interest and use in the observation that "I heard a fly buzz – when I died" might be understood in contrast to historically common sayings such as "He heard choirs of angels when he died"[24] than it would to observe that you can sing the poem to the tune of "The Yellow Rose of Texas," which was unknown to Dickinson. Death-bed stories abounded in Puritan New England. It might be more fruitful to suggest that both "I heard a fly" and "Yellow Rose" are singable to 4 x 4 or common meter, used in a majority of hymns sung in the churches of Dickinson's home town, but the text of "Yellow Rose" provides no parallels or historical context for Dickinson's poem. Both observations are in a sense true, but the historical one seems logically and emotionally justifiable, the other belongs in the realm of junk criticism.[25]

The function of this entire review of script acts has been to map out the challenge of representing print literature electronically in ways that take advantage of the medium to enhance the possibility that historical meanings, even author meaning, can be deciphered. If one begins with the notion that "text" is the inert spoor left by writers and serves as the spur to readers to perform meanings, one can do better than to say readers must fare as best they can. Understanding how writers encode

---

[23] *Radiant Textuality* (New York: Palgrave, 2001).

[24] This alter-reading was told to me by Price Caldwell as an illustration of one aspect of molecular sememics, described below.

[25] The term "junk criticism" is posited in relation to "junk linguistics" and "junk science" pilloried entertainingly by Paul M. Postal in *Skeptical Linguistic Essays* posted on the Internet at *www.nyu.edu/gsas/dept/lingu/people/faculty/postal/papers/skeptical.pdf* downloaded 4 July 2003.

meaning and how readers generate meaning actually identifies the kinds of information that electronic representations of print texts can provide for readers interested in historical meanings. Given this basic view of the communicative enterprise and the functional methodology of interpretation, it follows that written texts, whether holograph, scribal, printed, typed, scanned or otherwise digitized, can be treated either as textual events, tethered, just as speech is tethered, to time and place and originator, or they can be treated as a species of time machine untethered and moving through time, like the urn in Keats's poem that "shalt remain, in midst of other woe," serving new generations "When old age shall this generation waste." Indeed, it may be a measure of our good judgment that we can treat the same texts in more than one way.[26]

ELEMENTS OF SCRIPT ACT THEORY

If written texts are to be treated as "tethered" deliberate acts that exist beyond the act of origination to serve as the spoors that remain as witness of those acts and also to serve as the spurs for countless separate acts of reception, it follows that any copy of the written work serves in some precise ways as the spoors for the acts that produced that copy and simultaneously fails to provide evidence about the acts that produced the original or other copies. Reception responses to written texts are, then, responses to the copy being read, not to the work as represented variously by all its copies. This precision either may not matter or may seem not to matter. Readers are so used to the absence of information that would distinguish the copy being read from any other copy, that it is usually assumed that there is no significant difference and that any copy will do. Textual criticism has, for the most part, failed to demonstrate either to the general public or to the academic community that such views are misleading or inadequate. For the most part, scholarly editors have been seen by literary scholars as performing the sole service of producing established, error-free texts that will save the user from the most egregious pitfalls of using just any old copy and provide the prestige of using an established or standard copy. But textual critics have not been able to impress on either the scholarly or the general critical consciousness that

---

[26] One of our most dexterous critics, Jerome McGann, has written important books on both aspects of interpretation. See *The Textual Condition* (Princeton: Princeton University Press, 1991) on historical, contextual aspects of text; and see his *Radiant Textuality* on interpretive game theory.

response to one copy of the work may not be the same as response to other copies or to explain why and how that is so.[27]

A review of the elements of script act theory will make clear two propositions: first, that viewing written works as a historical series of discreet script acts makes a difference in how one reads, and second that providing all of the relevant script act information in one place, such as an electronic edition/archive or knowledge site for a given work, is so great a task that it is unlikely that any one scholar could provide it all for even one literary work.

An initial script act consists of a writer (an agent of text creation), inscribing a document (material object) at a certain time or during certain times (the temporal element), working at a certain place or places (the location or spatial element), with one or more purposes (the motive or intention element) for one or another expected audience about whose knowledge the writer makes assumptions (target readers), using a range of linguistic, lexical, semantic tools (the language element), in a range of skill capacities. This list does not suggest that the resulting writing conveys specific meanings or that its purpose, function, or achievement matches any putative intentions or is limited to them. It only acknowledges that script acts begin with an agent working at a time and place to produce a written document for some reason. It does, however, point to the contextual cocoon or sememic molecule[28] that has contingent influences on the act(s) of text generation. This molecule includes the text itself, the form and container of the text, and the range of enabling contingencies that the writer thought went without saying.

On the reception side, a script act consists of a reader (an agent of meaning generation or interpretation or performance of text); working at certain times and in certain places; imagining the sources and types of

---

[27] The point of textual criticism is NOT to get the text right and accurate; it is to examine the history of texts for all their clues and evidence in order to get a solid view of how they were created, deployed, manipulated, and appropriated so that we can better understand the history and significances of our books.

[28] The term sememic molecule is borrowed from Price Caldwell who invented it as a metaphor for the whole complex of interrelated elements bearing on meaning construction at the point of text generation; see "Molecular Sememics: A Progress Report," *Meisei Review* 4 (1989), 65–86; and "Whorf, Orwell, and Mentalese," *Meisei Review* 19 (2004), 91–106. Text generation is taken to be an event that develops within an evolving molecular structure of meaning as each word is added to a sentence, such that grammatical structures and historical and other contexts work together complexly for a writer in the act of composition. Seeing each point in a sentence as a node in a sememic molecule helps one see that the "not said" at each point is limited to relatively few and relevant alternatives governed by the molecule and not by all words belonging to some "part of speech" such as noun or adjective. Similar – not necessarily identical – complex combinations of elements work for the reader in the act(s) of interpretation.

work being read; and employing a range of linguistic, lexical, and semantic tools in a range of skill capacities. This list does not suggest that the reader either succeeds or fails to understand what the writer "had in mind" when producing the text. It only points to the fact that the contextual, contingent influences on the reader might not be the same as those that were in place for the writer at text creation. Readers might or might not notice the generic forms or the bibliographical form of the lexical text, and they might not have access to the same set of linguistic, and socio-economic or political contingencies that go without saying, but they will have supplied from knowledge or imagination an enabling set of contingencies that will make the text "make sense" or "work" for them.

Between these two types of script act lies the range of production acts – also script acts – involved in producing the manuscript, the typescript (if there was one), the proofs, the magazine or serial editions (if there were any), the first edition, and all subsequent editions, each produced by an agent or agents of transmission and (inevitably) change, working at certain times, in certain places, with varied ranges of linguistic tools and skills that affect the words, spelling, capitalization, fonts, page designs, and book design to produce the particular copy that any particular reader picks up to read. For most of the tasks involved in text transmission, a worker of some sort (secretary, editor, or type compositor) will first have to interpret the text and then produce some understanding of it in order to recompose or transmit it in the new form being manufactured. It is not a mindless process. Therefore, production personnel act first as readers performing reception acts and then become agents of generation, creating the new form. The consequences of their actions usually either go unnoticed altogether or are noted and buried in the textual apparatus of scholarly editions.[29]

Thus, access to transcriptions or images of surviving texts as arrays of documents archived in a web-site or library would hardly begin to make the work accessible to readers. Edited texts tracing the work of selected agents of text and deselecting the work of others would provide one kind of mediated access to the work. Relational readings could be enabled through links to variant forms of the text. Contextual elements could be provided in a variety of ways. Narratives of textual history, variation,

---

[29] A fuller discussion of these three aspects of textuality and of the relation between texts as matter, as concept, and as action is elaborated in Chapter 3 of my *Resisting Texts: Authority and Submission in Constructions of Meaning* (Ann Arbor: University of Michigan Press, 1997).

adaptation and appropriation would provide other kinds of guidance to the interpretive richness of the archive.

None of this matters in ordinary reading as it has developed in the print world; for readers have been trained to read the words and to ignore those aspects of written texts that are not readily available.[30] The script act complex, consisting of the written text and all its parts that go (or at one time went) without saying for its author and producers, highlights the dilemma that socially or culturally new readers find themselves in. Readers are used to ignoring the author, the circumstances of composition, the original or intended audiences, or the vicissitudes of production that might have affected the text of the copy in hand. Readers, as illustrated above, are adept at supplying coherent contextual support for interpretations, and so they readily produce satisfactory (though often adventitious) reading experiences. According to the logic of script act theory, however, if readers wished to access the full range of surviving evidence that pinpoints the acts of script generation, script production, and script reception relating specifically to the copy or copies of the work under consideration, they could not do it because most copies leave unsaid (unwritten) the elements of script acts that are supposed to go without saying. This is the challenge of electronic editions or knowledge sites.

---

[30] Indeed, even when these aspects are present in the form of footnotes or endnotes, many readers systematically ignore them.

CHAPTER 4

An electronic infrastructure for representing script acts

Type faces – like people's faces – have distinctive features indicating aspects of character.

Marshall Lee, *Bookmaking* (1965)

Humanity, technology,
is never merely good or bad – or worse:
 authentic or unnatural,
but somewhere in the greys our habits spread
 as the brain's best stab at rainbow.

W. N. Herbert, "Get Complex" (from *Cabaret McGonagall*, 1996)

This chapter is divided into two sections, reflecting the difficulties I have had in finding a balance between desire and fulfillment, between theory and practice. The first section maps out a conceptual space for electronic representations of literary texts, the second reviews a chaos of practical problems and specific cases that have yet to be resolved.

I A CONCEPTUAL SPACE FOR ELECTRONIC KNOWLEDGE SITES

There was a time when all scholars, textual and literary alike, desired one thing in a text: that it accurately represent what the author wished it to contain. The paradigm was God as author and sacred writ as text. Texts that were true to their author's intention contained truth that was worth every effort to get the text right. Textual scholarship in this model was devoted to two complementary but opposite propositions: that the text must be preserved from change, protected from the predations of time and careless or malicious handling, and that the text must be changed to restore the pristine purity it had lost through neglect and time. Correctness and control were the watchwords of this type of work.

The paradigm scholarly edition for such a view of work and text was a critically edited (emended) text to reflect the true text with an apparatus that showed the differing readings of authoritative source texts and a variorum of previous editorial or scribal conjectures and commentary.

Then God died, followed closely by the author. What had seemed like a cooperative enterprise between textual and literary critics to get the author's words right in order to get the author's meaning right fell first into a division of labor and then into a division of goals. Literary critics found that the difficulties and impossibilities of recovering an author's meaning were happily replaced by textual appropriations, reader responses, and the study of what texts could, rather than did, mean. Textual critics, though appearing to fight a rearguard action, discovered that texts were more than simply correct or erroneous. Textual shape was in flux, affected by authorial revision and by the acts of editors meeting new needs: new target audiences, censorship, and the tastes of new times. Tracing the history of these textual changes and their various cultural implications became an activity parallel to that of literary critics pursuing new ways to (mis)read texts.

In this new atmosphere the old paradigm scholarly edition would not do. The new paradigm has not yet been designed, though limited pro-totypes abound. Several questions about the new paradigm must be asked and answered:

What is the goal of a scholarly edition?
How can it be constructed?
How should it be published?
Who will use the scholarly edition?
How will it be used?
And perhaps most important for textual critics:
Who can or who should be in control?
Who will pay for the scholarship, construction, and dissemination?

These questions have no correct or permanently viable answers. Because of the multiple points of view and the multiple uses to which texts are now put, no text is per se more important than any other text for all purposes; and, therefore, there is no text that can be agreed upon as everyone's goal text for an edition. But it does not follow that any text will do for any purpose. A user who wants to know what hymns Emily Dickinson knew is not going to find the answer in the hymnal used today in Congregational Churches. Modern paperback editions of Shakespeare

are unlikely to give an idea about what eighteenth-century readers understood the plays to be. The goal of the scholarly edition will depend on the uses to which it will be put. Some texts are inappropriate for some uses.

From that point of view, the goal of a scholarly edition of any work should be to provide access to specific texts – not to the universal text. And of course the construction and presentation of each scholarly edition should specify which text is which. From that it follows that readers should be able to select from the texts the specific one that is appropriate for the kinds of questions that will be asked of it. Can all texts, in forms designed for appropriate uses, be provided in one electronic archive in a way that will not confuse users?

The answer to the questions "How can it be constructed?" and "How should it be published?" are increasingly clear: scholarly editions should be constructed and published electronically. The print alternatives must either be content with a single text – either falsely presented as a universally usable text or honestly presented as just one of several possible texts and inadequate for some critical purposes – or expand to multi-volume print editions of each work. This condition works fairly well for those authors whose stature commands the resources in funds and intellect and dedication to sustain multi-volume publication. Electronic editions, one must admit to begin with, require all the same research and dedication required by major print editions – and they may be even more demanding because the medium offers space and method for practical ways to give more. But the two main reasons electronic editions are now the only practical medium for major projects are that such projects are open-ended and can be added to and manipulated after their original editors have retired, and, second, that only this medium actually gives users the practical power to select the text or texts most appropriate for their own work and interests.

The electronic solution has the added potential to give end users both the textual materials and the tools that would give them possession of the electronic edition so that they could, each in his or her own way, enrich and personalize it – even more so than they now do with their dog-eared, underscored and interleaved print books. This idea, that users might customize editions according to their own views, has prompted two rather different responses among editors. One is that, in that case, why should the editor do more than to present an archive of texts from which users can select any one and do with it whatever they like. This response appeals to editors who do not actually want to edit and who say that editing is intrusive or that the editor's work should be in the background, preferably invisible to the reader. My view is that such editors duck their responsibility to give users a "properly edited" text and erroneously believe that there exist users who wish to do all their own collating and emending and checking of the facts. Such readers exist, if at all, in market-negligible numbers. This vision of an unmediated archive of texts does not fulfill the goal of creating editions that "users can appropriate, enrich, and personalize." And that brings up the second general response among editors to the idea of a user-controlled edition: that editing is an exacting and difficult discipline for producing accurate and comprehensive texts which must be protected from corruption by inept or unscrupulous or careless persons. My view is that it is not only true that people do what they like with texts, that is why they acquire them. It is not the texts that need protection from people, it is the integrity of the editorial work that needs protection, and that, I contend, can be achieved while giving the textual material and the tools that would give users possession of the editions. The tools I imagine here are not the basic tools for analyzing and editing documents to create a scholarly edition. That work is to be done by the editors. What readers should be able to do is second guess the editor, make local notes and changes in the emendations or new emendations, and create links, extract quotations, and trace themes using electronic tools associated with the edition. They should not continue to find that turning down page corners, underlining, and making marginal notes in a cheap paperback are easier than doing comparable things with the electronic edition.

Whereas in the earlier paradigm editorial control was paramount, in the new model edition, control should be passed along with the edition to its users. The main reason for this is that, whereas there may have been a time when the editor served the main interests of the user by providing a text that approximated a general view of what the text should be – a time when the words "standard text" and "established text" had general currency and meaning – it is now the case that users have differing specialized needs. This condition is not affected by the fact that many literary critics have no interest in the authenticity or condition of the texts they use, or by the fact that some literary critics are in principle opposed to the notion of the integrity of texts. It is, nonetheless, the case that for many sorts of literary inquiry and commentary, what text is used makes a difference. The publication of James L. W. West's edition of Theodore Dreiser's *Sister Carrie* created a furor in some critical quarters because, by eliminating the effects of Dreiser's friend George Henry and the effects on the text by the publisher's editors, West "created" a *Sister Carrie* radically unlike the *Sister Carrie* that had been known for eighty years. Any attempt to understand the original reviews of the novel would be confounded if studied in relation to West's new "established" text because reviewers hadn't read that book.[1] Controversy, perhaps even furors, arise when textual evidence produces radically different views of a work. Among the most publicized in recent years concern the textual condition of *King Lear* and the publication of Binder and Parker's manuscript edition of Stephen Crane's *The Red Badge of Courage*,[2] but the list has been expanded to include a great number of others with fewer differences at stake.[3] This does not mean that smaller unpublicized textual histories and textual differences do not matter. Many examples of small but significant variants were revealed in the series of reviews of classroom editions fostered by Joseph Katz in *Proof.*[4]

The point is that for critics who care which text they are using as a basis for the arguments they are making, a scholarly edition that offers them access to the right text for the task is preferable to a "standard" text that eliminates the elements of greatest interest simply because the editor did not anticipate such a user or because the editor disapproves of that form of inquiry.

Much of what follows is offered as analysis of the difficulties and potential answers to the question "How can a scholarly edition be constructed?" but the emphasis will be on why a full view of script act theory makes the forms of representation necessary and useful, rather than on technical or practical advice about hardware or software.

It is widely asserted that electronic technologies have changed the nature of textuality. The function of chapter three has been to draw one portrait of the nature of written textuality. One could conclude that textuality's nature has been constrained during the Gutenberg era, indeed, since the first commitment of text to paper. Manuscript and print texts both "speak" primarily linearly and singularly. Efforts to have these forms speak simultaneously, in chorus, radially, or by indexed random access have worked marvelously well in print for the committed few willing to learn the coding and turn the pages and hold the book with

---

[1] Donald Pizer, Review of the Pennsylvania *Sister Carrie, American Literature* 53 (January 1982), 731–7.

[2] Warren and Taylor, *The Divisions of the Kingdom*; Henry Binder, ed., *Red Badge of Courage* (New York: W. W. Norton, 1979).

[3] See Jack Stillinger's list of debated cases at the end of *Multiple Authorship and the Myth of Solitary Genius* (New York and Oxford: Oxford University Press, 1991).

[4] *Proof* 2–4, 1972–4.

fingers in multiple places at once. For the many who are unwilling to invest that type of commitment, the thrills of the single linear text suffice. And it is still an open question whether that will not continue to be the case, though the advent of DVD movies with editors' and directors' introductions, commentaries, alternative cuts, and outtakes suggest that, given sufficient ease and intuitive access, not only scholars but general readers would find multiple forms of works and information about "making" to be of interest. It can be questioned whether textuality, in the constrained form of print, has been allowed to reveal its nature fully.

It can still be argued that texts were not constrained by print technology but, instead, were designed specifically for print technology. This argument might hold that while electronic media have provided novelists and poets in the computer age with new visions about how and what to write, it would be inappropriate to drag texts written with print design in mind – indeed, written with no notion of any alternative "condition of being" other than print – into an electronic environment with some notion of releasing them from the constraints of print. Such acts might better be termed "adaptations" rather than "editions" or even "electronic representations" of print literature. But I believe that argument puts the opportunities and conditions of electronic editions too simply and starkly. In what follows I distinguish between the historical condition of print texts – which are "enshrined" in the notion of the textual archive (actual or electronic) – on the one hand, and the use of tools to investigate texts both as processes of composition and production and as instances of historical script actions. What is being "electronified" in an electronic scholarly edition is not the texts but the access to texts and textual scholarship. The potential effects are profoundly textual, both in the sense of changing readers' relationships to the text and changing their interpretations and uses of texts.

The reading strategies now taught in schools and universities, and the literary theories that explain and justify every conceivable appropriation and twist of text, may have seemed necessary as compensation for the ambiguities and uncertainties of textuality imposed by its print form and the consequent clumsiness of attempts at choreographed and harmonic arrangements in print. Scrolls by their form emphasize the linearity of works, enabling compact packaging but very clumsy movement from one part of the work to another. (Imagine a scroll with cross references or endnotes!) The codex (book with leaves, as opposed to scrolls) maintained the compact packaging and linearity but added "random access" to the extent that readers could keep fingers positioned strategically at various openings for quick reference.[5] If metaphor can allow one to clarify differences in how textuality could fulfill its "nature," one could say of the codex that it provided texts with an architectural habitation with very limited openness.[6] Its varied fonts, its footnotes, running titles and side notes, its appendixes and indexes, its illustrations, tables, charts, and maps, and more recently, its attached recordings, videos, fiches, and CDs all showed a remarkably inventive openness to organization, packaging, and readerly navigation. And yet, in the end, in the print world every book had a closing date, a production schedule, a publication date and then the making process ended. Every part remained fixed and immovable relative to every other part. The codex was flexible and extendable but only in the limited ways captured in the metaphor of architecture – once built, it could be added to or renovated, but not easily. Both actions required publication production acts from the ground up in order to enable structural change. Readers with both the original and the revised print edition could see and use first one form and then another and then the first again. But the normal impulse of readers would be to see one as the replacement of the other – as though a house had been torn down and rebuilt. Architecture is, then, perhaps the wrong metaphor in which to encapsulate the concept of textuality. Perhaps architecture is too small a vision.

We could try "infrastructure" with its evocation of roads, streets, alleys, bridges, sewage systems, electrical grids, traffic lights, wall plugs, and appliances each contributing in a flexible way, inviting by its openness the invention of new concepts of organization and new instruments for the enhancement of human action. It appears that electronic environments could aspire to work as an infrastructure for textuality – a concept that allows for multiple notions of what constitutes a text and what sorts of approaches to it should or could be taken and what instruments could be devised to enhance human actions in relation to texts. If texts, like food, water, clean air, and means to remove waste, are sustenance to the mind and spirit, nourishing, cleansing, beguiling, and enhancing human action, then texts must have many means of being brought to us and of being used. Dickinson's "There is no Frigate like a

---

[5] Anyone who has tried to read on microfilm a book with endnotes will immediately sense the advantage of codex over scrolls.

[6] I began thinking about electronic editions in terms of architecture, as the title of this chapter still attests, but I was persuaded of the limitations of "architecture" as a metaphor and of the usefulness of "infrastructure" and "coral reef" by Peter Robinson, Willard McCarty, and through them by Michael Sperberg-McQueen, each of whom has a more intimate acquaintance with the world of computers than I.

Book" might be paraphrased for electronic texts somehow. But how? It remains to be seen if an electronic architecture or infrastructure for written texts can be conceived and then devised that will alter the conditions of textual habitation and make texts stand forth in what will appear in practice to be a new nature of textuality.

The images of architecture and infrastructure both suggest human planning, strategies, and goals with humans developing the means for achieving them. It has been suggested that textuality might find a better metaphor in the coral reef.[7] A sense of natural development and symbiotic relations and mutually dependent developments in a hugely complex natural interaction under the control of no one in particular and eventuating in breath-taking beauty may be an attractive alternative vision. But I cannot go there. Texts are human inventions constituted by humanly devised sign systems and mechanical means of production and distribution. Their conventions are of human invention and agreement. Humans ruin rather than build coral reefs. It is true that language grows and changes in spite of French Academies and Webster's dictionaries, but insofar as humans create texts of great complexity and dexterity through the conscious manipulation of the conventions of writing, it seems necessary to provide conscious ways to enhance one's ability to comprehend the functions, meanings, purposes, and even intentions of their creation and manufacture. Coral cannot be prevented from forming on human structures placed in coral-friendly environments. Nor can misuse of tools – using a screwdriver for a hammer or a cooker to heat a house – be prevented. Unintended consequences and unintended uses are inevitable in all human action. But if we are to explore the textual potentialities of the electronic environment, we cannot leave it all to chance. Just look at the texts already proliferating like parasytic zebra mussels on the Internet, clogging the exchange of reliable information. In a coral reef it might be difficult to distinguish between a Project Gutenberg, a Rossetti Archive, and Chaucer's *The General Prologue on CD-ROM*.[8] Texts on screens look remarkably alike, despite profound differences in quality; and search engines tend to throw them up in lists prioritized by elements other than textual acumen or reliability.

[7] See Michael Sperberg-McQueen's comments come from his "Trip Report" on the "Text Analysis Software Planning Meeting" held at Princeton, 17–19 May 1996, at http://tigger.uic.edu/~cmsmcq/trips/ceth9505.html (accessed 19 December 2003).
[8] Project Gutenberg (http://promo.net/pg/), Rossetti Archive (http://www.iath.virginia.edu/rossetti/), Chaucer (http://www.sd-editions.com/).

The purpose of this chapter is, first, to imagine the difference that the enriched and more dexterous medium of electronic editions will bring to text presentations and, more important, to receptions of literary works; and, second, to suggest a space and a shape for developing electronic editions that will serve not only as archives but as knowledge sites that would enable the kind of reading imagined. The space and shape I will try to describe is one where textual archives serve as a base for scholarly editions which serve in tandem with every other sort of literary scholarship to create knowledge sites of current and developing scholarship that can also serve as pedagogical tools in an environment where each user can choose an entry way, select a congenial set of enabling contextual materials, and emerge with a personalized interactive form of the work (serving the place of the well-marked and dog-eared book), always able to plug back in for more information or different perspectives.

In spite of the advances already made in the medium of electronic texts, we have not fully understood or exploited the capabilities of electronic texts. Our slow adaptation to the medium arises in part from the narrow concept of textuality to which we have been habituated in print culture and in part from a too easy satisfaction with the initial efforts to transport print to marginally improved electronic forms. Attempts to create single comprehensive edition-presentation software may also have slowed progress by investing effort in closed systems not designed for expansion or adaptation beyond the purposes of the particular project at hand. In any case, it has resulted in many promising but limited or dead-end projects.

What developers of electronic scholarly editions to date have in common is the absence of a full array of interactive and compatible tools for mounting full-scale electronic scholarly editions. Because most of what we have learned about creating electronic editions comes from the work of individual scholars or small teams working in isolation on specific scholarly projects, the pieces of the puzzle are scattered and frequently incompatible. Each project is built on a particular platform (Macintosh, Windows, Sun, etc.), using particular text formats (word processors, typesetting or formatting programs, HTML, SGML, XML, etc.), to archive texts with a range of particular characteristics (hundreds of scribal manuscripts or just one authorial manuscript; a few printed sources or multiple authorial manuscripts; fair copies or heavily revised manuscripts or palimpsests, etc.), in order to produce editions conceived in particular ways (as databases for philological studies, as archives of manuscripts, as repositories of the "most authentic" or "most important" documents, as critically edited texts), with or without illustrative materials (paintings, drawings, sculpture, architecture, maps, charts), designed to show textual fluidity or textual stability. It is not surprising that each project has made choices for software or choices for arrangement or choices for access that depend both on the nature of the materials that are being edited and on the nature of the scholarly interests of the editors or the audience they perceive. It is a complex situation that has been and is being addressed but for which a generally accepted solution has yet to emerge. There is great hope that greater compatibility will be achieved with the TEI (Text Encoding Initiative) and XML (Extendible Markup Language) – encoding language that sets standards for data files and mark-up so that multiple tools can access the same data.

The chief characteristic of this account of the current state of things is that each developing scholarly project is tied fairly closely to a particular set of tools and markup protocols. One scholar's data is not easily accessed by another scholar's tools or adapted to new uses or different ways of structuring the data. This is so in part because texts and scholarship are often just as proprietary as the software used with them. Copyrights are relevant to the problem. Just imagine a new James Joyce *Ulysses* electronic edition with an archive of files representing every extant stage of manuscript from first drafts through marked proofs and revisions in later printings.[9] Imagine the archive to be fully linked so that variants can be accessed. Imagine it copyrighted and sold. And then imagine that another scholar/IT technician develops software that can take the archive and crawl through it in such a way as to show, at any speed the user wants, the process of writing for any given passage, so that the user can watch it grow and change. Give the user VCR controls for rewind and pause. And provide a window for commentary. Then ask, how can that new piece of software be used for *Portrait of the Artist*, or Beckett's *Stirring Still*, Cary's *The Horse's Mouth*, and Stoppard's *Dirty Linen* – assuming there were archived files of these works marked up and in a condition to be enhanced by added markup.

The world of electronic scholarly editions may be working towards it but has not yet achieved a condition in which scholarship is invested modularly into the development of marked archives, marked commentary and annotation, marked analysis of text variation and genesis in such a way that the results of scholarship could be employed modularly with a

---

[9] This is unlikely to happen, given the current attitude of the Joyce estate, which has used copyright recently to halt at least two efforts to start such editions.

variety of tools for display of static texts, for display of dynamic texts, for selection of texts, for manipulation of texts, for accessing commentary and annotations, or for personalizing editions for a variety of critical, historical, linguistic, or philological uses.

In most cases the electronic editions now on offer do not serve as models for the construction of new editions of works other than those whose basic characteristics are like those of the project already under-taken. Thus, stand-alone electronic editions of *Beowulf* or *King Lear* and works by Samuel Beckett and Marcus Clark have developed not only the files of text and scholarship associated with major scholarly editions but have created or aggregated non-interchangeable electronic tools for their use. The net result is an individualization of the project both in its materials and its modes of storage and retrieval. Even collaborative pro-jects and centers of electronic editing have produced limited and limiting results. The editions surrounding Peter Robinson's amazing work on Chaucer tend to be works with similar textual histories – Dante and the New Testament, not Shakespeare, Joyce or Thackeray. Likewise, the projects produced at the Institute for Advanced Technology in the Humanities (IATH) at the University of Virginia tend to be works for which illustrative material is of high importance (Blake and Rossetti) and where the concepts of archiving, imaging, and commentary is more valued than that of critical editing. This is not to say that these projects are less good than they could have been. Without them we would have a hard time imagining improvements.

This is early days, though the enthusiasm of those involved in the more elaborate prototype editions vents itself in statements like, "I think one can do an awful lot with XML and XSL, and I think what we lack in the infrastructure right now is a good, free XML search engine that would support Xpath and Xquery. If we had that, I actually don't think there would be a whole lot to complain about."[10] Well, we don't have that (or didn't when I wrote this), and we do not have several other important things – or we have them in isolated and incompatible platform-dependent forms. What we have now will not serve for very long tech-nologically and does not meet and never has met demands from a scholarly point of view. If one were to put together the extraordinarily

[10] This is a direct quotation from an email sent to me by a person who shall remain nameless and not held responsible for what was probably an unguarded and not just ill-considered statement. Unfortunately, it is not unlike frequent expressions of enthusiasm for electronic media. Since then others have said what we need is XSL-FO and XSL formatting. The list will continue to grow – as will our desires for and capabilities for new ways to access and display texts.

dexterous and beautiful presentations of electronic editions being done at IATH[11] with Peter Robinson's extraordinarily complex combination of text collation and beauty of presentation for the Chaucer and other medieval projects at the University of Birmingham,[12] and Paul Eggert's and Phill Berrie's collation and conversion tools, and authentication processes at the Australian Defence Force Academy,[13] and Eric Lochard's ARCANE authoring project involving an extensive array of charting, mapping, time-lining, and other types of verbal and graphic annotation and a panoply of output capabilities,[14] and the comprehensive organization of materials and access planned by the HyperNietzsche project[15] – in short, if one had comprehensive scholarly compilations of the documents of a knowledge area, beauty of presentation, imaging, collation on the fly, constant self-check for authenticity, writer's tools for annotational linking, multiple forms of output (to screen, to print, to XML, to WORD, to TEX, to PDF, to others), sound, motion, decent speed, decent holding capacity, user-friendly interface, quick navigation to any point (three clicks or less), and scholarly quality – and if one had these capabilities in authoring mode, augmenter's mode, and reader's mode, in a suite of programs with similar interfaces all workable on multiple platforms so that they were not too difficult to learn or to port from one set of equipment to another, and so that the tools developed for one archive could be easily adapted for use with another archive – then we would have something to crow about. We would also have something to write permanent how-to manuals about. Instead, what we have are multiple experiments – some of which do a very good job of surveying the ground and mapping improvements, as for example De Smedt's and Vanhoutte's Dutch electronic edition of Stijn Streuvels's *De teleurgang van den Waterhoek.*[16]

---

[11] Institute for Advance Technology in the Humanities: www.iath.virginia.edu/.

[12] www.sd-editions.com/.

[13] http://idun.itsc.adfa.edu.au/ASEC/aueledns.html.

[14] See Eric-Olivier Lochard and Dominique Taurisson: "'The World According to Arcane.' An Operating Instrumental Paradigm for Scholarly Editions," in *Perspectives of Scholarly Editing / Perspektiven der Textedition*, ed. Bodo Plachta and H.T.M. van Vliet (Berlin: Weidler Buchverlag, 2002), pp. 151–62. There are dozens more projects that I do not mean to neglect here. I selected these because I'm sufficiently familiar with them to know that each offers a desirable capability that is absent from each of the others. My surmise is that most truly sophisticated experiments in electronic editing provide some unique capability not available elsewhere.

[15] www.hyperl.org (accessed 18 November 2004).

[16] See Edward Vanhoutte, "A Linkemic Approach to Textual Variation: Theory and Practice of the Electronic-Critical Editions of Stijn Streuvels' *De teleurgang van den Waterhoek,*" *Human IT* 1 (2000) www.hb.se/bhs/ith/1-00/ev.htm.

Because the means in both software and hardware are still in a rapidly developing infancy, technical problems have dominated discussions of how to produce scholarly electronic editions. When an editorial project is defined primarily as textual scholarship in the hands of literary scholars who are amateurs in technology but who want electronic presentation and distribution, complicated textual issues often find only tentative technical solutions. Conversely, when a new editorial project is defined primarily as electronic rather than textual and is placed in the hands of technicians who are amateurs in literary and textual scholarship, beautiful and eloquent technical demonstrations present rather obvious, simple, or flawed notions of textual issues.[17] Casual observers will invariably be much more impressed by the technical genius of the latter than by the textual complexity and nuance of the former because casual observers do not actually use scholarship, they only look at it. The merits of a knowledge site are not to be measured by the reactions of tourists.

A full-scale electronic scholarly edition should allow the user to answer quickly and easily questions about the work that might affect how it is used.

A The documents

1 What are the important historical documentary forms of this work?
2 Can I choose a specific historical document as my reading text?
3 Can I choose a critically edited form of the work as my reading text?
4 Can I see photographic images of any of these forms of the text?
5 As I read any text can I pause at any time to see what the other forms of the text say or look like at that point? i.e., are the differences mapped and linked?
6 As I read any text can I be alerted to the existence of major variant forms? or all variant forms?
7 Can I alter any given reading text to represent my own emended version of it?
8 Can I read descriptions of the provenance of each document?

---

[17] One hesitates to point fingers, but Simon Gatrell's Thomas Hardy's Wessex site has textual sophistication that combined literary and textual criticism at its best but the technical appeal of a do-it-yourself barn construction (http://www.english.uga.edu/wessex/). Conversely, the Harriet Beecher Stowe project at IATH has the technical beauty and sophistication of a race car but leaves too many textual questions unexplored – a condition being redressed by Wesley Raabe's work at IATH (http://www.iath.virginia.edu/utc/).

9 Can I access the editor's informed opinion about the relative merits or salient features of each documentary version?

B The methodology

10 Can I read the editor's rationale for choosing a historical text as the basis for an edited version and can I find an explanation of the principles for the editor's emendations? Are all emendations noted in some way?
11 Is there an account of the composition, revision, and publication of the work?
12 Is there an argument presented for the consequences of choosing one reading text over another?
13 When variants are being shown, is there editorial commentary available about them?
14 Are ancillary documents such as illustrations, contextual works, letters, personal documents, or news items available either in explanatory annotations or in full text form?
15 How was accuracy in transcription assured?

C The contexts

16 Are there bibliographies, letters, biographies, and histories relevant to the composition or the subject of this work or guides to the author's reading?
17 Are there guides to existing interpretive works – from original reviews to recent scholarship and criticism?
18 Are there adaptations in print, film, or other media, abridgments, or censored versions that might be of interest?

D The uses

19 Is there a tutorial showing the full capabilities of the electronic edition? A guide for beginners?
20 Are there ways I can do the electronic equivalent of dog-earing, underlining, making marginal notes, cross-referencing, logging quotations for future use? Can I write an essay in the site with links to its parts as full-text documentation and sourcing?
21 What other things can I do with this edition?

Because there is no overarching goal or theory or analysis of what electronic editions can be, there has yet to be developed a sense among
scholarly editors working on electronic editions that they are contributing
to a system of editions that participate in a communal goal, nor, with the
exception of TEI and perhaps XML, has there developed a very widely
accepted sense of "industry standards" that would enhance the notion of
interchangeable modules for edition design and construction.[18] Consequently advice about particular software and hardware dates rapidly. And
nobody knows all the answers.

It takes a village

Creating an electronic edition is not a one-person operation; it requires
skills rarely if ever found in any one person. Scholarly editors are first and
foremost textual critics. They are also bibliographers and they know how
to conduct literary and historical research. But they are usually not also
librarians, typesetters, printers, publishers, book designers, programmers,
web-masters, or systems analysts. In the days of print editions, some
editors undertook some of those production roles, and in the computer
age, some editors try to program and design interfaces. In both book
design and electronic presentations, textual scholarship often visibly
outdistances the ability of these same persons' amateur technical attempts
at beauty and dexterity. Yet, in many cases, textual critics, whose business
it is to study the composition, revision, publication, and transmission of
texts, have had to adopt these other roles just to get the fruits of their
textual labor produced at all or produced with scholarly quality control. It
may even seem to some that it is the textual critic's duty, in the electronic
age, to become an expert in electronic matters, perhaps for the same
reason some editors became type compositors – they do what they have to
do in the absence of the support that would provide them with the
necessary team. On the other hand, it has also occurred that some very
adept programmers and internet technologists have undertaken editions,

---

[18] Significant efforts to create a sense of community in this regard have been developing within and
in connection with the Modern Language Association of America's Committee on Scholarly
Editions. See "Guidelines for Scholarly Editions" http://sunsite.berkeley.edu/MLA/guidelines.
html and http://jefferson.village.virginia.edu/~jmu2m/cse/CSEguidelines.html. See also, Report
from an Editors' Review of the Modern Language Association's Committee on Scholarly Editions'
Draft Guidelines for Electronic Scholarly Editions http://www.iath.virginia.edu/~jmu2m/cse/
Editors.rpt.htm and John Unsworth, "Reconsidering and Revising the MLA Committee on
Scholarly Editions' Guidelines for Scholarly Editions" http://www.iath.virginia.edu/~jmu2m/
sts2001.html (accessed September 7, 2004).

often with results in which the beauty of professional design surpassed the amateur textual scholarship invested. Such persons need a team as well. The division of expertise has led to the present situation – one in which the technological answers are limited to the needs of a particular scholarly project or to those of very similar projects in a single field.

As can be seen from the chart below[19] of a possible knowledge site (as opposed to an archive or a scholarly edition), it will require a community with a life beyond the lives of the originators of scholarly projects to maintain and continue such projects. I believe this will happen, just as communities have arisen to support libraries, scholarly journals, and specialized research institutes that outlast their founders, so will communities arise around knowledge sites. If a search engine like Google is a model for access to information – a model that truly seems like a coral reef in which every sort of life, low life as well as high, is tolerated – then the knowledge site, as a collaborative effort outliving its originators, can grow and develop through changes in intellectual focuses, insights, and fads and accommodate new knowledge in configurations that may augment or correct rather than replace the work that went before.[20]

Although strictly speaking scholarly editing focuses on the study of the composition, revision, publication, and transmission of texts, it yet behooves textual critics to be knowledgable about the computer technology because knowledge of the means of achieving the aims and goals of final presentations and functionalities will affect every decision being made from the beginning of research to the final enhancement or final abandonment of the project. Equally, textual scholarship requires the

---

[19] See pages 101–2.

[20] The coral reef image is taken from Michael Sperberg-McQueen who has used it frequently including in "New TA Software: Some Characteristics, and a Proposed Architecture": "We are not building a building; blueprints will get us nowhere. We are trying to cultivate a coral reef; all we can do is try to give the polyps something to attach themselves to, and watch over their growth." http://pigeon.cch.kcl.ac.uk/ta-dev/notes/design.htm (accessed 26 June 2004). It is picked up and elaborated by Peter Robinson in "Where We Are With Electronic Scholarly Editions, and Where We Want To Be": "As yet, we are not even agreed what path to follow towards this goal: should we try to create a single architecture, which all must use? Or, should we fashion something like a tool set, an infrastructure which may be used to make what editions we please? Or do we need something yet more anarchic: what Michael Sperberg-McQueen describes as a 'coral reef of cooperating programs', where scattered individuals and projects working 'in a chaotic environment of experimentation and communication' yet manage to produce materials which work seamlessly together. Unlikely as it sounds, and untidy as it may seem to those used to ordered programs of software and data development, with the neat schedules of work-packages so admired by grant agencies, this last may be our best hope. This model has certainly worked in the software world, where open source software developed in the last years under these conditions drives large sections of the community." http://computerphilologie.uni-muenchen.de/jg03/robinson.html (accessed 26 June 2004).

services of Internet technologists. And both types of expert need the input of those who have thought about how readers assimilate complex textuality. This is not a case of simplifying, dumbing down, or compacting complex textual situations; it is a case of providing access to textual complexity as a highway rather than as an obstacle course. Clarity, not simplicity.

Every textual scholar who has ever started a sentence with the words, "The goal of scholarly editing is . . . " has been accused of narrowness or waywardness regardless of how generic and bland the following statement may be. Nevertheless, whatever else it may also include, whether a book, a CD, a web-site, recorded texts, or some combination of these, or a new idea yet to be conceived, the goals of a scholarly electronic edition or knowledge site could or should include the presentation of a text or texts of a work, edited according to principles and methods explained by the editor in accord with the editor's understanding of the work's modes of existence. One could try for a more straightforward account – the truth and nothing but the truth about scholarly editing: the presentation of the texts, their variants, their origins, the production processes, their reception, along with commentary about these textual matters. However, the straightforward statement begs too many questions and seems not to acknowledge that the evidence of textuality – the extant historical documents – cannot be handled, transcribed, or presented in objective or neutral ways. Each editor, knowingly or naively, after having identified and analyzed every extant form deemed by that editor to be relevant, defines relevance and proceeds to transcribe, edit, and annotate, according to a particular "orientation to text." I described five orientations in detail in *Scholarly Editing in the Computer Age* as bibliographical, documentary, authorial, sociological, and aesthetic. Although editors may appeal to arguments from a mixture of these orientations, no single act of editing can conform to more than one at a time. Presentation of texts fulfilling the demands of one orientation distorts the record for those trying to access the texts from a different orientation. These differences may in some cases be trivial, but in others are quite important.[21] Even editors intending to mount all the relevant texts for a work on an electronic site must analyze those texts and provide an explanation of the relations between them. That is not possible without comparing the texts

---

[21] It would take too much space to rehearse the intricacies or significance of different orientations here. See Chapter 2, "Forms," in *Scholarly Editing in the Computer Age*, 3rd edn. (University of Michigan Press, 1996).

word for word, letter for letter, punctuation mark for punctuation mark, and comparing and analyzing the iconographic differences in the paper, type fonts, and page and cover designs. Already editors are beginning to deal with works that never existed in any but electronic forms, and their concerns may be different from those addressed here. The concept of a knowledge site developed here may provide ways to accommodate the entire range of orientations to text as well as the whole range of extant texts.

Electronic scholarly editions either already can, or promise soon to be able to, offer to both editors and edition users considerably more than was possible in print editions. That is, print editions were almost always faced with limitations imposed by economics of publishing, and by a split desire to serve a general reading public who wanted a simple but sound text and to serve a small tribe of scholars who needed the whole textual record. Print editions never actually managed to be all things to all people. The knowledge site imagined here, constructed modularly and contributed to by "a village" of scholars could never get itself printed as an integral whole, though most of its parts have been or could be printed in smaller units. It seems logical now, when undertaking a scholarly edition to plan to produce it as an electronic knowledge site with a variety of tools for accessing its materials and taking advantage of its incorporated scholarship. If there are to be print scholarly editions also, they should probably be thought of as offshoots from the electronic edition, targeted to specific audiences or for specific uses such as reading or teaching as opposed to prolonged and detailed study. Although historically the print edition precedes the electronic one, even at this early stage of electronic text development, it is becoming backward to think of creating a print scholarly edition and then retool it as an electronic edition.

There are several reasons for this about-face in the procedures of editorial scholarship. The primary one is that computer-assisted scholarly editing has already computerized every aspect of transcription, collation, revision, and record-keeping. The production of print editions by manual means is virtually unknown now. It is inconceivable that anyone would produce a scholarly edition using the equipment and procedures standard in the 1960s. Now, although the production of print editions from electronic data will probably never cease, it seems much more sensible to aim, from the beginning of research, at the larger possibilities of electronic publication for the full-scale scholarly work. It would be backward to aim now at a print scholarly edition because at almost every stage of preparing a print scholarly edition compromises are made and decisions are taken about what to leave out that do not have to be made for electronic editions. Instead of the compromise or the elision of material, in the electronic edition decisions have to be made about navigation – at what level and by what means will esoteric bits of information be accessible?

If one thinks of print editions as off-shoots from a major electronic knowledge-site project, one can think of them as targeted to specific audiences or markets, based on the best and fullest knowledge of textual matters but trimmed and shaped for specific users, particularly casual or student users, who deserve the best access to a work for their purposes.

But because we already have many valuable print scholarly editions and many editions in progress that were designed for print first, it is useful to think of the problems of conversion and even of using electronic products as supplements to already printed editions. For projects already begun as print editions, the process necessarily still proceeds from print to electronic form. Soon, however, that stage will be over.

Industry standards and modular structures

As mentioned above the only generally agreed upon industry standard for electronic scholarly editions to date is the TEI standard markup system. The World Wide Web and XML provide broad standards within which editors, programmers, and edition users currently provide or gain access to texts and related scholarship and within which they can develop and use tools for textual analysis and text manipulation. These qualify as standard in my definition simply because they apply across platforms and are used by many types of software. How these meetings will take place and how access will be achieved and how tools will be configured and deployed are all questions still being explored and answered only tentatively.

Though highly touted and potentially very serviceable, a serious down side of the XML (and HTML and SGML before it) standard is that it does not allow what is called overlapping hierarchies – that is, the ability to install two or more ways to structure and to look at the same work. For example, if one divides up a work by making the title, the chapters, the paragraphs, and the sentences serve as the units, one cannot then also divide up the work according to its material makeup – sheets, gatherings, leaves, and pages – because a paragraph may begin on one page and end on another. XML requires that one close everything that was opened in one category before opening a new one – if a paragraph opens on one page, it must be closed before closing the page and opening a new page on which the paragraph can continue, once reopened. This would not be a problem if everyone would just agree that an essay or a chapter consists of paragraphs and that their arrangement on pages is irrelevant – but we don't. Imaginative people have developed more or less clumsy ways around this limitation, but what is needed is a language and markup system that allows overlapping hierarchies. But the purpose of this section is not to berate the current system, but to imagine a technological environment and structure for presenting complex textuality in logical, clear, and user-friendly forms. Perhaps once it is imagined it can be built.

The disadvantage of industry standards, generally speaking, is that as research and development take place, regardless of the field, situations will arise in which one will want to do something that was not foreseen when the standards were set and that is not allowed by those standards. The advantage of standards, if they are flexible and versatile enough, is that they make it possible to share services and interchange parts without affecting the functionality of the whole or of other parts. A modular approach to the functions of an electronic edition/archive/knowledge site may help us achieve the flexibility and compatibility we want. An outline of the editorial and reader functions and the types of materials and sets of information that affect either the editing or the reading process is set out here as an indication of the areas for which software is needed. Much of the software already exists – that is, the ability of computers to handle the target tasks has already been demonstrated. Many of these solutions were developed in such a way that the basic materials of the edition/archive/ knowledge site could not be accessed and manipulated and added to or commented on without having to change from a PC to a Macintosh or Unix based platform and without having first to convert the text from XML or WORD to TEX or QUARK or something else in order to be able to run the software. Already the solutions thus developed, and new solutions to problems of access and manipulation of data, are being transformed as data (texts and commentary) have migrated to XML-encoded form and the tools have been altered to deal with such data in multiple platforms.

It may be worth repeating, before launching this overview, that I do not imagine any one reader will wish or be able to use or attend to all these parts at any one time. The point is to provide a place where different readers can satisfy differing demands at different times from the same set of basic materials[22] using an ever-developing suite of electronic tools.

---

[22] For a fuller argumentation of this point, see my *Scholarly Editing in the Computer Age*, 3rd edn. (Ann Arbor: University of Michigan Press, 1996), especially the chapter on Orientations.

It is also important to remember that this outline attempts to cover all forms that literary works take, and that any given literary work may lack some of the materials or its treatment may emphasize some parts over others. And some projects will begin with what its directors think most important and leave other parts to be developed by future scholars. The structure being imagined is open and extendable in all directions.[23]

Insufficient input has been brought to bear from studies of textuality and of how people either do or can read. We need a new profession to complement the professions of textual criticism and of electronic programming – to be found perhaps in the new field of informatics. It should be the profession of textual reception, exploring not only how people read and study texts but how they *could* study texts. Such a field of inquiry would develop a design for text presentation driven by how to create user-friendly access to all the materials and levels of signification inherent in textuality. Perhaps a department of computer humanities or humanities computing could house such a profession. My main point here, however, is not to imagine the mass development of readers or even one reader who would be interested in all the parts of an edition or knowledge site, but instead to imagine a heterogeneous readership wanting a variety of different things which can be accessed from a single but complex knowledge site providing access to a range of specific texts of a work and the tools to use them variously. The electronic scholarly "knowledge site" must be capable of handling every reader even though no single reader will handle all the capabilities of the knowledge site.

Materials, structures and capabilities

The chart below maps in the left column the range of materials and tools and relationships that a knowledge site needs to be capable of providing, and on the right the questions or actions readers might wish to undertake, as presented in the boxed questions on pages 92–3 above.

The challenge is to house the materials, to provide the interfaces and links that create a navigable web; to provide access in such a way that growth and development of the knowledge site is encouragingly easy; and to provide tools that allow individuals to personalize their own access to the work.

---

[23] It is not a criticism of this overview to point out that it provides space for materials or information that one or another critical approach finds unnecessary or even objectionable. It would be a weakness of the system if a category of material or analysis that someone wished to have was impossible to provide.

I Textual foundations

Basic data
Material evidence
Transcriptions of documentary data: ms and print texts
Digitized images of same

Readers should be able to read each extant document in isolation and in full, either as a transcription or as a digitized image or both.

Inferred data
Transcriptions of critically developed data, edited texts
Digitized image of designed pages for new text

New critical editions of the text, not necessarily just one, should be available, in both a firmly formatted form (like a book [.pdf, for example]) and as a searchable transcription.

Internal data links
Collations: linking points of variance
Emendations for critically edited texts
Additional material facts (hyphenation, fonts, formats)

Readers should have access to variant forms – both image and transcript – regardless of which text they are currently reading. Facts about the documentary texts should be available.

Bibliographical analysis
Physical descriptions of manuscripts
Bibliographical description of printed editions, printings and states
Description of and histories of design, format, handwriting, typography, etc.

Readers can obtain information about the material production and manufacture of the physical objects that are the manuscript, proofs, and books containing the text.

Textual analysis
Descriptions of revisions sites
Explanations of convergence and divergence in texts
Provenance and textual histories
Identification of textual agency (who did what, where, when, how)
Genetic analysis: composition, revision, production, manipulation, censorship, appropriation, etc.

Provides information about the composition and revision of the work at every stage of its development, appropriation, or adaptation. Identifies, so far as possible, the agent of change and the time and place of change and any contextual information that would suggest motives for change.

II Contexts and progressions

Contextual data (individualized for each stage of textual existence)
Historical introductions
Biographical (for author, editors, composition, and publication)
Explanatory annotations
Verbal analysis – style, grammar, word choices, genre, etc.

Provides as much access to the "things that went without saying" but that affect the uptake of the text. Without this material, readers tend to make up or assume things which may not be relevant to the script act in hand.

Social, economic, political,
    intellectual milieu
Links to full text archives of letters,
    diaries, ancillary materials
InterTextuality
Links to sources, analogues,   Provides a guide to those works
    influences, coincidences, etc.   against which or in connection
           with which the present work was
           written

Linguistic analysis
Dialect   Linguistic and stylistic analysis
Use of italics for titles, ships,   provide explanations for
    emphasis, foreign words, etc.   unfamiliar usages.
Use of quote marks, ditto
Naming
Syntax structures

III Interpretive interactions

Reception history
Reviews and criticism   The history of the work's reception
Literary analyses   can give context to any reader's
    Narrative structure   own reaction to the work.
    Genre
    Ideologies of gender, race, region,
       religion, politics, etc.
Cultural analyses
Adaptations
Translations   Provides the history of
Abridgments   transmutations of the work – in
Plays   description at least if not full text.
Radio adaptations   Capability for audio and motion
Movies   pictures needs to be available.
Other appropriations

IV User enhancements

New markup   Readers/scholars can introduce new
       analysis markup to the texts
Variant texts   Readers can emend and create new
       versions by mixing historical
       variants or introducing new
       emendations
New explanatory notes,   Readers can add information to the
   commentary   system
Personal note space   Readers can make notes and import
       quotations of text, audio, and still
       or motion images.

II PRACTICAL PROBLEMS

How will it be financed?

It was not my intention to analyze the costs or suggest a way to finance this approach. Rather, I wanted to analyze how script acts work so as to identify more broadly and deeply the desires and needs of readers and students of literature and to imagine the environments made possible by electronic representations in which such "thick engagements with texts" could take place. However, if the costs were so prohibitive and the mechanisms for support of the system so inadequate as to make the whole enterprise an exercise in science fiction, it would scarcely be worth our attention. What follows may or may not prove useful as a way to think about financing.

It appears to me that the financial considerations have four components that can be taken up separately but which in the end must be seen as coordinated or capable of being coordinated.

The first category involves IT development of software, coordination of software, maintenance of knowledge site computer files, and the never-ending need to migrate the system and its contents to new and better technology and to drop off discontinued technology. Dissemination methodology belongs here, though other aspects belong in category four. This category has both personnel and infrastructure equipment expenses.

A second category involves the scholarly development of the materials of each knowledge site, with its extensive bibliographical, textual, interpretive and interweaving, and proofreading and beta-testing tasks. This category has personnel, travel, photographic, and personal equipment expenses.

A third category involves the problem of review, refereeing, or gateway tasks that separate the wheat from the chaff and ensure the quality of knowledge site content. This category involves personnel and communication expenses.

A fourth category involves permission fees, copyrights, and royalties. In order for a knowledge site to make unique primary materials and copyright materials available for access, libraries, publishers, authors, and anyone with a vested interest in materials and the power to withhold that material must be addressed pragmatically – which probably means fees rather than just appeals to goodwill toward the intellectual community. Dissemination by some financially feasible scheme belongs here, though its technical logistics belong in category one.

Two points are worth making at the outset. The first is that the world of knowledge in print has found ways to finance the analogous categories of expenses: the world of publishing has invested and recovered enormous sums in printing and graphics equipment; the world of scholarship has supported large and small research projects that include most if not all the kinds of investigation needed for knowledge site creation; the world of academe in conjunction with publishers has created wide-ranging networks of referees and gateways to uphold the quality of scholarship; and the world of libraries, archives, book and manuscript collection, and copyrights have all learned to live with the financial arrangements that make their existence possible. Finally, in addition to the commercial aspects of this vast network of print-knowledge development and maintenance, there is the world of governmental, institutional, and private funding that is constantly adding financial support to the world of knowledge.

The first point, then, is that these worlds will all continue to play crucial roles when forms of re-presentation for scholarly work under the rubric "knowledge site" become electronic instead of print. These "worlds" support knowledge, knowledge generation, and knowledge dissemination. The fact of print, like the fact of electronic representation, has to do with medium not substance. What looks like the sale of a physical book is in fact the sale of text with intellectual value. It may be true that some publishers can sell physical books with false or inferior textual value, but that fact is not relevant to the world of knowledge – except perhaps as an irritation. The *quality* of real knowledge is the bread and butter of real publishing. Real publishers, real libraries, and real scholars are committed first to the quality of knowledge. But they must be financially sustainable.

The second point is that for the development and maintenance of electronic knowledge sites with democratic access (i.e., affordable to most people), a pricing system different from that current in the book and database world probably needs to be devised. Rather than the sale and purchase of a book at a given price, rather than the periodic payment of a subscription fee, and rather than the payment of a one-time or periodic license fee for receiving materials or for access gained to otherwise closed databases, a different approach is needed.

Academic institutions and funding agencies as well as the small world of scholarly editors have all failed as yet to come up with a full-scale solution to the complex problem of funding, training, development, maintenance, and distribution of large scholarly projects. Of course there are spectacular exceptions: the *Cambridge Bibliography of English Literature*, the *Dictionary of National Biography*, the *Oxford English Dictionary*. There are also spectacular success stories in the building of collections of materials – hundreds of collection successes in world-famous libraries. But from the democratic student/scholar's point of view these wonders are accessible in a limited number of places on earth, and for them the lack of funds to acquire collections or to travel to collections restricts access to written and printed knowledge.

The infrastructure and social system that would provide and maintain the personnel required and the long-term support that would make real progress in electronic knowledge sites possible has not coalesced. What is needed is the community of scholarship that over hundreds of years has developed around printed knowledge to conjoin in the development of electronic knowledge sites. Like small villages growing together into great cities, the boundaries of knowledge sites can merge and interact. It is a project for all scholars in document-based disciplines working together – as they always have – in conjunction with the existing support systems found in funding agencies, academic publishing, and library systems. But the primary focus needs to shift from the publication, dissemination, and maintenance of books, to the construction of electronic knowledge sites. For this to work a new player is needed – major world-class browsers, searchers, and linking systems capable of unlimited growth, lightning speed, endless maintenance, and world-wide distribution or access – for profit. It must be for profit, just as book publication is for profit; for, if it fails to maintain itself, it will fail the world of knowledge and scholarship.

All our textual production skills for the best part of the last 500 years have been devoted to print media and much of what has so far been done in electronic form consists of porting from print to electronic equivalents. The exploration of what can be done has been driven by photography, the movie industry, and librarianship. The exploration of how it can generate self-sustaining revenue has been driven by the history and practice of book production and sale. To me, the most likely development for revenue is not material sales or subscriptions but user fees. Licenses or the sale of CDs or database access do not reflect value received nor use generated; they involve a priori predictions of possible use value. But since accounting systems for tracking hits and charging "subscribers" are now well-developed technologies, pennies or half-pennies per hit, generated the world over, would enable libraries to provide their patrons with access to a much more comprehensive and useful electronic repository of knowledge than any single library, no matter how big, could afford to purchase and house. And royalties to contributing publishers, libraries, and scholars would also be tracked and paid based on use, rather than purchase or initial one-time fees. Actual use, not estimated value would drive the revenue. Users would always have access to sites in their most developed and updated form and would not be stuck with last year's purchase. And because contributions to the knowledge sites would have to be vetted by the world of scholarship, the materials in the sites would, for the most part, be more reliable than that which could be found on the Internet at large. Very large libraries with extensive holdings and large numbers of users would, by this system both pay a great deal in use fees and receive a great deal in royalty payments from the world-wide access to their own unique materials. Such payments would continue for as long as they continued to own the originals. Publishers and authors would stand to earn use fees for as long as their copyrights were valid. Small use-fees from all over the world would very likely exceed the income now generated by sale of books to a limited number of libraries.

It is worth pointing out that this system is compatible with open source and free access to knowledge sites in that no fee need be charged for access to materials that are not in copyright, not unique, or which have been donated to the public domain. The fee system would kick in only when a user tries to access protected information. At that point, the fee would be small enough to deter only misers and the indigent.

Other scenarios have been tried or suggested; many are now in place. My point is not that I have found the best or even a feasible structure, but rather that it appears possible to create a complex, comprehensive, world-wide, electronic representation of knowledge sites that are financially self-sustaining, and, thus, that can be developed, maintained, and function for many years – perhaps as many as Gutenberg's 500 years and counting.

Some language and software solutions

Despite its shortcomings, TEI conformant XML is currently the best language and markup for transcriptions and other text materials. Its primary shortcomings have been identified and revisions have been promised. Markup, for those to whom the concept might be unfamiliar, consists of a system of tags or marks associated with sections or parts or items in a text file. If a text file at its simplest consists of a stream of letters, spaces, and punctuation, markup provides identifiers so that various sorts of software can do a variety of things with the texts: identifying fonts (italics, etc.), formats (headings, indentations, footnotes, links, etc.), features (phonological, morphological, lexical, etc.), and a whole variety of associated items (variant texts, annotations, instructions, etc.). Markup can be rudimentary or rich; it can be solely bibliographical or linguistic or historical or it can relate to formats; or it can be a mixture of these. Different software accessing the same marked-up files might focus attention on some tags and ignore or simply be unable to "see" other tags.

Imaging, for the present time, has to be described in terms of its goals because the options are too many. What is wanted is high enough resolution to make the image at least as readable as the original; tests have shown that some electronic images are more readable than the originals. Color is wanted that will be represented with fidelity on different computer screens. Reproductions of reproductions may have to be considered, but folk wisdom and technical knowledge suggests that images made from originals would be better. Regardless of the solution, temporary though it may be, users have the right to know what was used as the basis of the image (an original or a reproduction) and what process was used that might have altered the appearance of the object on display. This includes knowing whether the image is of the text only or of the object (manuscript or book) upon which the text is printed. No one, it can be assumed, will be so naive as to mistake even a high resolution reproduction for the real thing. When they have seen a virtually real reproduction of the Rosetta Stone, they will not say they have seen the thing itself.

Software to collate texts has existed since the early 1970s, the best known and most versatile for scholarly editing being PC-CASE, MacCASE, and COLLATE. The latter two also provide mechanisms for creating links among variant texts. Other collation programs display variants but have yet to be coordinated with other processes for editing, such as the one developed for the John Donne Variorum (http://donnevariorum.tamu.edu/down/downpage.htm). Juxta is a more complex collation program still in development (http://www.nines.org/tools/tools.html).

ANASTASIA is to my knowledge the most versatile presentation software yet developed for scholarly editions. It gives access to images and transcripts of documents, links between variant documents, full textual apparatus, introductions, and explanatory notes. Less well developed at this point is JITM (Just In Time Markup). It incorporates text collation on the fly, a text authentication mechanism, and it enables an enhancement-markup capability for readers. JITM is modular and provides a kind of flexibility of approach that gives readers control over the materials, but its potentials are not fully realized and its user interface still (in 2004) leaves much to be desired. Numerous projects in process of development employ XML with newly designed interfaces (what one sees on the screen and how one selects from menus and links) to incorporate experimental ways to present scholarly editions.[24]

A consortium of scholars interested in the works of Friedrich Nietzsche has developed a suite of programs called HyperNietzsche, in which to house, link, and make basic texts and scholarship available for free. Its mark-up system, a variant of SGML with elements of TEI conformancy, and its networking system are currently tied to a concept of "open source" which requires that copyright be abandoned by all in exchange for copyleft to insure free access by all users. The software developed, the concept of how knowledge can be "constructed" from primary materials through multiple kinds of cultural and scholarly added value are in line with the principles developed in this book. Whether or not the participants can make the system work for free and endure through time remains to be seen. Its health is dependent on grant funding and the goodwill of the participants. As this project grows to serve the development of knowledge sites other than Nietzsche, its name will become HYPER, HyperResearch, and HyperLearning.

Eric-Olivier Lochard's ARCANE is a comprehensive, yet closed, system developed primarily for historical editions. It gives access to individual documents, provides for user enhancement for added commentary; is far more creative than any other system I've seen in its use of charts, mapping, and chronological progressions; and anticipates multiple forms for output to screen, to paper, and to files in various forms: .tex, .pdf, .doc, etc. However, it has no means of identifying variant texts.

These do not add up to the solution that is needed, nor, indeed, do I believe that a single comprehensive software solution is desired. These programs are among the most promising approaches because they are based on visions for scholarly uses, and they demonstrate some of the ways electronic editions can do more, and more conveniently, than print editions could. It is important to let individual projects develop according to the nature of their materials and the approaches to knowledge that they

---

[24] See Bibliography, below, particularly for the Nietzsche Project (D'Iorio et al.), Alexandra Brown-Rau's *King Lear* prototype, Dirk Van Hulle's Samuel Beckett project (as yet only demonstrated as a prototype); Marcel De Smedt and Edward Vanhoutte, *Stijn Streuvels, De Teleurgang van den Waterhoek. Elektronisch-kritische editie/Electronic-Critical Edition* (Amsterdam: Amsterdam University Press/KANTL, 2000 [CD-Rom]); Kevin Kiernan's Beowulf and Boethius projects.

find valuable for some time yet to come before any attempt is made to invent the cookie-cutter that all projects must conform to. But they should be encouraged to develop modularly, with more attention to the ways in which the bits and pieces of the edition can stand alone and especially to the idea that the text produced should be able to be adapted by others for other uses. There seems hope in the idea that what is needed is a front-end interface for users that will allow them to access multiple knowledge sites in a way that helps them past the problems inherent in the fact that each project uses a different markup language or structures its content files in different ways.

New and legacy projects

In this transition time, when electronic forms are challenging the reign of the "print book," scholarly editors divide into two different groups defined by the problems they face in developing electronic editions. One group, seasoned editors or inheritors of the legacy research materials of such editors, will already have many files of relevant texts in forms not yet ready for an electronic site, not yet properly marked for posting and perhaps not fully proofread and corrected. The other group, editors with new projects, faced with research materials wholly in print or manuscript form, need to develop computer readable files, and find analysis tools and file-manipulation tools appropriate for mounting an electronic site. Eventually, perhaps, the latter may be the only kind of scholarly editor, but I address first the problems faced by editors who already have computer text files developed for print or archival purposes. There is a surprising amount of carry-over value from the procedures developed for such projects for use with new projects. And many new editors will find that regardless of how many versions they intend eventually to post in full-text, and particularly for long prose fiction works, there are reasons to create, during the research phase, a preliminary archive of text files to enhance collation and quality control. Such files, like the legacy files of older editions, will then need later to be converted and marked for electronic site presentation.

Neither group has the luxury yet of a set of tools that will render unproblematic the process of electronic scholarly editing. The first task of scholarly editing is always a bibliographical project – finding original materials – a global search for unique as well as multiple copies. The full extent of *intra*-edition variation within and amongst multiple printings of any edition (copies produced from the same setting of type) must be determined – a task for which computers are practically useless, but which is enhanced by Hinman Collators, Lindstrand Comparators, and other optical devices such as the ones developed by Randall McCleod.[25] For detecting *inter*-edition variations, computers are very helpful – essential, really. But relevant texts must first be rendered as computer files – by typing, and/or scanning (more probably *and* than *or*, because most scholarly editors want image files as well as text files for display, and because scanning is still more error prone, though cheaper, than the work of competent typists). Text files must be proofread to ensure that they accurately reflect the source texts – by sight collation or computer comparison using products like COLLATE or PC-CASE or Mac-CASE or some other text comparison computer program designed to produce variants in a form easily converted to a presentation format, revealing and analyzing the relations among the variant forms of the work.[26]

A survey of truly sophisticated experimental electronic editions (excluding amateur productions such as found in Project Gutenberg and Chadwyck-Healey's poetry projects) reveals that most of them provide at least one unique capability not found in the others. And, because each is either tied to a particular type of software or hardware or because of the general limitation that still prevents fully-fledged full-function editions, the result is that, at the moment, no matter what course one takes, scholarly principles must be compromised with the result that some need or desire to provide some facet or other of the work will be sacrificed. In this sense, the situation for electronic editions resembles the limitations of print editions. One can still hope that in the future this will be less so, but one cannot help musing over the hype that has proclaimed electronic editing the panacea rescuing editors from the straitjacket of print editions. I think it is necessary and important to sound this practical and dis-couraging note because of the inflated claims of some enthusiasts for

---

[25] Optical collation is conducted with multiple copies of what appear to be identical books, the products of a single setting of type or, possibly, a new setting that apes a previous edition line for line. The discovery of stop-press corrections and variants between printings is best conducted by optical collation. The machines mentioned allow one to see two books at once in such a way as to highlight variation. Thus, a full page can be collated and all differences found in about two or three seconds.

[26] Some researchers, acting before thinking, have thought it clever to type or scan one text and then save the time and effort of typing or scanning additional exemplars that require collation, using instead the first text and emending it to reflect the differences they see in other texts. Because that procedure depends on human detection of differences, the computer is rendered useless as a collation device capable of cross validating human collation. Each material text must be transcribed separately in order for machine collation to discover variants that sight collation misses.

electronic editions. Yes, they are better. No, they are not good enough. And one reason is that a full vision of what is wanted has not been articulated either clearly or effectively. Perhaps not enough people yet want it; but in 1975 few people knew they wanted a desktop computer, and in 1991 who wanted a DVD player?

To some extent the composition and production materials that have survived for any given written work identify and delimit the editorial treatment most appropriate in handling the work and developing the electronic edition, but editors have a great many choices to make as well, and they will do so more thoughtfully and effectively if they have explored their options well. Editing is not a straightforward task, even in the hands of the most ignorant or unselfconscious or single-minded of editors. Works like Jerome McGann's *A Critique of Modern Textual Criticism* (1983), and *The Textual Condition* (1991) or like my own *Scholarly Editing in the Computer Age* (1996) and *Resisting Texts* (1997) explore the effects on editing resulting from a variety of assumptions about what a written work is and how the editor is to construct it and how the reader is to interact with it. David Greetham's *Theories of the Text* does not give any practical advice about how to edit texts, but it explores, so it seems, every conceivable implication and failing inherent in the ways that have been used to edit. Anyone embarking on an editorial project in English from the early modern period to the present without a working knowledge of these works of scholarship or the tradition of essays on editing in *Studies in Bibliography* and *TEXT: An Annual of Textual Scholarship* may well be an editor but more than likely is not a scholarly one.

These "prerequisites," so to speak, are all implied or stated in the "Guidelines for Electronic Scholarly Editions" put out by the Modern Language Association's Committee on Scholarly Editions (see n.18). Undergirding those guidelines also is the belief that for the complexity of presentation demanded by full-scale scholarly editions and for the long-range portability and survival of editorial work, editors should adopt the standards and procedures embodied in TEI (Text Encoding Initiative) for preparing SGML, XML, or comparable file markup. Editors starting from scratch can choose tools that already have these standards in view when they begin the tasks of rendering into electronic files the bibliographic forms that will eventually occupy the edition's electronic site. I cannot over-stress the importance for new editors that they explore the whole range of problems and tools needed, from the gathering of original editions, through their analysis by collation and annotation, to the final presentation on an electronic site. Failure to survey in detail every step of the process in advance will lead to grief over the production of files that lack some key component or that must go through some extra step of file conversion. Time spent planning the steps of the research and processes for mounting the electronic site will be time saved from wasted efforts and from the wasteful use of tools that produce incompatible results. Editors with legacy files from projects not originally designed for electronic presentation have now to face the problems created by the fact that they did not foresee an electronic site as the end product of their work. Their problems, as we shall see, are more complex than that of mere file conversion to TEI conformant XML.

A division of labor

Every scholarly editor and every publisher of scholarly editions, whether in book form or electronic, has a different experience base from which to assess or plan the steps in the process and to determine who does what. Some very elaborate and impressive projects have been accomplished primarily by one person who was editor, designer, programmer, and desktop publisher. Other projects involve teams of editors, expert programmers, webmasters, design specialists, and publishing houses that do a range of production tasks from copy-editing, file conversion, typesetting, and book or CD manufacturing to publishing, distributing, advertising, and marketing the end products.

This range of tasks suggests that any one editor's or publisher's practical experience is limited and that advice from any one source is similarly limited. Editors and publishers who have experience with many scholarly editions may well start with an aspect of scholarly editing frequently treated as a taboo subject: the money. It is not just the money to do the research, to travel to archives, to transcribe documents, to create image files, to proofread, to markup files, to compare texts, to compile all the data and then to prepare an edition, or an archive/edition, or a knowledge site; it is also the business of vetting the results, having third, fourth, or fifth pairs of eyes to check for accuracy, coherence, and usability. And then there are production expenses including the publisher's overhead. Even as a one-man desktop publication, it were folly to think that a scholarly edition could ever break even; it is first of all a labor of love and then of grants and subsidies.

And it is not just the money. Think for a moment about the support structures, the infrastructure, the institutions that support print scholarship. It is universities, individual departments, computing centers, internal and external funding, publishing houses, refereeing systems, marketing systems. And last but not least, libraries where the products of the print industry are maintained for decades and centuries. None of that was developed with electronic publishing in mind. The people, the institutions, the shared notion of the continued value of electronic editions are just developing. And by comparison with books, which when printed are relatively stable when unattended on a shelf, electronic editions are both subject to continued upgrading and subject to absolutely sure degradation through neglect.

But one should not be discouraged. The existence of hundreds of scholarly editions both completed and in progress suggests that there is enough love and sometimes enough grants and subsidies to get the job done. And yet I do not know of any project that has not compromised in some way between the ideals of the project and the practical necessities governed by money. To some extent this book is an exploration of ideals rather than practicalities – an effort to see what could or should be done, rather than advice about what to do now or what is done now. But one cannot ever forget the pressures to compromise, among which finances stands perhaps as paramount.

Editorial problems: a case study

As an example of the problems faced by an editor in the modern period of English literature, I offer my own experiences of preparing an edition of William Thackeray's works. The purpose is to give practical life to the abstractions of the foregoing description of aims and problems in creating an electronic knowledge site. It also reveals my own limitations as I try to deal with a topic and an opportunity of whose importance I am convinced and whose complexity is such that neither I nor anyone I have yet met or read has a sufficient breadth of knowledge to deal with adequately. It can be skipped without losing the theoretical structure for my arguments.

In summary, the Thackeray Edition Project in its aim to produce a print scholarly edition already had:

1 Working electronic files of the manuscripts and of every other relevant historical document. Some of these files were fully proofed and updated; others still contained transcription errors in the files, though their existence was documented in the working papers.

2 Collation files showing variants among the historical texts.
3 Electronic historical collations of all authoritative texts.
4 An electronic file of the newly edited critical text.
5 An electronic list of emendations in the new critical text.
6 Electronic files of historical and textual introductions.

In the case of the Thackeray edition and of a number of projects that used some version of CASE, all these are ASCII files, marked either by CASE-conformant mnemonic codes or by typesetting codes.

In short, from the point of view of one wishing to create an electronic archive, what we have is a rich mess. Only two or three text files for each volume in the edition were of "export quality" – the diplomatic transcription of the manuscripts, the transcription of the historical document chosen as copy-text, and the text of the critical edition. Files for other texts existed but were not fully corrected.

The producer of an electronic edition/archive faces a very different set of demands from those faced by print editors. These demands can be categorized by the stages of work required for anyone wanting to port the Thackeray edition files, or similar legacy files, into a web environment conforming to the demands of XML/SGML and TEI. And this task is not so simple as converting files from one form to another, which might be done automatically with a conversion program. To do so would produce XML files with the same limitation and errors of the original files.

Constructing an edition

The first category of problems is the one facing all editors who long for a comprehensive answer to the question: How should an electronic scholarly edition/archive be constructed? There is no compelling answer: there is no browser that has built-in capacities to handle variant texts, variant images, good user interface, proper deployment and presentation of ancillary materials such as annotations, links to off site resources, links to moving pictures and audio, and that also maintains for the user a clear sense of where one is in a tree of knowledge offering the fruits of an expanded/expanding notion of textuality. And to my knowledge only one relevant software package, JITM, incorporates a repetitive self-check to verify that updates have not corrupted the text inadvertently. And only two, that I know of, offer readers any significant role in interacting with the edition/archive to either enhance it or personalize it by shaping it to the needs of the user's own research and projects. There is not yet a good answer to the question: Whose software should one use? There isn't even a standard answer to the question: What file structure or tree structure should be used for files of basic texts so that the variety of next-wave text software will know where to find the textual grist for its mills?

TEI conformant XML (or, formerly, SGML) anticipates the development of adequate browsers and forefends the obsolescence of one's work by maintaining basic file markup that is easily exchanged between platforms and software.[27] Such sweeping assurances are, however, small comfort to WWW novices who see a formidable new user-unfriendly system to be understood and mastered in order to make possible the shift from legacy forms to SGML or XML-TEI. It is important to acknowledge that scholarly editors deep in the intricacies of textual criticism of an author's works find TEI and XML an irritating distraction and that IT experts glorying in the capabilities of electronic wonders usually do not take the time to understand the demands of textual critics and the intricacies of editorial theory. Enervating to those who have some understanding of both fields is the fact that fully functional SGML browsers were first promised some ten years ago, and now there are none. The brave new world seems always to fall on its face just at the moment of fulfillment, usually due to the obsolescence of some temporary feature in the prototype editions on offer.

And yet, if one is not to grow old and die while waiting for the new standards to sort themselves out and for the development of an integrated series of fully-capable editorial tools, one must embrace what we have, which is TEI and a score of stand-alone and frequently incompatible tools from which to cobble together the electronic editions currently within our reach. But our goal should be a score of stand-alone and fully compatible tools able to be used with a growing number of knowledge sites built around individual literary works. No one is likely to produce a comprehensive software solution, but together we can form a community of interchangeable modules in a flexible, expandable structure of software and edition constructions.

Translating legacy files

The second category of problems for porting CASE-conformant legacy files to TEI-conformant WEB files is the conversion process replacing the

---

[27] The most accessible presentation of this concept that I have read is Michael Sperberg-McQueen's "Textual Criticism and TEI" at http://xml.coverpages.org/sperb-mla94.html.

mnemonic codes and typesetting codes of their original designs with the TEI codes of a new design. That is not a one-to-one conversion process, as no doubt is already clear to most editors. The codes needed for CASE or other collation processes and for typesetting in the print world were conceived of as relating to the way texts *look*, i.e., formatting and fonts. The codes now needed for the web world need to be conceived of as relating to the ways in which texts *function*, i.e., semantic significance, and how they are structured. Where originally, for example, coding indicated 12 points of indentation following 2 points of extra vertical space, coding now needs to distinguish the beginning of an extract from the beginning of a letter or a poem or a list or some other form of text that functions or is structured in a particular way, and which, by the way, usually follows vertical space and is indented. Differentiation of function is required where before attention focused on what it looked like. Whereas a single italics code was used for all italicized words, it is now desirable to indicate whether the italicized passage functions as a book title, foreign words, a ship's name, emphasis, or some other function. The difference is not an easy one because the coding of appearance in context has been so integral to our ability to read that appearance and function often seem to be the same thing. The purpose of differentiating similar things is, as always in scholarly analysis, to let us see things more clearly, not to render them completely understood.

In some ways, such conversions are trivial. There is usually in the original file a marker where a marker is needed. But the marker is the wrong one, or it is used in two or three places that now must be distinguished from one another, or it exists distinguishably at the beginning of the passage to which it applies but only generically at the end, thus making it impossible just to search and replace.

Quality upgrades

The third category of problems for porting legacy files or new working files to the WWW is the need to impose quality control on every file. Files that were working files that did not have to be finally corrected now become presentation files. Thus, for the Thackeray edition, for example, the files that were marked mnemonically and not updated after the final computer collation have now to be proofread and updated again to ensure that they accurately reflect the historical documents they represent. Their flaws are minor, and their flaws are noted in printouts, but in the existing files errors remain as little unmarked landmines. The files that were finally and fully proofread no longer have the mnemonic codes but now have typesetting codes. Any program written to convert the coding of one set of files will have to be rewritten to apply to the other sets of files.

The question is: Is all that worth doing? or at least that was the question for me. I suppose each person answers it somewhat differently, but for me the answer was "No, not until the way forward is more clearly mapped and not until the conversion process becomes routine." Of course, neither of those things happens on its own. So, I pursued two separate efforts, each, one could say, ideologically opposed to the other.

Two electronic solutions

The first was to hire a computer literate research assistant and try to guide him through the process of converting into XML the legacy file used in typesetting *The Newcomes* – a file coded for typesetting using TEX. My sense of the formidableness of the conversion process derives from my layman's relation to TEI-XML, though I am quite comfortable with TEX. The fundamental idea of this effort was that the XML product should not only "contain" all the information already contained in the print scholarly edition but that additional enrichment markup should be added as opportunity arose. Furthermore, the form of ported information should be adapted to the strengths of the new medium. Thus, for example, if the print edition had textual revisions reported as footnotes, the XML version would have them as links. And if the print edition failed to report the bibliographical features of the work's historical source texts (because the expense outweighed the perceived benefits), that was no reason why such information could not be coded and added to the XML version.

The resulting file, as the experience of others has also shown, grew in size and messiness and diminished in verifiable accuracy. Of course we had been told that such would be the result, but for us it was a training course. It is important for any builder of an electronic text file to be aware of the potential not only for messiness but for serious integrity failure in this process. Because each enhancement of the presentation file is done on the same file, every act of enhancement has the potential to produce inadvertent change. Some form of verification is therefore required at each step of the way. Keeping back-up copies and logs of changes and running machine collations (see nn. 25 and 26) are among the ways that occurred to us, though there are probably far more sophisticated ways of which I am unaware. The dual problems of converting TEX to XML by hand and maintaining textual integrity led me to conclude this process was hopelessly flawed. Perhaps my experience will save others from learning the hard way.

The second effort is the more instructive one, though it too remains unsatisfactory. It involves the Just In Time Markup (JITM) system, developed by Phill Berrie at the Australian Defence Force Academy branch of the University of New South Wales.[28] Its ideology is quite different from the single, growing, messy, enriched XML file approach. Before proceeding I should acknowledge that the ways in which JITM frames the problems of electronic scholarly editing are not currently widely accepted and that its methods of constructing solutions is also not widely accepted. However, my experience of it convinces me that its opponents have much to learn from it. As in most fields, the competition for shelf space leads enthusiasts to exaggerate the shortcomings of approaches ideologically opposed to their own. I present what follows as a possible temporary solution that has great appeal to me as a textual critic because it focuses on the integrity of the editorial work, not because it offers beauty or dexterity of presentation at this point in its development. To me the important point is not the solution but the demonstration of scholarly care for details that matter.

Although JITM is still in developing stages (and what comprehensive system is not?), its design addresses a full range of scholarly interests from the textual to the explanatory and to the illustrative. In JITM the primary concern is for the "text itself" and the ways in which text is transcribed. But it is not by design committed to any particular pre-conception about texts that would limit it, say, to the preservation of a particular source document's rendition of the words and punctuation, the fonts such as italics and boldface, and the formatting such as block indentations and letter salutations and closings. Often scholars interested in the historicity or authenticity of texts are concerned with the provenance and variance of texts, their sources and their composition, revision, transcription, and production histories. JITM can, of course, accommodate such concerns, but it can also be used by scholars whose primary interests lie in linguistics or in historical or thematic concerns. Its facilities accommodate concern for explanatory annotations of obscure or dated materials that will help modern readers to understand the conventions and contexts of the time when the texts were created, revised, or reproduced, and it facilitates additional uses that can be made of literary and historical texts

---

[28] See http://idun.itsc.adfa.edu.au/ASEC/aueledns.html and linked web-sites.

for the study of linguistics or of typographic or design history or the relation between verbal and visual materials.

JITM helps scholars address these concerns for research into texts, and it provides an environment for Internet presentation of the texts and the scholarship by providing:

1 A durable home for text files and for scholarly enhancements;
2 A system for verifying continued accuracy of texts through multiple uses and multiple enhancements;
3 A file structure and coding system designed to enable migration of texts to future systems and migration of scholarly added-value from current systems to future systems;
4 A series of two-step interactive conversion tools enabling migration of legacy text files and legacy text enhancements from older projects into the JITM environment;
5 A text-relational tool (i.e., a collation system) that allows instant identification of variation among versions of texts; and
6 Text annotation systems to house all kinds of scholarly enhancements and analysis of texts, from textual and explanatory to linguistic and other analytical studies.

For the Thackeray project, had items 2 and 4 alone been in this list, it would have made JITM an attractive electronic tool. Item 2 offers a systematic approach to the problem of text integrity and item 4 provides a systematic way to make the extensive electronic archive of research texts and print-edition files available, at least for basic quasi-representation in Internet form. The rest of the functions of JITM make it one of the world's most versatile and forward-looking electronic text-handling systems.

The way JITM handles text files is to divide our interests in texts into categories so that relevant information is kept separately and provided on demand. A functional, base, ASCII text file with only the most funda-mental textual "content" (i.e., letters, punctuation, and spaces) is extracted and used as the basis upon which a variety of representations of the work can be built on demand or just in time. This base text is also represented by a mathematical formula invoked after each use of the base text to ensure that no changes have been made inadvertently. Upon its importation into JITM for the first time, SGML or XML markup is extracted and placed in parallel files or overlay files. Each markup file represents a category of interest in the work and can be selected separately or in tandem with other categories by a user who desires to see the text as rendered by and for those interests. Thus, a person interested in the first edition of the work would select a historical and representational set of markup to create a perspective of the work representing the first edition. Someone else might be more interested in seeing that text as analyzed by a linguist and will select appropriate markup files to enhance that kind of interest. A user might select perspectives representing manuscripts, other historical editions, a critical edition, and might branch out from any text to annotations of various kinds.

To import legacy files into JITM, the conversion tools used to substitute TEI conformant SGML or XML codes must be used first, so that the added value already contained in the legacy files can be saved automatically for reuse. But once lodged in the JITM system, new added value markup can be provided at any time without fear of inadvertently destroying the integrity of previous work. These added markups can be selected or deselected at will by the user choosing the perspectives to be generated from the stored and accumulating data. A prototype edition of Marcus Clark's *His Natural Life* using JITM, though still under construction, provides a sense of how this form of presentation gives flexibility to users.[29]

JITM is not without faults: the tools associated with JITM are in developmental stages, and are neither user friendly nor elegant. A users' manual and help files were not yet ready in 2004. Interface design is inelegant and "clunky." But JITM has the potential to address all these problems. More importantly, it currently functions on a MacIntosh (Apple) computer, and it operates within the HyperCard Software environment. This means that JITM is fully functional as a tool only in the Mac world though to viewers it is available with any browser on the Internet. Furthermore, perspectives generated by JITM are savable, portable, and browse-able HTML, SGML, or XML files. They can be displayed on any web-browser.

As an unexpected benefit of its divided-file structure, JITM provides a preliminary way to deal with conflicting overlapping structural systems, a currently fatal weakness in the SGML-XML implementations. In cases where the selection of multiple markup files results in a perspective in which there would be conflicting overlapping structures, the user will be informed of this fact and given a choice of viewing first one and then another perspective because XML is unable to use both at once. Either form can be saved for separate use.

[29] See http://idun.its.adfa.edu.au/publications.html.

As an editor with thirty years of experience in scholarly editing and computer use, however, I will not invest very heavily into final presentation forms of an electronic edition/archive until the problems inherent in the current capabilities have been better addressed. SGML/ XML needs revamping or replacement to allow multiple overlapping structures. Likewise, the way transcribers describe textual elements and deploy them (either as structural hierarchies or as one-off entities) in order to skirt this, SGML limitation needs to be carefully thought through because kluged (i.e., clever, ersatz) solutions within the limitations of SGML, developed as "temporary fixes," are likely to haunt us when a markup system that recognizes and enhances overlapping structures becomes functional.

The example of William Thackeray's works

The editorial problems posed by William Thackeray's prose works and the strategies for dealing with them – collecting original documents, collating, emending, constructing apparatuses to show textual histories and identify those responsible for them, deploying these materials both at the foot of text pages and in appendices, and verifying the accuracy of the work – have been the business of a major editorial project begun in 1976 and resulting, to date, in eight volumes published between 1989 and 2005. Of a projected twenty-three-volume print edition, only eleven will be published as books, unless someone sees a need for a book form of the "volumes" in the remainder of the edition. The editorial policies, the arguments supporting them, the changes in both policy and method of deployment, and the processes for achieving comprehensive coverage of materials and accuracy of research and edition preparation are amply discussed in the textual introductions to the published volumes and are not rehearsed here.[30]

The Thackeray edition, like dozens of other scholarly editorial projects involving prose fiction, has accumulated millions of bytes of text files representing manuscripts and historical editions as well as new critical scholarly editions. Our situation is, I believe, like that of other editors of print scholarly editions who have such files; for we face three serious tasks if we decide to create electronic web-based or CD-based editions/archives

---

[30] *Vanity Fair* (1989), *Henry Esmond* (1989), *Pendennis* (1991), *Yellowplush and Gahagan* (1991), *Newcomes* (1996), *Barry Lyndon* (1998), *Catherine* (1998) – the first four published by Garland; the latter three by University of Michigan Press.

of our projects. The first involves the significant enterprise of learning how to convert legacy text and apparatus files to TEI conformant SGML or XML, deciding what software to employ in that process, and working through the arguments about how to house the emergent text files so that they will be beautifully and usefully presentable and yet remain dexterously portable to future electronic environments. The second, related to that, is the task of making and then implementing the decisions about what functions and structures within the text are to be specially marked. This is a problem for all editors, new and old, for typists and scanners and print editions were never in the habit of or capable of analyzing for presentation the differences in function between one type of italics and another or between one type of quotation mark and another – for the expression of which there never was an opportunity until the capabilities of SGML/XML and TEI markup made it possible. Neither did they pay any attention to the conflicting overlap of bibliographical structures, organizational structures, and semantic structures – which were never conflicting until the limitations of SGML/XML made them so. The third task involves verifying the accuracy of the legacy text files that, in the world of print editions, dropped from interest and were left "unmaintained" once they had served their purposes in the research for the print scholarly edition.

William Makepeace Thackeray began publishing occasional pieces in London and Paris in the 1830s, came to fame with the publication of *Vanity Fair* in 1847–8, and died the author of eight major novels at age 52 in 1863. His works fill twenty-four substantial volumes.[31] His manuscripts, with some notable exceptions, are incomplete and tend to be scattered in a number of libraries in England and America.[32] They indicate that Thackeray, like many journalists, relied upon compositors to impose conventional punctuation and capitalization, but that he was a careful penman whose spelling required little or no checking. The manuscripts also show that, while most were written under the pressure of deadlines and are not heavily overwritten, Thackeray revised his work not only by adding and subtracting passages to adjust to prescribed lengths for serial

---

[31] There is no comprehensive bibliography. My checklist of Thackeray's books in the CBEL3 is supplemented by Edgar Harden's *A Checklist of Contributions by William Makepeace Thackeray to Newspapers, Periodicals, Books, and Serial Part Issues, 1828–1864*, No. 68 ELS Monograph Series. (Victoria, B.C.: English Literary Studies, University of Victoria, 1996).

[32] See Colby and Sutherland's census of Thackeray Manuscripts in *Costerus* n.s. 2 (1974), supplemented in the same issue by Lange and by various listings in *The Thackeray Newsletter*.

publications but also by rewriting sentences for sense, cadence, echoes of similar words, and myriad minor stylistic effects.

Thackeray was an artist as well as a writer, and much of his major fiction contains the work of both his pen and his pencil. For *Vanity Fair, The History of Pendennis* and other major novels, Thackeray drew vignette illustrations for chapter initials, and he drew illustrations of the novel's actions for drop-in illustrations in the text. Both of these types of drawings were produced as woodcuts. He also drew full-page illustrations on steel plates for reproduction on a different stock of paper to be inserted in each installment. The results are illustrated books unlike many illustrated novels, because one could argue that the "work of art" in so far as novels are works of art – consists of both text and illustration.[33]

My textual work on Thackeray is best represented by the four volumes of my edition that were published by Garland and, to date, the three additional volumes published by the University of Michigan Press. I have also written a history of the edition, tracing the changes in editorial theory, policies, and practice that have attended that work from 1969 to 1995 – a period in which five different publishers contracted for the edition and during which I wrote *Scholarly Editing in the Computer Age* primarily for the purpose of clarifying the changes that had to be made in the Thackeray edition to bring its policies and procedures up to date.[34] I also wrote *Pegasus in Harness: Victorian Publishing and W. M. Thackeray* to trace the financial and textual relations between Thackeray and his publishers.

I will not repeat any of those histories here, beginning instead with a brief description of the uses of electronic equipment and programs for that edition as a prelude to the considerations now under way to construct an electronic edition/archive for the works of Thackeray. The tale I tell may be somewhat more useful to editors of print scholarly editions who used the computer extensively for research and for production of camera-ready copy. But the principles involved in developing a match between the methods, technologies, and data gathering of the beginning

---

[33] The major discussions of Thackeray's illustrations are in Nicholas Pickwoad, "Commentary on Illustrations" in *Vanity Fair*, ed. Peter Shillingsburg (New York: Garland, 1989) and in *The History of Pendennis*, ed. Peter Shillingsburg (New York: Garland, 1991); J. R. Harvey, *Victorian Novelists and their Illustrators* (New York: New York University Press, 1971); Patricia Runk Sweeney, "Thackeray's Best Illustrator," *Costerus* n.s. 2 (1974), 84–111; and Anthony Burton, 'Thackeray's Collaborations with Cruikshank, Doyle, and Walker," *Costerus*, n.s. 2 (1974), 141–84.

[34] For an account of how editorial policies and funding developed for the edition see "Editing Thackeray: A History," *Studies in the Novel* 27 (Fall), 363–74; reprinted in *Textual Criticism and the Common Reader*, ed. Alexander Pettit (Athens: University of Georgia Press, 1999).

of the project with a clear view of the demands of the end product on an electronic site are important to all editors. The accumulated archive of legacy text files, useful temporarily in a project meant for print, might serve as the foundation for new electronic editions/archives – even though they may have insufficient and relatively primitive coding already embedded and though some of the files may not have been finally proof-read and corrected.

Some practical software problems

The scholarly edition of Thackeray's works is not unlike many editions undertaken in the 1960s through the 1980s in that it tried to adapt emerging electronic technology as rapidly as possible. The development of CASE (computer assisted scholarly editing) programs made it both possible and desirable to produce electronic files for each of the historical documents deemed authorial or potentially authorial.

I will skip over our experiences with punch cards and printers restricted to upper-case letters and graphic plotters adapted as printers with upper and lower case letters. The relevant factor is that we created machine-readable text files that have managed to migrate from punched card, through 9-track reel-to-reel tapes, to 8.5in., 5.25in., and 3.5in. floppy disks, and finally to the hard disks and CDs of today. Perhaps the luckiest accident of those early days was that our particular campus was dedicated to machines that had already chosen ASCII, rather than IBCIDIC, as the basic encoding language for verbal texts, because ASCII is still the basic language of TEI /SGML/XML.[35]

The development of CASE was also important to the electronic future of the Thackeray edition because its collation routines and its handling of diplomatic transcriptions of the manuscripts made it desirable to create computer transcriptions of each historical form of the work. CASE, supported by NEH and Mississippi State University, was adapted by a number of NEH funded editions in the USA and by others in Australia. Over time the programs were converted from their original electronic home in the PLi language of Univac computers to IBM, DEC10, and

---

[35] CASE, originally developed by Susan Follett as a Masters degree project, was revamped by Russell Kegley who added a total of nine routines for handling text files to enhance research and production of print scholarly editions on a UNIVAC mainframe. Boyd Nations ported the programs to PC-CASE and Phill Berrie adapted them to MacCASE. I do not know the names of the many other programmers involved in developing other versions for PRIME, DEC, and IBM mainframes.

PRIME mainframes, and then to PCs and Macs. Each conversion sloughed off some capabilities and developed new ones. But the important thing to note is that for each project, CASE made it desirable to produce computer readable ASCII files of each historical form of the work deemed to be of potential interest.

The capabilities and methods of CASE have been described in print elsewhere.[36] For our purposes, it is sufficient to know that for most projects, Computer Assisted Scholarly Editing consisted of three important concepts. First, the computer mechanisms for discovering, recording, and storing variant forms of the work and for discovering and listing the variants among those forms encouraged editors to create computer-readable transcripts of each potential source text – thus, CASE users already have electronic files for each different authoritative form of the work. Second, the process consisted of a progression of steps in which the output of one set of routines became, after verification and correction, the input of advanced routines in a series of steps that would culminate in the production of files used for typesetting the new edition text and apparatus. And third, the process from beginning to end incorporated verification and correction procedures tending to render the final product more accurate than had ever been true of old systems that relied only upon repeated proofreading.

However, there was, from the point of view of electronic archive/ edition builders, a serious flaw in the beauty of that three-part concept. The flaw consisted in seeing only one text – the one destined to drive the typesetting machines for the new edition – as the center of attention and full maintenance. All other computer texts were considered to be useful up to some point in the process after which they were left aside in a repository of stored files. Those mothballed files can now be seen as a legacy that might be refurbished, saving greatly on the amount of labor that would be required to start over from scratch. In retrospect it was too bad that some files in the scholarly process were deemed no longer useful and therefore not maintained or updated regularly; for, when one contemplates the electronic edition/archive of the future (a future which is already here), one sees the need for electronic files of each historically important form of the work.

---

[36] Miriam Shillingsburg, "Computer Assistance to Scholarly Editing," *Bulletin of Research in the Humanities* 81 (Winter 1978), 448–63; and Peter Shillingsburg, "The Computer as Research Assistant in Scholarly Editing," *Literary Research Newsletter* 5 (1980), 31–45.

CHAPTER 5

Victorian fiction: shapes shaping reading

Such dim-conceivéd glories of the brain
　　Bring round the heart an indescribable feud;
So do these wonders a most dizzy pain,
　　That mingles Grecian grandeur with the rude
Wasting of old Time – with a billowy main,
　　A sun, a shadow of a magnitude.

Keats, "On Seeing the Elgin Marbles
for the First Time" (1817)

Given the general, perhaps abstract, surveys of chapters three and four, about the complexity of script acts and problems of developing an electronic infrastructure to contain its knowledge sites, it is now time to turn to a different aspect of the complexities of moving print literature into electronic forms – to confront in one area the sheer enormity of and seemingly insurmountable obstacles facing such an enterprise. And yet, if the project is not conceived comprehensively and grandly, the results will fail to satisfy more from the failure to attempt a miracle than from its impossibility.

Much of literary theory and criticism of the past two or three decades has, perhaps ironically, been devoted to making us aware of our "situatedness" – of the ways in which our present time, our geographic and cultural place, our interests, our acknowledged and unacknowledged ideologies, and our personal experiences and skills or lack thereof limit, direct, and focus our critical insights and our sense of history. Without arguing against the concept that what we are we are, many historians and literary scholars have nevertheless tried to recoup historical perspectives because we see, at the very least, that attempts to collect and arrange evidence of the past provides a clear difference in perspective on and understandings of text from those that are produced when such attempts are not made. And if one feels a sense of the present as a strong influence on understanding, can their present have been less important to those generating the texts we now find important to read and study? And it is not just a sense of history that is essential to those of us who teach history and literature. Keats's sense of it before the Elgin Marbles is evoked not by the imagination but by the physical remains from the past. Books – original editions – convey significance by their age as well as their texts, though it is a factor impossible to capture in a modern paperback reprint.

To give a simple practical illustration of this sense of history one can imagine the kind of understanding and criticism brought to bear on Victorian fiction by a person who lacks such a sense – and I meet them all the time in my classrooms. Imagine readers of Victorian fiction – and you can substitute the literature of any genre and any period – who see only modern paperback editions, and who do not and have not read widely in Victorian writings of other kinds, such as domestic and military histories, philosophy, science, education, politics, industry, and exploration, which are readily found in the periodicals of the time. Clearly such readers can develop a very lively appreciation for Victorian fiction and will either skip the parts that are opaque to them or will make up adventitious inter-pretations, which from the limited perspective that generated them will be considered adequate and perhaps inevitable or even brilliant. If we suppose the ignorance of our imagined readers to be complete, having also failed to read modern works of criticism and history dealing with the Victorian period, we have before us a completely unfettered reader, engaging with a text untethered from its origins, and thus uninhibited from making up interpretations in reference to imaginary contexts, and, presumably, quite happy in this condition. Such readers are, of course, not ignorant of their own time, place, and personal, social, and political interests and experiences, nor are they entirely devoid of linguistic readerly skills, and from that perspective it appears that their reading experiences of Victorian fiction are quite satisfactory.

It may be impossible, except imaginatively, to posit an alternative, ideal reader with a sense of history adequate for the task of reading Victorian fiction from a fully knowledgable perspective; for, while the ignorant creature just imagined in the abstract does in fact exist in nearly over-whelming numbers, the ideal reader probably does not exist anywhere at all. Nigel Cross, writing about the Victorian "common writer," suggested in 1985 that "A glance at the annual list of literary thesis titles confirms that there is scant interest in more than a handful of nineteenth-century writers. Such a narrow focus betrays a fairly thorough ignorance of the social and economic conditions of authorship and publishing."[1] Twenty

[1] Nigel Cross, *The Common Writer* (Cambridge University Press, 1985), p. 1.

years later the situation has changed. John Sutherland's *Stanford* (or *Longman*) *Companion to Victorian Fiction* has focused attention on over 700 novelists of the period. The *New Cambridge Bibliography of English Literature*, 3rd edition, and the *New Dictionary of National Biography* are enlarging our access to novels and novelists formerly dismissed as minor. Indeed, the annual lists of dissertations is demonstrating that literary critical trends have responded practically to a shift away from categorizing writers as "major or minor" and from aesthetic appraisals, moving instead towards a less evaluative approach that emphasizes what might be called historical curiosity – an interest in the sociology of writing, publishing, and reading. This new perspective evinces an equal fascination for minor as for major writers and in fact tends to give preference to the previously ignored. This is a step in a historical direction and tends to diminish the play of aesthetic judgment.

But let us put this change into a somewhat larger perspective, focusing on the enormity of the historical enterprise and the plethora of historic evidence.[2] The Victorian period is famously the Age of the Novel. Educated estimates suggest that 40,000–50,000 novels by some 3,500 different authors were written and published in England between 1830 and 1900.[3] Nigel Cross, using census information, estimates the number of persons who considered themselves to be writers in 1800 to be about 550 and in 1900 to be about 9,000. For the century, Cross estimates that there were 20,000 self-styled writers. Of these it would be conservative to suggest that only 3,500 ever wrote a novel that was actually published.

Let us suppose that one set out to become an adequately informed reader of Victorian fiction with a clear historical sense and unmediated contact with the evidence surviving from the period. There is, as yet, no comprehensive bibliography of Victorian novels. Nor is there a comprehensive repository of Victorian fiction. The Wolff Collection at the

---

[2] This chapter and the next can be seen as subsequent enlargements of my earlier essay, "The Faces of Victorian Fiction" in *The Iconic Page*, ed. George Bornstein and Theresa Tinkle (Ann Arbor: University of Michigan Press, 1998), pp. 141–56. There I tried to imagine typical reactions by contemporary Victorian readers to the books in their new pristine off-the-shelf bindings, as a contrast to reactions of students on a modern Victorian literature course encountering the texts today as modern paperback books.

[3] Simon Eliot, *Some Patterns and Trends in British Publishing, 1800–1919* (Occasional Papers of the Bibliographical Society, No. 8, 1994), sections A and C; and Richard Altick, *The English Common Reader* (Chicago: University of Chicago Press, 1957). Gordon N. Ray estimated over 40,000 in *Bibliographical Resources for the Study of Nineteenth Century Fiction* (Los Angeles: Clark Library, 1964). John Sutherland estimated 50,000 in "Victorian Novelists: Who Were They?" in *Victorian Writers, Publishers, Readers* (New York: St. Martin's, 1995), 151–52. Sutherland provided individual notes on just under 900 authors in *The Stanford Companion to Victorian Fiction* (Stanford: Stanford University Press, 1989).

Ransom Humanities Research Center, University of Texas, has over 7,000 novels dating from 1830 to 1900. The Sadleir Collection at the Clark Library at UCLA, the Parrish and Metzdorf Collections at Princeton, the libraries of the University of Illinois, the University of Toronto, and in Britain the Bodleian Library at Oxford and the British Library are the most famous collections of Victorian fiction known to me. Margaret Harris compiled a list of nearly 1,600 "three-decker" novels in the University of Sydney Library.[4] But supposing our determined historical reader devoted a life to visiting these collections and reading the novels in original form (assuming for the nonce that such a thing could happen), what forms of Victorian fiction would this reader be likely to find and what likely to miss?

Our reader would find all the first editions, second, and subsequent editions, mostly in fine condition, of the standard authors, say the top twenty-five to fifty authors as measured by the evaluative scales of popularity, moral greatness, and aesthetic appeal of the last century. Also available would be first editions and a minimal scattering of subsequent editions of works by less well-known authors. The total number of different novels available in these repositories would not top 10,000-15,000, in my estimation. So, then, what would our avid and ambitious reader not find, besides the 35,000 novels not represented at all? Fiction serialized in newspapers and provincial literary magazines, dauntingly surveyed by Graham Law.[5] Such fiction dropped from sight during a time when it was considered to be both minor and marginal. Thousands of novels that never existed in more than one edition of about 150 to 300 copies. Thousands of novels that were scarcely published at all because the costs of production were all met by their authors and thus there was no incentive for the publishers to distribute the work. What about fiction republished in revised and abridged editions? Book collectors and libraries have specialized in first editions for so long that significant and permanent losses have occurred for second and subsequent editions. Such editions were altered sometimes in dramatic ways, but they are important historically even if only slightly altered – one could argue they are important even if not altered at all. And one should not forget the historical significance of another class of books that libraries and book collectors tend not to collect: books in poor physical condition (foxed,

---

[4] Margaret Harris, *A Checklist of the "Three-Decker" Collection in the Fisher Library, University of Sydney* (Department of English, University of Sydney, 1980).
[5] Graham Law, *Serializing Fiction in the Victorian Press* (London: Palgrave, 2000).

goosed, shaken, dog-eared) whose condition nevertheless evidences the number and kinds of readings they had received.

Without even touching on the problems of accessing the historical contexts of the novels in other publications of the time and in the plethora of histories of the Victorian period published since then, it is already clear from the sheer numbers of original editions and their sheer lack of survival that comprehensive historical knowledge even of the primary materials is impossible to us. A dramatic shift away from the central concerns of literary historians and critics is represented by some studies of publishing and authorship from outside the traditional field of literary history and criticism, where the primary focus has been on the history of ideas, of genres, of plots, structures, and narrative techniques, of literary biography, and of literary tastes and critical values. Gaye Tuchman and Nina Fortin, sociologists by training, undertook a statistical sampling method to develop a sense of the gender distribution and earning power of Victorian novelists.[6] Tuchman and Fortin were interested in the economics of authorship and the social implications of economics on the relative roles of men and women in the profession. This move from the literary to the economic represents another aspect of the trend away from Arnoldian literary appreciation of the best that has been thought and said and towards more general historical investigations. One comes away from the Tuchman and Fortin study, however, with a profound sense of dissatisfaction because the conclusions seem based on too small a foundation: one that took into consideration about 700 writers, just under half of them women, and which relied, necessarily, on the choices and accuracy of reporting of many secondary sources, and a study that focused primarily on writers published by Macmillan, whose archives formed a significant base. It is cautionary to note that, while such a study represents a far broader sampling of data than is usually encompassed by literary students of Victorian fiction, its conclusions still seem inadequate and narrow.

Likewise, Marxist approaches have tended to emphasize the modes of production and the economics of book making and book distribution as forces greater or perhaps more interesting than "genius" or than "literary taste" in directing the kinds of books that are written and published. In the past two decades important books have been written about the economic and production relations between publishers and authors such as

---

[6] Gaye Tuchman and Nina Fortin, *Edging Women Out: Victorian Novelists, Publishers, and Social Change* (London: Routledge, 1989).

Dickens, Thackeray, Tennyson, Hardy, Rossetti, and Dodgson (Lewis Carroll).[7] None of these is particularly Marxist, but two studies by N. N. Feltes have presented secondary evidence about publishing history in a Marxist framework. Feltes's studies are, frankly, disappointing from a historical perspective because the conclusions do not arise from an examination of the evidence, but instead the evidence is selected and arranged to support the preselected conclusions.[8]

One might say, however, that such disappointments about historical constructions are inevitable regardless of the perspective or methodology employed because there is too much evidence, yet its gaps are too hard to access, and every construction of the past is "situated" in the present. One could conclude that no satisfactory history of Victorian fiction can be constructed. But that is because of the impossible and impractical nature of the goal being posited for book history or for history itself. Perhaps it is passé to point out that the business of the history of the book is limited and that its limitations are not a reason for despair.

A practical illustration of the difficulties and rewards of historical investigations is in order. In 1842 Baron Bernhard Tauchnitz in Leipzig, Germany, began a publishing venture that finally failed ten years after World War II – in 1955. He called it "The Collection of British Authors," which by the outbreak of the War had published 5,372 works, keeping many of them in print for the entire period of its existence. One must turn to The Modern Library from Random House, the Everyman's Library, and Penguin or Oxford Classics in the twentieth century for endeavors of a comparable scale. In his day, the Baron had no enduring competitors. The inception and growth of his series parallels the development of the British Empire – a relevant context in at least two respects. The first is that the British Empire spanned the globe in ways that created a global market-demand for the English language and for British literature. Englishmen were invading the four corners of earth in what now is generally viewed, usually with disapproval, as moral, economic, military,

---

[7] Robert Patten, *Charles Dickens and his Publishers* (Oxford: Clarendon, 1978); Peter Shillingsburg, *Pegasus in Harness* (Charlottesville: University Press of Virginia, 1992); June Steffensen Hagen, *Tennyson and his Publishers* (London: Macmillan, 1979); Simon Gatrell, *Hardy the Creator* (Oxford: Clarendon, 1988) and R. L. Purdy, *Thomas Hardy: A Bibliographical Study* (London: Oxford University Press, 1954); Robert Keane, *Dante Gabriel Rossetti: The Poet as Craftsman* (New York: Peter Lang, 2002); Morton Cohen and Anita Gondolfo, eds. *Lewis Carroll and the House of Macmillan* (Cambridge: Cambridge University Press, 1987).

[8] N. N. Feltes *Modes of Production of Victorian Novels* (Chicago: University of Chicago Press, 1986) and *Literary Capital and the Late Victorian Novel* (Madison: University of Wisconsin Press, 1993). See my review of the former in *JEGP* 87 (1988), 262–5.

cultural, and racial – what can we say? – imperialism. Englishmen, we now say, thought they were right and that that gave them the right. The second is that the Empire created the transportation routes by which British literature invaded the four corners of earth. And while it is true that British publishers exported their magazines and books, both in the forms designed for home consumption and in specialized colonial editions, and while it is also true that the Baron declared he had no intention of making his editions available in England or its colonies, that did not keep his books out of every port of call along the routes or from the non-British tourist destinations for English readers. In the end it was Baron Tauchnitz of Leipzig and the Collection of British Authors that supplied the bulk of casual reading of British literature outside of England and the United States for world-wide consumption by Englishmen and by others who wished to read British literature.

The absence of an international copyright law (and one should note that there was an absence of pretty much any International Law in the nineteenth century – unless one holds that imperial powers imposing their will on colonial subjects constituted international law – a view which few if any actually now hold) – the absence of an international copyright law made what Baron Tauchnitz did both possible and, one might say, necessary – both beneficial and exploitative.[9] The German saw the opportunity and exploited it. He was ruthless in beating out his competition. He traveled to England to meet with authors and publishers; he brought "bribes" and contracts; he obtained exclusive contractual rights to publish English books on the Continent of Europe on dates frequently preceding the date of publication in England. He purchased advanced proof sheets and in some cases manuscripts in order that his books would appear in the bookstores before any of his Continental competitors – such as Jugel in Frankfurt, Galigniani or Baudry in Paris, or Robertson and Schroder in Brussels – could even obtain a printed copy to reprint from. By the time competitors could print their so-called pirated (though not in fact illegal) editions, Tauchnitz already had his cheap paperback versions in the stores of Germany, France, Italy, and the approaches to and egresses from the British empire. The first publisher gets the most sales.

This part of the story is recounted, deliberately, in disapproving terms to show that the initial praiseful remarks could easily be turned against

---

[9] Simon Nowell-Smith, *International Copyright Law and the Publisher in the Reign of Queen Victoria* (London: Oxford University Press, 1968) provides a classic account.

the entrepreneur. The point has more to do with the fact that historians of the book have a responsibility not only to the facts but to the relations between the facts and their times and ourselves. What looked in the 1840s like an opportunity and indeed a service to both British authors (who were unprotected by law outside of England) and global readers (who desired abundant and cheap reading material), might now look like imperialism and greed at the expense of indigenous literatures.[10]

We owe a great debt to Ann Bowden and William Todd for the bibliography of the Tauchnitz books, a 1,078-page compendium of titles interspersed with factual accounts of the firm's people, places, and achievements.[11] At the publication of its 2,000th book in 1881 and at two anniversaries of the venture's beginnings, the fiftieth in 1892 and the seventy-fifth in 1917, the Tauchnitz firm published celebratory retrospectives with hundreds of laudatory passages culled from the letters sent to the publisher by British authors. And there have been a few essays on the Baron and his venture published in scholarly journals over the years. But what is most intriguing about this story is what is not and apparently cannot be known. The letters archive, attested by the anniversary books, was apparently bombed in World War II. About sixty letters to the Baron survive in the Berlin State Library, some of them thanking him for sending a copy of his 1,000th book, published in 1868, and the rest of them relating to the celebration of the publication of the firm's 2,000th book, in 1881. Unlike the letters excerpted in the celebration volumes, these surviving letters contain little of literary or historical significance – a fact that makes the loss of the others more lamentable.

Todd and Bowden, in the bibliography, point to the evidence that books from the Collection of British Authors, which from the beginning had included American works and eventually was renamed the Collection of British and American Authors, were to be found in hundreds of public libraries in the United States, Australia, and South Africa, though now they are a very rare find in such libraries. People simply read these cheap books to death; and libraries, with the exception of a few books that were

[10] It is not certain that Tauchnitz editions did in fact affect the production of indigenous literature anywhere, but the cheap availability of English literature in Australia and America in the nineteenth century was complained of mightily by authors in both those countries. One should hasten to add that it was primarily American publishers, and primarily Harpers (not Tauchnitz), that often chose to print "free" English texts not protected by copyright, instead of American authors, whom they had to pay.

[11] William Todd and Ann Bowden, *The Tauchnitz International Editions in English 1841–1955: A Bibliographical History* (New York: Bibliographical Society of America, 1988).

rebound, discarded them. The evidence of Tauchnitz's global impact is disappearing.

A more important aspect of the works, from a literary point of view, is that the Tauchnitz volumes may contain authorial readings that exist in no other form. That is to say, I discovered when working on William Thackeray's *The History of Pendennis*, that the last sentence of the Preface and, in the final chapter, a derogatory name for Blanche Amory, who was not the book's heroine, exist only in the early printings of the Tauchnitz edition of that book. The Baron's pursuit of advanced copy for his firm netted him versions that, because they did not incorporate final corrections, preserved earlier readings discarded from the British editions and perhaps otherwise totally lost. In the absence of manuscripts and proof sheets, Tauchnitz editions are the sole surviving witness. If this could happen for *Pendennis*, why not for other books? The main problem is that the only way to find out is to collate Tauchnitz editions with the British (or American) editions. Not only is that a huge task that few historians of the book have undertaken, it raises another very difficult problem.

The Baron, in his wisdom, instituted from the beginning the practice of dating his books only once. All subsequent reprints carry the same title page date. This I discovered the hard way when I moved from one library (in Basle, Switzerland) to another (in London) mid-way through the collation of *Pendennis* and noticed that the Tauchnitz volume at the British Library, dated and printed and bound identically with the copy I had begun with in Basel, actually contained the text of the cut down, revised version first published six years after the date on the title page. Fortunately the BL had two copies – one of which proved to be the early version. Editors of the Clarendon Dickens editions were not so lucky, either not thinking to look at the Tauchnitz editions or finding only later reprintings of no particular interest and assuming them to be what the date on the title page proclaimed them.

These textual consequences for the systematic misdating of Tauchnitz reprints extend to any use of them by a scholar or critic who for whatever reason assumes the date on the title-page to be accurate. On the positive side it can be said that users will always have a sense of when the work was first published, but they will also always have the false sense that the text they hold dates from that year. Todd and Bowden provide a key to other factors, particularly the wording of imprints, that help identify actual publishing dates.

Was the Baron an imperialistic opportunist and exploiter or a beneficial patron of the arts? Was he both of those things? Is there a difference between a patron and an exploiter? Is anyone's opinion about these things more valuable than anyone else's? Each of these questions has an answer, or more than one, that can be or has been supported. But first, there is a lot of work to be done – finding early editions and collating them with their motherland texts – and in the end we have to acknowledge that the archive of letters and records, which might have documented the negotiations and identified the printers' copies used by Tauchnitz, has been destroyed and that we will never know the ways in which its preservation could have helped.

A consideration of the historical goals of book history and textual criticism may help clarify what is possible and what might be gained as the product of such work. Several aspects that frequently are confused in considerations of "history" must be distinguished: What actually happened in the past is not the same as the evidence that survives; nor is it the same as accounts of what happened, either written as a record at the time of the events or recollected by participants at a later time, or written by non-participants (historians) from research into the surviving evidence and surviving first-hand accounts. Perhaps it is only lay persons who fail to distinguish between what happened in the past and accounts of what happened in the past. The former (what happened) is not accessible to us with certainty; accounts of what happened are accessible but are never comprehensive or unassailable. Although available to us only through inference from the evidence and incompletely and perhaps inaccurately through accounts, we know in general terms that what happened is that writers wrote, usually with pen or pencil on paper, and submitted manuscripts to publishers, who usually selected works for publication and through various means influenced what the writers wrote or how they revised. Publishers directed the printing and binding of books and arranged for distribution and sales to buyers of books. Buyers in their turn either simply shelved their new commodities or read them and disposed of or stored the physical objects. Similar processes continued through second and subsequent editions. And the useful life of each book included the actions of subscription librarians and subscription library users, and others who borrowed, stole, or otherwise acquired some type of possession of the book. And in some ways the most important thing that happened is that readers reacted to what they read, fortunately frequently in writing, thus giving a social life to the actions of author, publishers, and booksellers. We *believe* these things happened because we have accounts of such happenings and because we have the physical evidence that such things happened. What we *know* is that the accounts and the evidence exist; what we believe is that these accounts and evidence lead us to more or less accurate or useful understandings about what happened.

It is, however, distressing to see book historians conveying mis-information. In preparing this chapter I read the false and/or misleading facts that stereotyping was introduced in 1827 and could be produced by using plaster of Paris, electrotyping, or paper flonges as molds, thus greatly facilitating the production of multiple printings of books over time. Well, yes and no. Stereotypes produced with plaster of Paris were introduced sporadically by printing houses in the second and third quarters of the century; electrotyping came a few years later and was used more for illustrations than for letterpress; and paper flonges as molds came even later, closer to 1870 than to 1830.[12] What principle of selection makes it important to know that there are three ways of producing stereotyped plates but not important to indicate when each method was developed? And was it just ignorance or a principle of selection that left out the fact that pages printed from stereotyped plates made from plaster of Paris molds are slightly smaller than pages printed from the standing type from which those plates were molded, while pages printed from electrotypes are of identical size? How important to our enterprise is precision in these matters? How important to our work is accuracy about extant evidence when absent evidence, for the significance of which we can say nothing precise, is a constant problem? Is it important to know that for some books duplicate sets of plates were cast? Is it important to know that through time corrections were made to stereotyped plates causing variants between books printed from the same set of plates? Is it important to know that when the first, perhaps corrected set of plates wore out, the second, probably uncorrected set would be brought out from storage for use, thus in effect restoring an earlier version for later printing?

I am not discouraged by this state of affairs. It is just the state of affairs in which we all work. Bibliographies, scholarly editions, histories of the composition, revision, and transmission of texts, histories of book pro-duction, histories of book distribution, reviewing, and reading – all of it is subject to the limitations of evidence. And our reading of Victorian fiction is affected by our ignorance as it is by our knowledge and by the particular editions we read – whether a modern paperback or an original edition. Yet, it is useful to distinguish between these, just as military

---

[12] Philip Gaskell, *A New Introduction to Bibliography* (Oxford: Clarendon, 1972) provides detailed accounts.

historians do between historic sites and historical monuments. The fact that physical objects and places are important to our sense of history is borne out by the popularity of historic sites and historical monuments as tourist destinations. But there is an important difference between the site where an action took place and a monument erected to commemorate an event that may have taken place somewhere else. What, for historians of the book, is the difference between an original edition of a book and a modern reprint? Which is historic and which is merely historical? And how do either of these help us to conjure history itself? (What actually happened, or what was actually written, or what the author wanted the text to be? and what original readers understood?) Script act theory holds that these bits of knowledge and ignorance have a direct bearing on interpretation: reading is influenced if not governed by the way "the not-said" specifies "the said."

This chapter points to the idea that a knowledge site has no natural boundaries, that the pursuit of knowledge is both grand and impossible, and that the creation of useful electronic knowledge sites will be the work of communities of scholars over many years during which continued development of the site will increase its scope and usefulness until, perhaps, the artificial boundaries of one knowledge site will grow to meet the growing boundaries of others.

CHAPTER 6

The dank cellar of electronic texts

And what a congress of stinks! –
Roots ripe as old bait,
Pulpy stems, rank, silo-rich,
Leaf-mold, manure, lime, piled against slippery planks.
Nothing would give up life:
Even the dirt kept breathing a small breath.
Theodore Roethke, "Root Cellar" (1948)

I am, however, assuming competence.
Willard McCarty, "Modelling" (2003)

As this chapter was being drafted, I read "Root Cellar" by Theodore
Roethke about a place, "dank as a ditch,"[1] where the remains of stored
vegetables served as the foundation for a rich complex of new developments, not all of which seemed very attractive; the olfactory sensations,
the "congress of stinks," did, however, represent on-going life. In
reviewing the remarkable expansion of electronic texts available on the
Internet, I concluded after a two- or three-week survey that roughly one
tenth of 1 percent of the available texts on the Internet were reliable for
scholarly work – 99.9 percent of the texts were who knows what. The
word "cellar" means storehouse. And when it comes to root cellars, the
word "dank" is not necessarily pejorative. But there is something antiseptic in popular images of electronic texts, archived, as they seem to be,
in a luminous box or cellar above a keyboard: they are dry, they resist
handling except through some remote medium, one does not press the
flesh of electronic texts, and therefore one does not leave on them an ever
accumulating deposit of body oils and odors as readers do on books in a
library. So, "dank" in reference to electronic texts brings an unfamiliar,
organic, biological ambience into this antiseptic world, suggesting that

---

[1] Theodore Roethke, *Collected Poems of Theodore Roethke* (New York: Doubleday [1966]), p. 38.

electronic texts might breed, or grow, or develop molds or viruses of various sorts. Roethke's poem suggests that even here the vitality of life is evident, but most of us want more than just any kind of life from our root cellars.

This unsought notion of a dank cellar of electronic texts initiated a train of thoughts – the first being that even this early in the electronic revolution the world is overwhelmed by texts of unknown provenance, with unknown corruptions, representing unidentified or misidentified versions. These texts frequently result from enthusiasm for computers and the Internet in particular. Texts are easily scanned, either as images or by optical character recognition (OCR) software and posted on the World Wide Web; thus, almost anyone can easily become an editor, producer, and publisher. From comments at conferences and advice given on the Internet, I conclude that the big worry is not authenticity, verification, or attribution. It is to avoid posting texts of works still in copyright. Where new scholarly editions of works exist, this warning means that the ersatz editor cum publisher of an electronic text will pick a handy older edition, frequently a cheap reprint, as a source. The reasons to publish such electronic texts could be egotistical, but for many the reason may be altruistic instead: to make available for free the fruits of some labor and some technology where the alternatives might be to purchase a book or visit a library or go without any text at all. Furthermore, an obvious advantage of having computerized texts is that they can be searched, excerpted, and indexed without the use of 3 by 5 cards or pencils; but these excellent qualities of electronic texts have tended to generate an enthusiasm that neglects concerns for textual accuracy and provenance. The perfume of fecundity produced by the rank glut of such texts on the Internet is tainted also by a distinct under-scent of decay and disease. But this view need not detain us, for it merely replicates objections voiced in every generation since the fifteenth century – objections to the unbridled proliferation of corrupt and corrupting printed texts. It is an old process now made easier.

A companion to that thought is that our students are therefore exposed to texts that are untethered from their origins, from their original dates, original publishers, original typefaces, and original page arrangements and weights. These are the residual marks of what can be called the "eventness" of texts, the clues to the cultural contexts that informed the writing and reading of the works when they were fresh. Electronic texts that do not include images of the source text pages – that is, most electronic texts – thus erase all sense of "bookness" from the works, leaving text only in a new way, disturbing to anyone mindful of texts as representative of the individual and social actions of authoring, publishing, reading. And even if the physical clues to the origins of texts were known by our students, who have access to other sources of information, the texts of most electronic editions have often been poorly prepared, poorly proofread, and improperly vetted or not vetted at all; so that inadvertent readings lurk unmarked like verbal landmines to sabotage the pursuit of learning. Students eager for free texts and happy with the advantages of the computer medium are not naturally inclined to ask the necessary questions about provenance and accuracy. The unsophisticated replication of texts on the Internet, like the proliferation of relatively cheap paper texts, reflects a widespread assumption: that a literary text consists only of letters and punctuation and will mean the same thing wherever and however it appears. That false assumption also underlies the construction of classroom anthologies, as mentioned before. But communication theory and critical reflection suggest that each bibliographical event, like each verbal utterance, is significantly affected by its constituting context and medium. As students of texts, we care about provenance, contexts, histories, bibliography, and the accuracy of texts because all these affect how we read and how we understand the text. We must teach our students these things anew every year. Of course this criticism of student texts, like the first criticism, is very familiar, because we have voiced them of cheap reprints for years.

A third thought is that contemplating the spreading "mold" of electronic "pulp texts" might generate a hysterical attempt on our part to police the Internet or to set up a national or international text-vetting bureau or to publish in some official organ a list of approved electronic editions. After all, there is precedence for doing such things in the Modern Language Association's Center for Editions of American Authors and Committee on Scholarly Editions. But such organizations in the past have not stemmed the tide of unreliable reprints. Nor will they, in my opinion, make a dent in the flow of bad or unsafe and undocumented electronic texts.

The activity of scholarly editing in electronic media does not require that desperate remedy; for scholarly electronic text editing and archiving can be conducted with firm attention to its own house, to its own root cellar. There is, after all, not much difference between the electronic world and the print world concerning the relative availability of corrupt and reliable texts. Unreliable, unvetted reprints outnumber scholarly editions in the print world by proportions similar to the ones I am guessing at for electronic texts.

Turning, then, from the at-large world of electronic texts to the smaller one of electronic scholarly editions, we can find a good deal of thought and a developing body of practice that presents both a more hopeful and yet more problematic picture. I am not a historian of this movement, but a thumbnail sketch of it as a background may give this train of thoughts a boost. Electronic texts date back twenty-five years and more, but the electronic book as an end in itself – that is, not as a temporary form to use, for example, in creating a concordance or for typesetting a book – is a phenomenon of the very late 1980s and 1990s. Its short history is remarkably varied. Its early manifestations now make us smile: ftp sites from which one could download an ASCII text file without italics or other formatting seemed adequate to many people who thought their personal libraries would be greatly increased at little or no cost. This scheme reduced the rich complexity of the codex into a flat stream of ASCII characters. Then virtual worlds arrived, and "Saturday Night Live" satirized the virtual book with images of a book shown on a screen where keyboard commands turned codex pages. Like microfilm and facsimile projects – though actually not a bad place to start – this scheme demonstrates a paucity of imagination trapped in the world of physical objects and photography.

In 1993 with the help of Graham Barwell, Paul Eggert, and Chris Tiffin, I drew up a description of what I then thought would be an ideal electronic book, one that took advantage of developing software to provide textual experiences not available in codex forms and stepping gingerly beyond developing software to imagine other possibilities not yet available in prototype form. It was my first excursion into fantasy fiction. That description was widely circulated on the Internet, presented at a convention of the Modern Language Association of America (MLA), and subsequently expanded and published in *The Literary Text in the Digital Age*.[2] Some of its ideas found their way into the MLA's Center for Scholarly Editions' guidelines for electronic editions. I am happy to say that some ideas imagined then have since become possible, though others have not, and other desirable elements we did not imagine then have been developed.

The most ambitious development spawned by the demand for sophisticated electronic editions has been the Text Encoding Initiative (TEI) for use in SGML and XML markup systems. As explained in chapter

---

[2] "Principles for Electronic Archives, Scholarly Editions, and Tutorials," in *The Literary Text in the Digital Age*, ed. Richard J. Finneran (Ann Arbor: University of Michigan Press, 1996), pp. 23–35.

four, TEI provides standards and logical structures with which to build electronic texts that accommodate the rich complexity of language and the physical structures of books. Among the important practical projects implementing that markup language and doing in the short term what could be done to make the fruits of scholarly editing available in electronic form is the Model Editions Partnership conducted by David Chesnutt, Susan Hockey, and Michael Sperberg-McQueen. Other very important projects are the Rossetti Archive being developed by Jerome McGann; the Chaucer projects by Peter Robinson; the New Testament project by David Parker, Peter Robinson and others; the Emily Dickinson project by Martha Nell Smith, Ellen Louise Hart, and Marta Werner; two Ezra Pound projects by Patti Cockran and by Richard Taylor; the Women Writers Project at Brown University directed by Julia Flanders; the William Blake Archive by Joseph Viscomi, Robert Essick, and Morris Eaves; the Piers Plowman Archive by Hoyt Duggan; and various projects connected with the JITM (Just In Time Markup) system developed by Phill Berrie and Paul Eggert for the Australian Academy Library.[3] Ambitious projects that resemble in some ways the model in chapter four, include an electronic version of the Cambridge Ben Jonson Works edition, not yet published, and the HyperNietzsche Project, which is in early stages yet but is designed to become a fully fledged knowledge site.[4] There are others, but I mention these to call attention to serious, imaginative projects that make available research tools of genuine value, not only for the foundational scholarly work on the authors and texts involved but because they are pushing the envelope of electronic possibilities, asking more and more of the medium in an attempt to conceive and define what is meant or can be meant by the electronic edition, as opposed to a print edition.

But it was both thrilling and sobering when Jerome McGann and Peter Robinson began focusing their attention not on the glitzy achievements of their projects, though both have done so, and not on the difficulties

---

[3] Many of these projects were mentioned in chapter two. For the Model Editions Partnership see www.adh.sc.edu; for McGann's Rossetti Archive see www.iath.virginia.edu/rossetti/fullarch.html; for Robinson's Chaucer see www.canterburytalesproject.org/index.html; for Smith's Dickinson see www.emilydickinson.org/index.html; for Flander's Women Writers Project see www.wwp.brown.edu; for Viscomi's Blake Archive see www.blakearchive.org/main.html; for Duggan's Piers Plowman see www.iath.virginia.edu/piers/archive.goals.html; for Berrie's JITM see idun.itsc.adfa.edu.au/ASEC/JITM/publications.html. See also http://www.selc.ed.ac.uk/italian/digitalvariants/home.htm for an ambitious project to "reopen the kitchen" of writing for selected Italian authors.
[4] Jonson http://uk.cambridge.org/literature/features/cwbj/project/, and Nietzsche http://www.hypernietzsche.org.

and long hours that have dogged their work, though they could have done that, too,[5] but on the way in which their projects had forced them to think about texts in new ways, to ask new questions about textuality, and perhaps most interestingly, to ask new questions about what the archive was to do. Interestingly enough, Robinson's new tack has been to acknowledge the need for the guiding presence of the editor as electronic archives became more and more detailed and complex as representations of historical texts. McGann's new tack has tended toward game playing, using the computer's multiple capabilities both for refinement and con-tortion, to force new engagements with texts as they have never been seen before.[6] I found these developments in their work especially interesting for two reasons. The first was nostalgic. In 1977–8 when I spent a year with a programmer developing the nine programs known as CASE (Computer Assisted Scholarly Editing) – programs developed to aid the textual research of transcription, collation, and textual apparatuses and to prepare input for typesetting machines – the main thing I discovered was that my methodology for scholarly editing was not carefully thought out. I discovered that, whereas in science if one is careless one's lab might explode, in the humanities if one makes a mistake it generally goes unnoticed – until one has to develop computer programs that will replicate or organize the work. Then one discovers the meaning of the word "discipline".

One great value of modern work on electronic archives lies in its process, in what the work teaches the worker, rather than in the accomplishment of the product. McGann described the difficulties of accommodating the Rossetti material to the SGML markup language, a task that stretched his understanding of the structural complexity of the works he was handling (for example, he was learning to look at the paintings in ways made possible by digital reproductions and enhancements and distortions made possible by software like Photoshop) and the structural constraints in SGML (particularly its inability to handle overlapping structures, since it can only operate in a single hierarchy of structures). Similarly, Robinson

---

[5] McGann's and Robinson's remarks were made in the "Voice, Text and Hypertext at the Millennium" conference at the University of Washington, 29 October – 1 November 1997. For McGann, "Imagining What You Don't Know," see *Voice, Text, and HyperText*, ed. Raimonda Modiano, Leroy Searle, and Peter Shillingsburg (Seattle: University of Washington Press, 2003).

[6] Notice for instance the differences between Robinson's Wife of Bath Prologue project in which he sublimated the editorial role and his Hengwrt MS project where the presence of the editor is more palpable. (See Stubbs and Robinson, The Hengwrt Chaucer Digital Facsimile CD [Leicester: Scholarly Digital Editions, 2000].) And see McGann's *Radiant Textuality: Literature After the World Wide Web*, New York: Palgrave, 2001.

admitted what did not please him about his own very impressive *Wife of Bath* prototype for the electronic Chaucer. In describing what he was to do differently at the next stage, there was a similar emphasis on how doing the work and struggling with the inadequacies of the software led to new understandings of the significance of Chaucer's work and of the responsibilities of the editor. What Robinson discovered was that the neutral, objective, CD presentation and description of eighty-eight Chaucer manuscripts with approximately ten million hyperlinks (most of which were generated automatically by his software) ran the high risk of burying the user. His solution, in subsequent Chaucer projects, was to provide the reader with explanations of the significance of the parts, to provide frankly interpretive signposts, and to express editorial opinions about the value and significance of the materials presented.

That is an important development for the debate on editorial theory and practice. It brings me to the second reason I was pleased to learn of the developments in McGann's and Robinson's projects. It used to be, thirty years ago, that an editor imposed his or her understanding of the textual situation onto the edition, edited it boldly, and expected appreciation from readers for having provided, as a finished product, an edition on which readers could rely without having to investigate it for themselves. The justifications for such editorial actions stressed the objectivity of the work and the honesty of the apparatus. But self-deception in scholarship never lasts for long, and idealist, intentionalist editing was recognized for the subjective, dominating, reductive activity that it was. In its place more recently arose the apparently "truly" objective pursuit of the electronic archive with objective, high-resolution digitized reproductions of original texts, objective and antiseptic parallel texts, and hyperlinks to related materials. And Peter Robinson – who to do him justice never said that what he was doing was objective, but who tried to minimize the presence of the editor in the *Wife of Bath* CD-ROM edition – now says that such a neutral approach in a complex edition might bury the reader who needs the editor to exert a guiding hand. Amen. We have once again discovered that scholarly editing is not best served by editors whose main goal is to efface their presence from the project but rather by those who confidently and boldly assert their presence, demanding that readers recognize the scholarly edition as a contribution to criticism. Editing is by nature and by definition interference; it cannot be done objectively. It should be undertaken boldly, and should be reported straightforwardly and with the characteristic humility of first-rate criticism that offers itself to be considered and tested and used, if possible, as a tool in the arsenal of other critics. There is room for alternative editions; there is room for different (competing) editorial guidance through the textual evidence of one work.

In the last few years scholarly editors at conferences on electronic editions have been focusing their attention, naturally enough, on the ways to produce electronic editions more than on the implications those ways might have on the study of texts or on the pursuit of academic interests that such a shift in medium entails. Technical advances happen so frequently in computing that such presentations and demonstrations may be with us for many years to come, but a corrective is needed for that general trend. It is only natural that the practical considerations of electronic text-production should absorb the attention of electronic text producers, for there is so much to deal with: choices of hardware (where every new year's model is capable of so much more than the model you bought) and choices of software (where the cleverest and niftiest capabilities entail, as likely as not, proprietary coding that locks the edition into one form of access). To these one can add the many problems entailed in developing or learning a text-encoding system that will overcome the problems of new developing and evolving hardware and software. And it has been necessary for scholarly editors also to devote a great deal of attention to design: What shall the screen page look like? How shall hypertext links look and work? How should windows pop up and disappear or fade into the background? How shall we incorporate sound and motion in our texts? Where are the boundaries between scholarly editing, archiving, and pedagogy? Or are those boundaries disappearing?

These important concerns are likely to continue to absorb a great deal of attention, and we must not be distracted from them by temptations to scream out against the rapid proliferation of unreliable texts prepared (loosely speaking) by people who have not bothered to think long or hard about textual matters. Their fan-enthusiasm for their authors and for the internet must not distract us into inveighing against them or smiling approval on their "gifts" to the world.

We need more people thinking deeply about ways in which texts translated into new mediums lose old functions as they acquire new functions and how interactions with texts in the electronic world differ from interactions with print editions. My concerns are with the relations – practical and conceptual – between print and electronic editions.

Central to this thought is that no editorial task, whether in print or electronic medium, is merely the reproduction of a text. Stated positively,

all editorial tasks entail more than the mere transfer of words and
punctuation or images from one form to another. Every such transfer
creates something new and so radically different from its original that
scholarly editors for centuries have felt the need to write introductions for
their editions to explain what has happened. I leave aside here introductions that claim the new form is better or more accurate or more real
or more useful; I call attention only to the need for an introduction that
explains the differences between original and newly edited texts.

The need to introduce new editions arises, I think, from our understanding of how texts operate – or to be more accurate, of how humans
operate with texts. Texts are, after all, merely arrangements of symbols
presented in certain formats and preserved in a specific medium. Humans
undergo considerable training in interpreting the symbols, and reading
experience teaches them much about the implications of the formats and
media in which they encounter the symbols. Meanings are generated by
readers who have learned to deal with symbols and formats. Change the
symbol and the meaning changes; change the format and the implications
are changed; change the contexts of interactions with texts and the
importance and significance of the text changes.

These truths confronted me in a physical way when I visited the
Metzdorf, the Parrish, and the Taylor collections of Victorian fiction at
the Firestone Library in Princeton and, shortly thereafter the even more
extensive Wolff collection at the Harry Ransom Humanities Center at the
University of Texas. What follows here is intended to add both complexity and interest to the longer review of the example of Victorian
fiction in chapter five, above. I was working on a paper[7] concerning the
appearance, the formats, of Victorian fiction and was fortunate to be
introduced to the stacks of the Parrish and Wolff collections and to have
multiple copies of single titles brought to my work table. The sensations,
the look, the feel, the odors, the textures, the colors, shapes, and sizes of
the books all have a bearing on what follows, though the most over-
whelming sensation I felt as I looked at 7,000 Victorian novels in
the Wolff collection was that of ignorance. After thirty years work on
Victorian authors, I know next to nothing about Victorian fiction, for
that large room of books is but a minor representation of the 40,000 or
50,000 novels published between 1830 and 1900. Yet, vast as it is, Wolff's
collection of books stands in stark isolation from the books that they

---

[7] "The Faces of Victorian Fiction" in *The Iconic Page*, ed. George Bornstein and Theresa Tinkle
(Ann Arbor: University of Michigan Press, 1998), pp. 141–56.

jostled in the days when they were fresh off the press. Where were the books of agriculture, history, geography, exploration, navigation, mining, economics, art, music, biography, science, religion, politics, cookery, and domestic economy? How could I come to know the meaning or importance or significance of any one of these books without knowing what other books were published by its publishers or what other books were reviewed together with it? Must I go to Austin, Texas, and get permission between the hours of 10 a.m. and 4 p.m. to see no more than five books at a time to get a sense of what Victorian fiction was? I tasted and smelled and felt enough of original books in the context of their peers to know that it makes a huge difference to our experience of texts – a difference that does not and will not manifest itself in paperback reprints, in scholarly print editions, or in electronic books as currently conceived.

Nor can the interests I developed in the subject be easily satisfied by existing bibliographies or descriptions of collections, though the Wolff bibliography, Michael Sadleir's *Nineteenth Century Fiction*, and descriptions of the Rauri MacLean collection in Toronto are illuminating, impressive, and mind-bending once one has developed a hunger to know. Nor can existing histories of writing, publishing, and reading, or even a few visits to major collections of Victorian fiction provide more than appetizers, experienced at too long intervals. Additional descriptions of the "faces of Victorian fiction" of the whimsical sort I wrote will not do much to provide students or colleagues with the materials needed to develop a sensitivity to what Victorian fiction looked like or what its appearances meant to contemporary readers.

As mentioned in chapter five, my visits to the Metzdorf, Parrish, Taylor, and Wolff collections and perusal of descriptions of Sadleir's books and of MacLean's collection led me to conclude that these rich resources have two very serious flaws: they are by necessity sequestered from most students and interested scholars who do not live near to these libraries; and each collection is, by virtue of its selection principles, a distortion of the history of Victorian fiction. What bookstore in Victorian England shelved only first editions? Which shelved only novels? How can such collections represent the "eventness" of Victorian fiction?

Robert Lee Wolff's collection of Mary Elizabeth Braddon's works, for example, included many reprints of her best-selling *Lady Audley's Secret*, though it failed to include a first printing of the first edition. For most of his authors, Wolff's collection holds only the first edition. His collection fails to include all the reprints, even of *Lady Audley's Secret*, and therefore his bibliography of Victorian Fiction, which is really a catalogue of the books he owned, leaves out much of the printing history of Braddon's book. This is not a criticism of Wolff's magnificent work. It is a description of the state of affairs that developed at a time when collectors' interests were driven by concerns different from those that would drive an electronic "Knowledge Site" developed according to the concerns laid out in this book.

Gordon S. Haight's description of the editions of George Eliot's *The Mill on the Floss*, for a different kind of example, provides a comprehensive record of "authorized" productions of that work from 1860 to 1881. It provides a better visualization and understanding of the production objects and texts of *The Mill* than can be found materially as books in any one library in the world. But even such a listing and description and analysis is bounded by the compiler's interest – in this case, in the "composition and revision life" of the work. Haight's account does not include the evidence of the very active continued "reading life" of the work represented by the multiple unauthorized editions in America and Germany nor the multiple unauthorized editions everywhere that proliferated after the author's death.

Of course for most Victorian fiction there was only one edition ever. But there is no bibliography of Victorian fiction that is comprehensive as a record of Victorian consumption of native fiction. Obviously, the boundaries of such a project are artificial and could be extended.

My long-standing commitment to editing the works of W. M. Thackeray and my newly discovered interest in the "Faces of Victorian Fiction" led me to imagine a resource that is the kernel of an impossible dream proposal. It is to pursue systematically the establishment of an electronic archive of Victorian Fiction, beginning with images of original editions in contemporary bindings, and then including digitized texts, and later expanding to include textual, production, and other historical annotations, as well as texts newly edited by bold editors. I imagined an opening home page, not unlike a door to a storage root cellar or library into which the user entered a virtual bibliography: a shelving area that appears to hold lifelike books – arranged at the touch of a button chronologically (so I could see all the novels published in 1859), or alphabetically by author, or grouped according to publisher, each publisher's output arranged in the order published or by author, or perhaps grouped according to original publisher's price, or by format (all two-volume books sold at twelve shillings a volume separated from all the three-volume novels sold for thirty-six shillings, for example). In my dream I saw a merging of the book collections assembled by Parrish, Taylor, Wolff, Metzdorf, Sadleir, and MacLean, with additions from the Bodleian, and the British Library. And from my keyboard I could pull any book from the shelf and read, and search, and see parallel texts, and read historical and textual annotations, and have textual cruxes in verbose or background mode, and hyperlinked to – to you name it – film and stage adaptations, translations, and all the associated reviews and commentary.

And yet that is not enough to satisfy my craving. Special collections in libraries distort our sense of the marketing and textual history of Victorian fiction. Every book ever published had a first edition, but the most widely read books were produced in multiple editions. Special collections tend to emphasize two qualities that belie the historical record: First editions and fine condition. The result is that the evidence of reading is not preserved. Books that are much reprinted are seldom preserved in those reprinted forms. Copies that are much read, are seldom preserved because of the used condition. So, my dank cellar of electronic Victorian fiction must include cheap reprints and shaken and mauled editions as well. And before waking from this nightmarish vision of delight I should note that this proposal does not pretend to incorporate the contexts of Victorian fiction or literature on a broad scale as does George Landow's Victorian Web.[8] I imagine there being a variety of links between the Victorian Web and the "Victorian Fiction" archive as well as other relevant web sites.

But I come back from that vision of an end product to a point mentioned earlier: to the research involved in constructing such a library, to the bibliographical investigation, to the careful observation of the text in its various physical forms, each representing textual acts at points in time. There is no bibliography we can merely scan into a database; there is no collection of texts we merely need to photograph. What this grandiose scheme requires is what every electronic scholarly edition requires in a smaller way: basic textual scholarship, bibliography, textual criticism, critical acumen in the writing of introductions and explanatory notes, sensitivity to voices in the text, and the courage to express the best thinking the scholar has about the significance of the evidence at hand.

To conclude, root cellars are very necessary units and they house the sustenance of life. But they need constant attention, annual cleaning, restocking, and shelf repair. Scholarly editing is not ever finished; and it is done well or ill and redone well or ill, and it is constantly being confused by lay persons, students, and even members of academic professions with

---

[8] The Victorian Web, www.victorianweb.org (accessed 3 December 2004).

reprintings of every sort. Our task, I think, is to keep our cellar restocked, properly labeled, properly preserved, and as free of mold, viruses, and tainted fruit as careful scholarship can ensure. I do not mean we should keep out the cheap reprints; I mean only that no text should pretend to be other than what it is. Whether it is a cheap, shoddily prepared text or a scholarly edition, let it present itself as such – at least in our root cellar – and not pretend, in either case, to be "the work itself." We cannot rid the world of mold and debris, but we can refrain from creating it, and we can keep it out of our cellar by circulating our stock, by providing accurate descriptions of text and provenance, by adding to old scholarly editions new ones, boldly and straightforwardly edited, not intended to last for ever but intended to feed the minds of the next generation for a few years until they see how best to feed themselves and their progeny.

CHAPTER 7

Negotiating conflicting aims in textual scholarship

Two roads diverged in a yellow wood
    Robert Frost, "The Road Not Taken" (1920)

The Cottage which was named the Evening Star
Is gone – the ploughshare has been through the ground
On which it stood; great changes have been wrought
In all the neighbourhood: – yet the oak is left
That grew beside their door; and the remains
Of the unfinished Sheep-fold may be seen
Beside the boisterous brook of Green-head Ghyll.
    William Wordsworth, "Michael" (1800)

This chapter is about losses.[1] It is written in the context of positive hopes and claims about books. Book collecting and archive building form a part of its context. Special collections and rare book collections in libraries and collections formed by book lovers anywhere, for example, accentuate the positive when they focus on what they own and what they have preserved, but it is inevitable that the subject eventually turns to what they do not own and what was lost before it could be saved. Literary criticism forms another part of the context, accentuating the positive by focusing on insights and on the discovery of new or neglected talent, but it is inevitable that the subject eventually turns to faded insights, outmoded critical fads, or the rejection of formerly held ideas in the light, or should one say the flash, of new ones. And what is said here about books and book editions applies equally to electronic scholarly editions and to the electronic knowledge sites I so much hope will be developed.

Textual criticism and scholarly editing have provided their share of the positive. Phrases like, "establishing the facts," "placing the work in its

---

[1] An early version was published in *Problems of Editing*, ed. Christa Jansohn, Special issue, *editio* (Tübingen: Niemeyer, 1999), pp. 1–8.

contexts," "making the work accessible to the scholar, or to the student, or to the general reader," "providing reliable texts," and "winning the seal of approval of the Committee on Scholarly Editions of the Modern Language Association of America" all suggest positive advances. It is too late to dredge up the older hopes embodied in the phrases "the science of detecting errors," "the calculus of variants," "definitive editions," or "editing the work in such a way that it will never need to be done again," which were common in the 1960s but now strike many of us as exaggerated. There is a hint of similar hope in the new language of those who describe the electronic scholarly edition or electronic archive, which, we are told (indeed, I say it myself at times), will make it possible to present the work in all its significant forms and will eliminate many of the editorial choices that were necessary because of the limitations of the print medium. But I think accentuating the positive, without focusing sufficiently or meditatively upon the losses, has led textual critics and scholarly editors to over-reach and to claim to have done more than the facts will support.

It seems to me possible that an explanation for conflicts between editorial schools about the "proper aims" of scholarly editing and an explanation for the conflicts in the mind and heart of any individual editor over what should be the aims of his or her own scholarly edition might lie in our habit of accentuating the positive hope that our new edition will serve, if not everyone and if not for ever, at least for nearly everyone and at least for our lifetime. I suppose there is something noble about such aspirations; there is at least something ambitious about them. We support such talk with the principle that it is better to think big, to strive for great things. And as long as we ride the cusp of the newest enthusiasm, rather than meditate upon the achievements of the works already edited and settled comfortably on the library shelf, as long as we look forward and not backward, the value of positive thinking and of enthusiasm for the great achievements to come will seem necessary and useful.

But as we look back upon the achievements and gains of former positive, enthusiastic, hopeful scholarly editing, we have much to learn about losses. It is not difficult to find, in the essays and conference papers of scholarly editors and theorists about editing, language suggesting that former editors didn't quite see the error of their ways. Many of us remember the lapel button Herschel Parker used to wear to conferences. It proclaimed that W. W. Greg's Rationale of Copy-Text was too Rational, and we remember Jerome McGann's remark, reported by

W. Speed Hill, that "the copy-text school of editing" was "dead as a Dodo," and we have noted Donald Reiman's morally indignant frontal attack on critical editing in pursuit of authorial intentions in his *The Study of Modern Manuscripts* and in a paper against "theoryism" he presented at a conference in 1997.[2] In every case, it would seem, the failing of scholarly editions that do not measure up to modern expectations is that their editors got something wrong. The concomitant hope, it seems, is that the modern editor will get it right, finally.

But we should stop to note that, when these older editors were the modern editors, they spoke in the same way about their predecessors. A. E. Housman, the poet and classical editor, in the 1920s berated the "asses" who had edited before him. Ronald McKerrow in the 1930s berated the aesthetic picking and choosing among variants practiced by dilettante editors, his predecessors. W. W. Greg in 1950 pointed out the tyranny of copy-text to which McKerrow had fallen victim. Fredson Bowers in the 1960s showed the ways in which Greg's system for editing Renaissance texts needed refining and revising for application to later American fiction. In the 1980s Herschel Parker and Jerome McGann, each in a very different way, undertook to explain what was wrong with Bowers's approach.[3] Each generation seems to hope for the best answer and finds the efforts of older generations to be inadequate. Soon it will be our turn to have failed.

I would suggest that a meditation upon losses would help us as textual critics and scholarly editors to stem the flow of scholarly editions from the shelf of honor to the dustbin of superseded editions. How hard is it to see that the new editions fail to do some things that the superseded editions did or that otherwise could have been done but were not?

---

[2] If memory serves, Parker sported the lapel button at the April 1985 STS, and perhaps elsewhere. Hill's review of Dave Oliphant and Robin Bradford's *New Directions in Textual Studies* (1990) appeared in *TEXT* 6 (1994), 370–81. For Reiman see *The Study of Modern Manuscripts: Public, Confidential, and Private* (Baltimore: Johns Hopkins University Press, 1993); his paper was delivered at the "Voice, Text, and Hypertext" conference at the University of Washington in October 1997.

[3] A. E. Housman, "The Application of Thought to Textual Criticism," *Proceedings of the Classical Association* 18 (1922), 67–184; rpt. in *Selected Prose*, ed. John Carter (Cambridge: Cambridge University Press, 1961), pp. 131–50. R. B. McKerrow, "The Treatment of Shakespeare's Text by His Earlier Editors, 1709–1768," *Proceedings of the British Academy* 19 (1933), 89–122. W. W. Greg, "The Rationale of Copy-Text," *Studies in Bibliography* 3 (1950–1), 19–36. Fredson Bowers, "textual preface" (Vol. I) and "Textual Introduction" (Vols. I and II) for *The Centenary Works of Nathaniel Hawthorne* (Columbus: Ohio State University Press, Vol. I 1962; Vol. II 1964). Hershel Parker, *Flawed Texts and Verbal Icons: Literary Authority in American Fiction* (Evanston: Northwestern University Press, 1984). And Jerome McGann, *A Critique of Modern Textual Criticism* (Chicago: University of Chicago Press, 1983).

Oh, but new enthusiasms cry, we don't want editions to do what those old editions did. For example, we don't want an edition that represents the aesthetic tastes of editors in the 1890s; we don't want the clear reading text representing some 1960s editor's notion of what the author's final intentions might have been; we don't want a clear reading text of a historical edition from which the influences of the production process have been purged. Well, how long do we suppose that the current fashion of disdaining these achievements will last? And how long will it be before we start hearing that scholars do not want multiple texts, historical or otherwise, for the works they wish to interpret? Or that they do not want to sift through a range of artifacts glimmering from the screen of a computer? And, if I had the imaginative power to predict future editorial delights, I would tell you now for what new textual goals our editions will be abandoned.

So, again, I say, let us meditate upon losses – upon what is lost when a work is edited. Full stop. One does not have to edit in a certain way in order for there to be a loss in the process. One merely needs to edit. I do not know of a single case in which an edited work did not represent a loss of something. No edition is a full representation of that which it attempts to edit. No edition was ever or will ever represent a work adequately. Full stop. The positive. The hopeful. The perfection. The adequacy. The triumph of scholarship. They will not occur.

Let us make a short, representative list – it would take too long to make an exhaustive list – of the losses. First, the paper, ink, cloth, leather, and smell of the original edition is gone from the edited one – and with them the sense of a former age in which all these things were new. Second, the font, the width of margin, the shape or style of the running heads, and in some cases the feel of pages indented by standing metal type or textured by ink, or characteristically marred by broken types or uneven inking. The absence of these things might be even more acute in electronic texts than printed ones. With them goes a loss of the ravages of time, the changes of technology, and the mingling of grandeur with the rude wasting of old time. Next, the typos and the outmoded or merely eccentric punctuation and spellings stand now corrected, leaving the reader with no need to exercise the creative allowance and forgiveness that attend most readings of most new books. If our new edition provides a clear reading text of a critical edition, only one text of the work is embedded in the textual texture. Other readings are at the foot of the page or in a table at the back. And if they are at the foot of the page, we should add to what is lost the clear page of the original from which all evidence of false starts and revisions have been eliminated by the miracle of print and the machinations of the proofreaders and compositors. If there are revised versions of the work represented in the new edition, the sense of the uniqueness of the originals may be lost. If the various revised editions are represented in full in an electronic text, the immediate ability to compare revisions side by side may be lost.

This begins to sound like Robert Frost's poem "The Road Not Taken." No matter what the editor does, some equally good alternative is therefore not done; some alternative view of the work is lost. And every reader or rising young editor seeking to make a name will focus attention on what was not done and was therefore lost; and he or she will proclaim the need for new and better editorial principles, mindless of the fact that just ahead two roads diverge in a yellow wood, only one of which can be taken.

One can take issue with my statement that "some equally good alternative is therefore not done." Having seen the error of those ways, say the new editors, we have chosen the one that is the right one. And the new theory and method ride the cusp of new enthusiasm. But we should meditate upon the roads not taken. The new road may very well be best for some purposes, and there may be many who share your purposes and need to go down that road. But why must one call the equally good alternative road, that better serves or served other purposes – why must one call those errors? Could it be that the new enthusiasm, which will soon no doubt entail losses of its own, must attack the old in order to make room for the new? Why not settle for the good that can be done in the new way without distorting and tarring the good that others did in their other way?

The new editors could respond: "We have not chosen a single new way. Our electronic archive allows each user a choice of versions. Each historical text is presented in digital image, just as it was in the original. And the work as a whole has been linked, so that the variants between any text and its alter-texts can be traced at the click of a mouse. And a new critical edition, representing the author's intentions has been prepared. And historical, textual, and critical annotations have been prepared. And all this is available on the World Wide Web, so persons in any place on earth, far from any research library can log in and use the scholarly edition." And I would agree, of course, that that is very good. But my purpose is to focus on the losses, to point out that no matter how good that is, there are some things it does not do.

Aside from the fact that the web-site does not feel or smell or weigh the same as the originals it otherwise so fully and adequately represents, let us just focus on two ideas: that the web-site provides a critical edition as well as the historical edition; and that a web of links provides the connections among the parts of the archive. And let us take them in reverse order, so that we will ascend in order of importance. Linking in any electronic hypertext is accomplished by someone noticing something and creating a link or by some program identifying boolean similarities and constructing links automatically. In the latter case, the program recognizes similarities for conjunction according to a logic provided by a critic and a programmer who together thought it would be a good idea. In fact, every link in every hypertext is the result of someone having thought it was a good idea. It follows that in order for there to be a link, someone had to think it would be a good idea first. And from that it follows that any reader following links at will through an electronic archive will be retracing steps laid out by someone who has thought it out ahead of time. This is not necessarily bad. I'm not sure that I think there is an alternative to it. But it does raise the question, does it not, about whether the editorial work has been objective? Isn't that, after all, the argument for putting all the material forward with as little critical judgment as possible? Is it not the case that every editorial job, even the electronic archive, is critical in nature?

But perhaps that is splitting hairs. The level of critical intervention is minuscule in the electronic archive and, of course, the reader is free to seek connections unmarked by existing links. Well, then, in pursuit of this meditation on loss, could it not be argued that objective neutral editorial principles have created a rich and tangled web that produces information overload? That the result will be fully useful only to the very few people willing to take the time to figure out how to use it without being confused, and that most people who use it will misunderstand what they are doing? Is that not a loss? Again, it seems to me not necessarily bad – but a loss in fact, either of its vaunted objectivity or of a desirable clarity.

Let us turn to the second and more important issue: that, in addition to the historical texts gathered in the virtual archive, a critical edition is also presented. Now of all the viable critical principles one could follow, which is the dominant one chosen for the archive's critical edition? Will it present, like the Northwestern Newberry edition of Melville's *Moby-Dick*, a melding of two historical texts, each misrepresenting the author's intentions in different ways? Will it correct not only the demonstrable typographical errors but the errors of historical or geographical facts, like the Cambridge edition of *The Great Gatsby*? Will it adopt the author's changes but not the managing editor's changes, as I did in the Michigan edition of Thackeray's *The Newcomes*? Or will it conclude that no critical edition is required because the author exercised such good control over the publication processes of the original editions as is argued for the Virginia Electronic Archive of Dante Gabriel Rossetti? Or will it be argued that any modern editor's effort to second guess a genius author, such as William Wordsworth, by restoring a manuscript reading he, bless his heart, had rejected, would be a travesty, as Reiman argues in *The Study of Modern Manuscripts*? I have yet to hear anyone suggest that the electronic scholarly archive should have a critical edition of each sort added to the collection of historical texts. But why not? In what sense is it a gain to have in an archive a historical text that was poorly produced and represents the hasty and not-so-careful editorial work of a commercial publisher rather than the thoughtful, careful work of a scholarly editor – who just happens to pursue editorial goals with which you don't agree?

There are no universally applicable answers to these questions; each project editor will ask and answer them in some particular way that will serve particular purposes and fail in some other way. My point is now what it was at the outset: that no matter how we edit and no matter how big our archive becomes, the result entails losses.

And the moral that I draw from that observation is the one with which I began: that when we come forward with a new way to edit that accomplishes that which was not accomplished before, we resist the temptation to say that our new way is better or that the old way was diminished by errors of concept and inadequacy of procedure. The new way also fails to do that which someone else wants it to do; the new edition may also contain errors of fact or conception. But each edition, including this new one, may do something that is worthy of attention.

This is not to say that editions never fail or should never be ignored or reviled. They fail seriously when they claim to do that which was not done. They fail when the work is inaccurate. They fail when the purpose for which they were designed is not served by the result. But they do not fail just because the purpose for which they were designed is no longer the ruling fad. With one exception, if an edition fulfilled its aims at some point in the past, it still fulfills those aims now. And readers might forever find those editions useful in representing those aims. The exception is the obvious one. If the aim was to serve as the standard edition for all time, it will not. That is a "con game" that cannot succeed long for any edition. I suggest we stop trying to play that game.

What do I suggest instead? That as scholarly editors we do as clear a job as we can, up front in our editions, to describe our aims and give

instructions on how to use the work. This might entail warning readers
about what our new edition is not. It is not the work itself. It is not
uncritical or objective in its representation. It represents a critical
arrangement of, or omissions from, the historical record. And I suggest
for readers, especially scholarly readers – who expect to say things about
the work that are worthy of attention – that they learn to read scholarly
editions and understand what they are and what they are not. Perhaps it
will not affect what they say about a work, but I have a few examples of
folks who didn't bother and who thought it would not matter.

A *PMLA* essay on Thackeray's *Vanity Fair* focused readers' attention
on the narrator's prefatory remarks in "Before the Curtain" about the
showman of the fair and the accompanying frontispiece illustration of a
clown contemplating his reflection in a cracked mirror and compared
these images from the front of the book with the novel's closing illustration of the box of puppets being put away upon the conclusion of the
show. The point of the comparison was to show the continuity of
thought and image from beginning to end of the novel, suggesting the
unity of the novel. The critic seemed unaware that the novel was a
serialization in which the title-page plate, the preface, and the concluding
chapters – in short, all the parts he was referring to from the beginning
and end of the book, were drawn and written and published together as
part of the final number, nineteen months after the commencement of
installment number one, a fact that completely undermines the
assumption upon which the "insight" was based.[4] More recently another
critic complained about Thackeray's explanation of his orthographic
shenanigans in *The Yellowplush Papers* in the installment titled "Skimmings from the 'Dairy of George IV.'" on the grounds it came too late in
the sequence of the footman's English essays. This critic was using a late
collected edition in which the "Skimmings" installment had been moved
by an editor from its original position in fourth place to the twelfth (next
to last), where, of course, the explanation came too late, though not by
Thackeray's choice.[5]

These two examples from *Yellowplush* and *Vanity Fair* are rather
embarrassing, though perhaps benign, illustrations of how ignorance of the
facts of a book's history can render the resulting "critical insights" point-
less. By contrast, the question of whether Thackeray's use of authorial
commentary in *Vanity Fair* was deliberately ambiguous, leaving certain

---

[4] Robert E. Lougy, "The Structure of *Vanity Fair*," *PMLA* 90 (1975), 256–69.
[5] To my knowledge, the essay, which I saw in manuscript, was never published.

inferences pointedly up to the reader, or whether such "intrusions" on the narrative were merely conventional and heavy-handed, can be investigated in the manuscript revisions showing the author toying with the commentary, giving and then withdrawing "authorial" speculations and, in the end, in fact, seeming to mislead the reader on purpose, so that the authorial commentary becomes jokingly untrustworthy.

The argument supports the speculation that Thackeray deliberately trusts the reader to point the moral without assistance. One could remain skeptical of my assertion that the narrator is deliberately refusing to load the dice one way or another – skeptical of the idea that the author systematically trusts the reader to distrust the narrator systematically. One could still conclude that the author was inept or just ambiguous unintentionally. But the following evidence should lay that possibility to rest.

When Sir Pitt, in Chapter 10, tells his son, Pitt, not to preachify while Miss Crawley, the wealthy spinster aunt, is visiting, the first version in the manuscript of the discussion that follows reads:

> "Why, hang it, Pitt," said the father to his remonstrance. "You wouldn't be such a flat as to let three thousand a year go out of the family?"
> "What is money compared to our souls, Sir?" continued Crawley *who knew he was not to inherit a shilling of his aunt's money.* [Italics added]

The last phrase, in the narrator's voice, "who knew he was not to inherit a shilling of his aunt's money." was canceled in the manuscript. This revision makes the accusation instead become Sir Pitt's, who says: "You mean that the old lady won't leave the money to you." However, after the father's retort, the manuscript revision continued in the narrator's voice to make a bald assertion about the characters:

> "What is money compared to our souls, Sir?" continued Crawley.
> "You mean that the old lady won't leave the money to you" – *this was in fact the meaning of Mr. Crawley. No man for his own interest could accommodate himself to circumstances more. In London he would let a great man talk and laugh and be as wicked as he liked: but as he could get no good from Miss Crawley's money why compromise his conscience?. [sic] This was another reason why he should hate Rawdon Crawley. He thought his brother robbed him. Elder brothers often do think so; and curse the conspiracy of the younger children wh. unjustly deprives them of their fortune.* [Italics added]

This narratorial commentary, telling the reader the exact moral standing of both father and son, is canceled at some point between manuscript and proof and replaced by a musingly ambiguous question. In proof the passage appeared as follows:

> "Why, hang it, Pitt," said the father to his remonstrance. "You wouldn't be such a flat as to let three thousand a year go out of the family?"
> "What is money compared to our souls, Sir?" continued Crawley.
> "You mean that the old lady won't leave the money to you" – and who knows but it was Mr. Crawley's meaning?

When the last version appeared in proof, someone (probably Thackeray) drove the doubtfulness home by adding italics to "was" so that the first edition reads: "and who knows but it *was* Mr. Crawley's meaning?" The effect is not only to cast additional doubt on the narrator's overt and cancelled statement but to intensify the suspicion that both Crawleys, young and old, pious and wicked, are corrupt to the core.

I would conclude from these revisions that Thackeray meant to push onto readers the responsibility for "knowing" the unknowable about the characters or at least for deciding for themselves. This "critical insight" is no less an interpretation than the first two (about the similarity of vision between the Preface and the last chapters of *Vanity Fair* or about the effect of the comment on orthography in *Yellowplush*), but unlike those, the historical records actually support rather than contradict the conclusion.

I would conclude, furthermore, that knowledge of the sort scholarly editions can provide has the potential to influence critical insights in ways readers cannot afford to miss. But is there a perfect way to arrange the materials of a scholarly edition? Anyone who thinks there is probably happens also to agree with the critical biases that are privileged by the alleged perfect arrangement. Is there a way to eliminate the editor's critical biases? A meditation on losses would, I hope, make us less sanguine about the achievements of any new scholarly edition and more charitable about the particular uses of the ones ageing on the book shelf.

CHAPTER 8

Hagiolatry, cultural engineering, monument building, and other functions of scholarly editing

Wondrous indeed is the virtue of a true Book ... like a spiritual tree ... it stands from year to year, and from age to age ... ; and yearly comes its new produce of leaves ... , every one of which is talismanic and thaumaturgic, for it can persuade men.

Thomas Carlyle, *Sartor Resartus* (1832)

Because scholarly editing takes a great deal of time, is often tedious, requires meticulous care over masses of minute detail, involves decisions that can easily go wrong, is seldom rewarded by wealth or early promotions, and because every fifty years or less some new hot shot editor comes along demanding that the work scholarly editors have been doing needs complete overhaul and replacement – because so little reward seems to come from so much investment of time and intelligence, I am led to ask: Why do we create scholarly editions, why do we spend our time and our lives in this way?

This chapter has three main sections.[1] The first, called "The everlasting no," rehearses a variety of motives for scholarly editing that have been or should be discarded: they include hagiolatry, monument building, cultural preservation, and cultural engineering. Section II, called "The center of indifference," addresses what we lose and what we gain by discarding the high sounding but weak, false, and decayed motives rehearsed in Section I. And Section III, called, ironically enough, "The everlasting yea," presents some conclusions about what scholarly editing, stripped of its pretensions, actually can and should strive to achieve.

I   THE EVERLASTING NO

I present the following meditation on motives for scholarly editing as a confessional: reasons for editing I have held and discarded. The first is

---

[1] A version of this chapter appeared in *Voice, Text and Hypertext*, ed. Raimonda Modiano, Leroy Searle, and Peter Shillingsburg (Seattle: University of Washington Press, 2003), pp. 412–23.

that scholarly editing might be pursued out of some sense of self-importance or some delusion about the importance of editing. One could start with references to A. E. Housman who famously chose what he considered to be a third-rate writer to edit in order to create a more perfect work and lasting monument, first-rate writers being too difficult to edit perfectly. We could ask how many people know Housman as the editor of the works of Manilius or in what way Housman's significance as a thinker and writer and scholar is memorialized in that edition. While pondering that question, one might ask how few people purchased and cited in their subsequent scholarship my Garland edition of William Thackeray's *Vanity Fair* of which about 300 copies were printed or my edition of Thackeray's *Pendennis* of which 180 copies were printed. Of course, one then needs to sort out whether the value of an edition or of any work is to be gauged by the number of people who respond positively to it or by some less subjective standard – remembering that we live on a planet with approximately six billion people and in an age when the phrase "objective standard" is considered an oxymoron.

In a whimsical chapter of *Resisting Texts* I survey a range of possible meanings of scholarly editions: the meanings of the binding and weight and type. I thought perhaps the 350-year acid-free paper was an attempt to preserve the editor's work as much if not more than the author's work. And if we ask how much money we make as scholarly editors or how many people are "out there clamoring for our new editions," it might be tempting to think that we do what we do because, at least within certain small circles, we gain reputations and feel virtuous. Those are well-deserved rewards for scholarly editing when it is done well, but is that the extent of it? Would we be satisfied if we do what we do solely for the personal rewards found in doing it? I have invested too much of my life in scholarly editing to be able to stand the idea that the Thackeray edition now in progress will fulfill its function in the world by making my name known as Thackeray's editor or by legitimizing my participation in academic conferences.

So perhaps we should spurn the cynical view of scholarly editing as a self-serving activity and adopt a more noble view – one in which the editor serves the author and the author's public by worshipful actions that protect the work from the author's own neglectful or ill-considered actions regarding revisions, or that protect it from the predations of fools and quacks (other quacks, plague take them) who have undertaken to edit it, or actions that resurrect and perpetuate the memory of authors whose reputations have dropped below the horizon of modern consciousness. In pursuing such goals, editors have adopted strategies that minimize readers' awareness of the editorial presence in the text; for, of course, it is the *author's* work that is important. But that is no reason why, in professional communications with each other, we should continue to pretend that we are objective, scientific, principled scholars whose pursuit of truth produces the foundation rocks for significant criticism. The solid rocks of textual scholarship we have hung round our necks weigh about the same as millstones, not just from the weight of paper, but from the weight of cultural significance with which they have been freighted. I don't think the extreme tediousness or length of scholarly commitment to editorial projects is fully justified by these notions of noble actions on behalf of authors, because in the end they don't stand close scrutiny.

To take up and dismiss two more items in my chapter's title can be quickly compassed. Hagiolatry, the sanctification of literature or authorship, has been battered sufficiently in other critical circles to keep us from justifying our work publicly the way we did years ago when phrases like "preserving and restoring our cultural heritage" were spoken without blushing. In recent years it has become far more common for editors to provide access to historical texts than to provide an established text that renders the textual problems and complexities transparent. It is more likely that editors will speak of placing a text in its context than that they will claim to have established the definitive edition of a literary work. It is common for editors now to refer to their work as acts of criticism or as one of several viable editorial acts. And yet paper editions continue to be issued in the formats developed to preserve, once and for all, the definitive editions of the 1960s. I am not complaining about that, just suggesting that there is a disjunction between what we are now saying about the paper editions and the formats in which we package them.

By the phrase "cultural engineering" in my title I refer to the way in which collective efforts to produce scholarly editions can be seen as driven by the cultural preconceptions of the class of people from which scholarly editors derive – it has been said often enough, for example, that the majority of CEAA-approved editions were of the works of dead white males. Indeed, most of the editors are, or soon enough will be, dead white males also. But the phrase "cultural engineering" could refer to the possibility that collective editorial efforts shape or change cultural preconceptions. I do not, however, think of scholarly editing as one of the leading-edge professions in social and cultural revolutions. An increase in the number of scholarly editions of women and minority authors, post-colonial texts or folk writing is more likely to be the result of cultural forces driving editing than the other way around. An increase in the number of electronic editions is also more likely to be the result of cultural forces dragging us into cyberspace than it is that forward thinking scholarly editors are pushing the envelope of electronic innovation. Or perhaps there has been in the breasts of some editors the notion that their editions would help cement a cherished author's place in history or would even spark a resurgence of critical interest. Scholarly editions of William Gilmore Simms, Charles Brockden Brown, and William Makepeace Thackeray have had such effects – on a scale so small that no one has noticed. I am hard pressed to name a major twentieth-century edition that has revolutionized an author's reputation and critical standing. I recall Gary Taylor arguing at a Society for Textual Scholarship conference that perhaps a new edition of Thomas Middleton, or better yet several editions, might restore Middleton to the critical stature and popular reputation relative to Shakespeare that he once enjoyed. But I am not convinced that these motives for editing – that we rehabilitate authors' reputations or that we alter cultural awareness – rise above wishful thinking or even self-deception.

The sea changes in editing, made possible and even necessary by electronic media for editions, also reveal motives that ring false. When the first serious attacks on the notion of *definitive texts* were mounted, editors first defended their work by declaring that it was the *edition* not the *text* that was definitive. What the scholarly edition made possible, they said, was the serious study of texts and their variants because the list of emendations made possible the reconstruction of the copy-text and the historical collation made possible the essential reconstruction of other authoritative texts. Thus the text and apparatus combined to present a definitive source for study of the author's text and check on the editor's work. One hesitates to ask how many persons have actually used a scholarly edition to reconstruct a copy-text, or how many, bent on reconstructing other authoritative texts, found everything essential to such work in a historical collation. In fact the scholarly print edition could not sustain the burden of being called a definitive edition either; too much had to be left out because it was too expensive to print or because the technologies of printed editions made it impractical. Students interested in the bibliographical matrixes and cultural contexts of works demand more than print editions can supply. Much as they were clear improvements over the less thoughtful editions of the past, these new *editions* turned out to be no more definitive than the *texts*.

Some of the current arguments for electronic editions sound ominously like renewed attempts by editors to be definitive. One claim for electronic editions is that they are archives of texts. The editor's meddling hand has been curbed one stage earlier than was possible in any printed work. The computer makes possible, we are told, the juxtaposition of all the relevant texts in their linguistic and bibliographic variant forms. Thus a library of electronic texts, linked to explanations and parallels and histories, becomes accessible to a richly endowed posterity. To the extent that such archives contain accurate transcriptions, high resolution reproductions, precise and reliable guides to the provenance and significance of their contents, and the extent to which they are comprehensive, to that extent they are "definitive" – until the next generation of critics and scholars with new interests notices some other aspect of texts that scholarly editors of the past (by then that will be us) took for granted and ignored. But already, information overload has set in. The comprehensiveness of the electronic archive threatens to create a salt, estranging sea of information, separating the archive user from insights into the critical significance of textual histories.

II   THE CENTER OF INDIFFERENCE

I should pause to say that I don't think this line of argument leads to the conclusion that electronic archives should not be undertaken. The same cogent arguments for the accumulation of major libraries apply to the accumulation and preparation of major electronic archives. The arguments for the creation of library catalogues and other reference works, exploring the significance of libraries and archives, remain cogent as reasons to accumulate and explain textual histories of individual works. But there is something imposed upon editorial work by the drive for objectivity and comprehensiveness and endurance that leaves the results in some important way unsatisfactory. My task in this section is to try to track down the source of that dissatisfaction and to gauge its importance.

One approach to this problem is to ask what textual critics and scholarly editors lose when they give up the words "definitive," "objective," "established," "standard," "authoritative," "exhaustive," "comprehensive," and "complete". What do we lose if we acknowledge some pretty well-known but shushed facts about scholarly editions: that they are infrequently cited in critical articles, infrequently used as classroom texts, infrequently cited in term papers; that copy-texts and alter-texts are more easily and satisfactorily reconstructed by obtaining a photocopy (or an authentic exemplar) than by examining emendations tables; that nobody can or will read electronic texts of long prose works let alone an electronic archive of them; that in order to use an "unedited" text or archive to discover how a work was written and what difference that makes to a reading of the work, one must collate and compare and analyze the relevant texts? What do we lose if we acknowledge that our best editorial efforts and the best efforts of our publicists will soon join the largely silent chorus of has-been editions, discredited in the light of new ways of conceiving texts, textuality, and textual scholarship? What do we lose if we grasp firmly the contradictory truths, first, that the reader must do the textual work for herself in order to fully appreciate and understand the significance of variations in texts, not only linguistic and bibliographic but contextual, and, second, that if the scholarly editor does not do it for the reader, it probably will not get done?

First, let me say what I think we do not lose: We do not lose a reason to edit texts, or to preserve them, or to archive them, or to annotate them, or to examine them for their linguistic and bibliographic histories or their cultural, economic, and generic contexts. We do not lose a reason for trying to discover as much as can be known about how texts have become and how they have worked. And, perhaps the most important thing that is *not* lost, even when we give up this list of noble sounding terms, is the desire or necessity to be accurate in our work.

But we do lose a lot of excess baggage, inflated rhetoric, electronic hype, a false sense of importance and accomplishment, and the narrow grounds from which to bash the work of other editors. I assert that we lose these unnecessary things, though I do not intend to prove that it is so. But I speak from experience. And with these happy losses, I say, we gain a great deal of freedom. What a relief it is to an editor to be able to express an opinion without having to claim it as the standard opinion, to be able to assume that the user of an edition can and should know that an edition is a work of literary criticism, anchored in evidence, but to be used skeptically. How refreshing it is to be able to create an edition that represents no more than our best ability to respond to the textual evidence we have found. How light the burden becomes and interesting the chase when we cease to pretend objectivity in building monuments to the literary heroes of yore. How many times have scholarly editors failed to follow an enlightened instinct because the rules of definitive editing prescribed some other action?

I recall as an example, Gordon Haight's Clarendon edition of George Eliot's *Mill on the Floss*. Haight, as mentioned in chapter six, did a superb job of locating and identifying primary materials and articulating the compositional and publication history of the *Mill*. The introduction to the Clarendon edition provides a convincing and well-written account of how Eliot had read the proof for one edition but not another, how she had prepared copy for a third edition by marking up a copy of the second edition, and how the printers (or publishers or someone) had in each edition incrementally toned down and conventionalized the dialect spelling in the speech of her countrified characters. Faced with a textual situation in which the author had taken an active role, and believing that Eliot might have deliberately passed up the chance to reimpose dialect spellings, the editor prepared a text representing a fusion of Eliot's and the printers' work on the text. Although surviving documents include a manuscript, the first edition, the second edition (for which Eliot read proofs but did not supply copy), and a copy of the second edition with Eliot's manuscript corrections and revisions for the third edition, nevertheless, the editor chose as copy-text the third edition, which Eliot had not proofread. Why did the editor pick the first completely non-authoritative text as the copy-text? Because, he said, as much as he personally preferred the dialect spellings of the manuscript or even the slightly toned down versions in the first edition, nevertheless, the third edition represented a more corrected version and might incorporate Eliot's surrender to the publisher's and perhaps the public's need for more conventional spellings. Haight actually sounds sorrowful as he expresses his regret at the loss of authorial forms, and he sounds nearly apologetic about the typos introduced in the third edition which he now had to emend, thus calling special attention to the most trivial variants in the whole textual history. But he was impelled, by some notion of the rules of editing and of definitiveness, to make an editorial decision that few other people would have made, or if they did, they would not have made it for his reasons. Quite frankly, had Haight followed his critical inclinations, his edition would have accidentally conformed to the editorial norms of his day even more than it did as a result of his effort to do the normative thing. But that is a separate problem. That is to say, I am not now focusing on editorial acts taken by editors who do not fully understand their business or who do not articulate well either what they have done or why they have done it. I am instead focusing on the effects on texts worked by a "desire to do right" or a desire to "be definitive" or to eliminate individual critical judgment from editions. Those desires too frequently have led editors to reject their own best thinking in favor of what they believe to be the prevailing rules of editing, which are designed to inhibit the exercise of individual judgment – and thereby gain longevity for the edition. Forlorn hope.

And, of course, there are reasons to behave in that way. I have already elsewhere told the story of how my edition of Thackeray's *Vanity Fair* was rejected by the MLA's Committee on Scholarly Editions in the year I retired as chairman of that organization. In matters such as these it is good to remember that there is an inside view and an outside view, so that my assessment of that debacle is not likely to be the only one, but from my point of view the CSE that year wanted a conventional edition more than it wanted one that was sensibly edited. I remember the inspector wanting me to reject the manuscript as copy-text because it survived for only a part of the book. I suspect that the underlying reason was that the inspector in any case preferred editorial policies that regularly chose printed copy-texts over manuscript ones. There are, I know, outspoken advocates of that position in the profession, but the rationale proposed by the CSE inspector was not one of the ones frequently heard today. It was merely that the mixture of manuscript and printed copy-texts produced an inconsistent texture for the work – a fact I had explicitly brought to his attention in my introduction and dismissed as not compelling. Another CSE inspector and committee approved essentially that same edition a few years later.[2]

As I see it now, the desire for consistency, like the desire for definitiveness, is a force driving towards an edition with a reading text that could stand for the work itself – one in which the editor had fulfilled the perfection that author and publisher must have wanted and would have achieved had they had time and a research grant. Most scholarly editors have now abandoned such hopes, but there are two radically different ways in which to do so. Some editors retreat to the archive, increasing their insistence that the editor's personal judgment be curbed – believing that the exercise of individual judgment is what caused the problem with those misguided attempts to achieve textual perfection. The other is to recognize that editing inevitably involves the exercise of individual judgment, that texts have always been in some sense unsatisfactory, and that the best work of any editor, like the best work of any critic, will before long appear dated and in want of replacement. What a relief to be able to produce an edition that represents the editor's best thinking, rather than his or her most conventional thinking. What a relief to acknowledge that the purpose for the new edition is to arrange the evidence in a way that lends coherence to the editor's best insights into the

---

[2] An extended account of the Thackeray edition is in my "Editing Thackeray: A History," *Studies in the Novel* 27 (1995), 363–74.

author, the text, and the cultural milieu of text-creation – or of some other combination of forces the editor has identified as relevant. What a relief to cast off the burden of trying, in the scholarly edition, to establish the text as a standard for all time.

My sense of relief is based on the acknowledgment that there are two components of an edition that must be kept distinct. The first is that editions incorporate evidence. The second is that editions incorporate editorial insight. Evidence is found, not created. It is what it is. We cannot do anything *about* evidence. But we can do things *to* evidence. We can represent (or even misrepresent) it. But every act of (re)presentation is an act of criticism, an act of interpretation. Every new edition, every digitized image, every hyperlink establishing a relationship between bits of evidence is interpretational. Editorial insight can be narrow or comprehensive, convincing or unconvincing, well- or ill-articulated, but it remains insight and is not to be confused with evidence. The important thing to remember is that the evidence cannot be presented without interpretation and that editorial insight is a necessary component of editions. I suspect that sounds anathema to some editors – except those in denial, charitably thinking that I do not believe what I am writing.

I could list any number of writers on editorial practice who pay lip service to the notion that editorial insight and interpretation are necessary components of editions but who immediately turn to the rules of editing designed to prevent editors from exercising individual judgment. The essays in *Contemporary German Editorial Theory* are, for example, occupied primarily with explanations of how German editorial practice acknowledges the difference between "the artifact" (which is hard evidence – the physical document) and the "aesthetic object" (which is an editorial or reader's construct – the thing witnessed by the document) and then imposes rules that will prevent the exercise of individual judgment – that would prevent any efforts to edit the text in order to produce a text that better represents the aesthetic object.[3] Hans Zeller, for example, proposes the imposition of blanket rules designed to avoid the worst excesses of intentionalist, idealist editing – but at the terrible cost of adopting uncritically the introduction of textual faults even by unauthorized (re)transmitters of the text who have acquired "authorized"

[3] Hans Walter Gabler, George Bornstein, and Gillian Borland Pierce, eds., *Contemporary German Editorial Theory* (Ann Arbor: University of Michigan Press, 1995).

status just by not being noticed. Zeller was unhappy with the result of his own recommendations – as well he should be. He wrote:

> A new problem presents itself here which I regard as fundamentally unsolvable. It is best known through M. Bernays's (1866) discovery of the fatal effect of Himburg's corrupt pirated editions (1779) on Goethe's revision of his *Schriften*, specifically on the *Werther* of 1787. In the textual comparison with the initial edition of 1774 the corruptions are so blatant and scandalous that one would hesitate to allow the principles developed here to apply to this text.[4]

"Fundamentally unsolvable," Zeller says, because the only way to solve them is to abandon the principles developed for the purpose of preventing editors from doing what they think is best. That is pure sophistry combined with cowardice and perhaps a modicum of pomposity about the objectivity of scholarly editions. The barriers to solving Zeller's problems were erected by Zeller and by other editorial theorists pursuing definitiveness (by whatever label they prefer) and opposing individual judgment in the false belief that objectivity was the goal of scholarly editing. If it is, woe be to us all.[5]

My point is that the fundamental dissatisfaction one feels about scholarly editions is not that they don't get the recognition they merit, but that they have pretensions they cannot actually fulfill. We do not feel comfortable pretending to accomplishments that are false. We know they are false – whether the public does or not.

III   THE EVERLASTING YEA

When Thomas Carlyle got to his everlasting yea, he found doing work to be better than being purposeless in life. But I cannot bring myself to say that editing is better than being purposeless. I lived too long in the land that produced the song, "I ain't doing nothing but I'm not quite done," to believe that editing is a cure for purposelessness. Carlyle's everlasting yea did not entail a belief that anything made by man would last for very long, but like Carlyle, I think we can develop a positive attitude toward

---

[4] "Structure and Genesis in Editing: On German and Anglo-American Textual Criticism," in *Contemporary German Editorial Theory*, ed. Hans Walter Gabler, George Bornstein, and Gillian Borland Pierce (Ann Arbor: University of Michigan Press, 1995), pp. 95–123.

[5] I expressed this charge in "A Resistance to Contemporary German Editorial Theory," *editio* 12 (1998), 138–50. Its publication prompted a response which puts Zeller's argument in a better light: Bodo Plachta, "In Between the 'Royal Way' of Philology and 'Occult Science': Some Remarks About German Discussion on Text Constitution in the Last Ten Years," *TEXT* 12 (1999), 31–47. I take these issues up in greater detail in the next chapter.

editorial work that can stand scrutiny. As usual, it comes with names and distinctions that, for me at least, remove the confusions and dissatisfaction involved in mistaking one thing for another or in using one name to refer to two unlike activities.

When we look at the textual condition, its materials, its events, its players, and its mental states, we see many things that need to be done, many things that are the scholarly editor's responsibility, many things that have been called editing. But some of them are not editing, though editors frequently do them. If we separate out these activities, we can see why one person's view of the editing task might fail to satisfy another person's needs.

First, there is collection of evidence, making libraries and archives of the artifacts, material documents, and mechanically reproduced images of them. Without this foundation of collection and archiving, editors could not claim to be historical. This archiving activity is not, however, editing. It is collecting, describing, cataloguing, and indexing.

Second, though there is nothing particularly sequential in this list, are the acts of introducing and annotating texts. These activities have been called editing for as long as any other activity. They are important activities, and in recent years have come into their own as the vehicles for insights into the cultural, social, economic, and political contexts of texts. But introduction writing or annotation writing are not textual editing. It can easily be argued that a textual editor who has not annotated the text for its cultural and other contexts is not in a position to conduct textual editing with much sophistication, but annotating is not editing.

Third, the evidence of texts must be represented in reproducible form such as editions, both print and electronic. Since every act of representation of evidence not only entails loss but is critical and interpretive, we must strive for clarity about what we did and about why we did it, erring on the side of excess when presenting supporting materials and explanations, and when pointing out the relations between documents or between the text and historical events and places. We strive for accuracy and clarity not because they will insure the longevity of our editions, but because accuracy and clarity are the foundations of good scholarship and good criticism. We can never forget that the compilation of a scholarly edition is the interpretive best thinking of an editor and is NOT the establishment of a text for all time. Representing texts, delineating their textual and formal histories, and sorting out the agents of change in those histories is editing. No two editors would produce the same results. It is not science.

Fourth, I am particularly concerned that the critical, interpretive consequences of archiving, annotating, and editing not be lost as needles in a haystack of apparatuses. We should emphasize forums for the presentation of the best insights of textual criticism. I have said many times that editors spend enormous energy exploring the textual richness of the works they investigate and then hide the best things they discover in a clear reading text and a pile of evidence in an apparatus. What we have discovered is richness and the relevance of textual criticism; yet we do not write enough critical essays explaining the ways in which our work affects our understanding of the texts we edit. We do not write enough reviews of scholarly editions showing how textual criticism changes our reading of texts. We do not bring textual and editorial insight often enough into conference sessions other than those devoted to textual criticism. We spend too much time talking and writing to each other. This fourth matter is not editing, but it is something I think more editors should undertake.

In their very different ways, Hershel Parker and Jerry McGann have done as much as any of us to focus attention on the interpretive significance of textual histories. They have accomplished this primarily through critical analyses of texts, rather than through the production of the works they have edited. It is the essays and books they have written that have brought the consequences of textual insights to the wider attention of literate people. My view is that Parker has been less influential than his basic insight deserves because his method of presenting it demands assent more than it exercises persuasion. McGann's far more influential position is marred, in my view, by a tendency shared by some Historical-Critical (i.e., Germanic) editors, to allow blanket decisions to override the exercise of better judgment in specific instances. But both writers have written passionately, entertainingly, intelligently, and knowledgeably about the effects that variant forms of texts have on understanding and interpretation. If the people who do the real work of examining texts closely will also write about the interpretive consequences of their hard won knowledge, the difference between understanding texts and dancing around them, or taking airy flights from them, as many critics do, might become more evident in our profession.

CHAPTER 9

The aesthetic object: "the subject of our mirth"

In what follows, therefore, I shall be trying to explain why I stand with [Herschel] Parker (and against [G. Thomas] Tanselle) in maintaining the distinction between historical and literary work, and why I support Tanselle (as against Parker) in Tanselle's view of the distinction between private and public documents. My own view of literary work, and hence of how to go about editing it, rests on this pair of distinctions. Furthermore, the distinctions highlight the centrality of literary texts for understanding the textual condition.

Jerome McGann, *The Textual Condition* (1991)

Still, after years of regular exchanges at conferences[1] on German editorial problems and theories and in the pages of journals of textual scholarship like *editio* and *TEXT*, there remain misunderstandings (which is unfortunate) and disagreements (which may be inevitable) between Anglo-American editors and German (and other continental) editors about certain key issues in the production of Historical-Critical Editions, or Scholarly Editions, as they are known to Anglo-American scholars.[2]

---

[1] Between 1998 and 2003 I attended six conferences devoted to textual scholarship and editorial principles and practice in the Netherlands and Germany, and key German and Dutch scholars from those conferences presented papers at the biannual meeting of the Society for Textual Scholarship in New York. A continuing theme at these meetings was the differences between Historical-Critical editing and various forms of Anglo-American theory and practice. The resulting papers are given in the next note.

[2] The central documents of this discussion are: *Contemporary German Editorial Theory*, essays translated into English and edited by Hans Walter Gabler, George Bornstein, and Gillian Borland Pierce (University of Michigan Press, 1995). My reaction to these materials was first delivered in The Hague and printed as "A Resistance to German Editorial Theory," *editio* 12 (1998), 138–50. Bodo Plachta's response, presented in New York at the Society for Textual Scholarship Convention, was published as "In Between the 'Royal Way' of Philology and 'Occult Science': Some Remarks About German Discussion on Text Constitution in the Last Ten Years," *TEXT* 12 (1999), 31–47. My subsequent response, "Orientations to Texts," in *editio* (2001), was presented at the German editing conference in Lingen (2000). In addition, my contribution to *Text und Edition: Positionen und Perspektiven* (Berlin: Erich Schmidt, 2000), edited by Nutt-Kofoth, Plachta, van Vliet, and Zwerchina, has a bearing on the exchange of ideas, "Anglo-amerikanische Editionssissenschaft: Ein knapper Überblick." Other important contributions include Dieter Mehl,

In general terms the misunderstandings and disagreements seem to focus on the goals of scholarly editing and the concepts of authorization. At the core of the difficulty is, I believe, the distinction between the textual artifact and what Gunter Martens has called the "aesthetic object" – between physical documents and the art that they witness or represent.[3] This distinction was discussed briefly in the previous chapter; here it forms a background to explorations of other distinctions leading to disagreements over theory and practice in scholarly editing. Both German and American critics make that distinction, but we seem not to assess its importance in the same way. I offer here the hypothesis that our differences in methods and goals arise in part from differences in the basic materials with which we work.

Two observations might help to explain Anglo-American views. First, when envisioning or abstracting the aesthetic object from the artifact, readers can distinguish between their own notion of the aesthetic object (in the moment of reading) and what may have been the author's notion (at the time of writing). I am not saying we can know the author's view, only that we can distinguish between our personal aesthetic preferences and a different view that we attribute to the author on the basis of patterns of revision, on the author's statements, and on long acquaintance with the author's works. Both authorial and personal notions of the work of art are, however, abstractions from the document – from the text on the page – and thus both are constructs enabled by critical judgment. Anglo-American scholarly editors generally reject their own aesthetic preferences in favor of the aesthetic preferences attributed to the author, striving to emend to fulfill authorial preferences not the editor's personal aesthetic preferences. Nevertheless, individual critical acts of construction are involved, no matter how well intentioned the editor. And German historical-critical editors reject the notion of emending a documentary text in order to fulfill anyone's notion of an intended aesthetic object. Their approach is, therefore, fundamentally documentary rather than

---

"Editorial Theory and Practice in English Studies in Germany," and Bodo Plachta, "Teaching Editing – Learning Editing," both in *Problems of Editing* biehefte zu *editio*, ed. Christa Jansohn (1999). If one takes a longer view, this exchange of ideas across the Atlantic can be said to have begun with Hans Zeller's "A New Approach to the Critical Constitution of Literary Texts" in *Studies in Bibliography* (1975) and was continued significantly in Hans Walter Gabler's edition of James Joyce, *Ulysses* (1987).

[3] Gunter Martens, "(De)Constructing the Text by Editing: Reflections on the Receptional Significance of Textual Apparatuses," in *Contemporary German Editorial Theory*, ed. Hans Walter Gabler, George Bornstein, and Gillian Borland Pierce (Ann Arbor: University of Michigan Press, 1995), pp. 125–52.

intentionalist; the work is defined in relation to documentary witnesses, not in relation to the aims of those who created the documents.

The second observation is that, because differences are perceived between the textual artifacts and the aesthetic objects they represent, readers often act as if the textual artifacts are inaccurate or inadequate or corrupted or all three. Consequently, Anglo-American editors do not entirely trust the artifact, and from thence comes a reduced tendency to accept the authority of each and every reading in the document. Anglo-American editors often see their role as mediating between the fallible and inaccurate document and the more accurate or satisfactory aesthetic object. The aesthetic object, both German and Anglo-American editors agree, is what readers actually engage with at the level of meaning, style, and effect; but, as I understand it, German editors, by and large, would not try to provide readers with a new text claiming to be a closer approximation to an author's "aesthetic object" than is the text in an existing document. That is, they would not tend to emend a base text or copy-text in order to make it more closely approximate the aesthetic object, and the primary reason appears to be because individual interpretation would have to be employed. Instead, such editors strive to present readers with the historical artifacts and the physical information that can be used as a basis for individual interpretive engagements with the aesthetic object that is implied by the artifacts.

One might ask, then, why Anglo-American editors have focused for so long and with such intensity on the "aesthetic object," to use Martens's term. In fact the Anglo-American tradition would never adopt that term, for we also wish very much to avoid the idea of "aesthetic" editing. We use instead such terms as "authorial intentions" and "eclectic editions." For Continental editors, the words "intention" and "eclectic" are not good words, either; but Anglo-American editors have thought them to be superior to the term "aesthetic" because that word conjures a goal or aim in editing that places taste and improvement above respect for documentary evidence or authorial or other authorized acts. "Aesthetic editing" suggests an editor with a taste for improving what the author did. Anglo-American editors reject that completely unhistorical view – as, of course, German editors do also.

A look at some specific American and English textual histories reveals some characteristics in those histories that help account for why Anglo-American editors so often continue editing (emending) even after they have established what constitutes the textual artifacts – the place German editors tend to stop. Why do we wish to push beyond the artifacts to edit the aesthetic object? Is there something about American and English texts that is commonly different from German and Dutch texts that would cause editors to want to edit the author's intentions rather than to rest content with accurate representations of textual artifacts and a mapping of their relationships? Why is there that tendency in American editors?

One suggestion is that Anglo-American editorial traditions derive primarily from work with Shakespeare's texts, while German traditions derive primarily from work with Goethe's texts.[4] Two editorial problems with greater differences could not be selected as national norms. For Shakespeare there is not one single extant literary manuscript; for Goethe there are many. For Shakespeare it cannot be determined that he made any effort to get his works published (in fact the opposite seems to be the case); for Goethe the evidence is that he participated either in fact or in spirit with the attempts to publish his works. For Shakespeare the history of textual criticism has been to correct and improve the textual failures and disasters that attended the earliest attempts to publish his works; for Goethe textual criticism appears to defend and clarify the processes that led to the creation of the early texts. About Shakespeare's methods of composition and revision we know nothing; about Goethe's we know a great deal. An obvious, though not necessarily accurate conclusion to draw from these contrasts is that the Ango-American editorial tendency, set in train by the problems of editing Shakespeare, has been interventionist, while the German tradition, informed by the problems of editing Goethe, has tended to be descriptive and organizational – because at bottom Goethe's historical texts have been satisfactory and Shakespeare's have not.

The fact that there has been a strong German tradition of editing Shakespeare perhaps should have, but seems not to have had, a counter effect in Germany. It is also a fact that Anglo-American editorial practice on modern literature is blessed with many works for which there is just as much extant manuscript material as has survived for Goethe, which perhaps should have had, but seems not to have had, a counter effect on Anglo-American editors. Though useful to suggest national textual origins, we must seek additional explanations for the continued divergence between Anglo-American and German editorial theory and practice.

One such explanation – again difficult to demonstrate without extensive, detailed surveys of the writings of many authors – has two related premises: that German authors on average presented publishers with more carefully finished manuscripts than did Anglo-American authors, and that

---

[4] I was reminded of this idea in conversation by H. T. M. van Vliet.

German publishers (compositors) on average tended to reproduce their copy more accurately, perhaps because they felt more confidence in the manuscripts they worked from. While I do not have personal experience editing German texts, I accept this general observation from discussions with many German editors met at conferences. Like all generalizations, exceptions are easy to find, and one, already mentioned in the previous chapter, involves Goethe's own texts. *The Sorrows of Young Werther* was first published in 1774 and became almost immediately the bible of *sturm und drang* romanticism. Its account of the hopeless love of a young man for a married woman, ending in his suicide using pistols obtained from the woman's own hand caught the imagination of all Europe, leading to many piratical republications – in particular, the hastily, carelessly, indeed, abominably produced editions of a publisher named Himburg. Fourteen years after its first publication, Goethe prepared a new edition of *Werther* for his collected works (1787). By this time several things conspired to make Goethe alter the work, reducing its most provocatively romantic elements. Instead of choosing the 1774 first edition or the original manuscript, Goethe began with the corrupted 1779 Himburg edition. The result is a very important, thoroughly revised *Werther* in which Goethe's new work is mixed in with many readings that originated by accident in Himburg's piratical edition. What "authority" is to be found in this edition? How does this document "witness" the work of art? Did Goethe "intend" every word and point of punctuation in the new edition, including the perpetuated readings introduced in the Himburg? If an editor is to produce for modern readers the revised version of the work, is it justifiable to remove the Himburg errors by restoring the correct readings from the original, 1774, edition? Or should the editor say that Goethe had a chance to correct those errors; and the fact that he did not confers upon them not only the documentary authority they have from the fact of their existence in the revised document but the authorial blessing, tacit though it is, of having passed under the author's eye. Do we have the right to assume he did not see what he was looking at? As mentioned before, one German editor has written, "In the textual comparison with the initial edition of 1774 the corruptions are so blatant and scandalous that one would hesitate to allow the principles developed here [in an essay on editorial procedures] to apply to this text."[5] The point is that this

[5] Hans Zeller, "Structure and Genesis in Editing: On German and Anglo-American Textual Criticism," in *Contemporary German Editorial Theory*, ed. Hans Walter Gabler, George Bornstein, and Gillian Borland Pierce (Ann Arbor: University of Michigan Press, 1995), p. 116.

Goethe textual problem is very much like the common textual situations found in Anglo-American texts, but the German tendency to respect the documentary text and distrust the editorial itch to correct has led in this case to an expression of dissatisfaction with German editorial principles but has not led to a revision of German principles of emendation. An Anglo-American approach to this problem would begin with different premises, derived from greater familiarity with the breakdown of good intentions in the creation of texts.

A range of small examples might support this view of production processes that have led Anglo-American editors to distrust printed texts. One famous example concerns Herman Melville's novel *White Jacket* about a sailor whose sense of guilt and unworthiness forms a focus of attention. Sailors wore white jackets, and this sailor's jacket was soiled – as apparently was also his soul. At one point in the novel he falls overboard. In one of the most famous critical books on Melville at the mid-twentieth century, the critic F. O. Matthiessen quoted the description of the sailor's fall in which are the words: he was brushed by a "soiled fish of the sea." Matthiessen declared the word "soiled" to be a choice of genius of which only Melville would be capable. The metaphoric resonance with the theme of guilt is perfectly captured in this word.[6] Unfortunately for Matthiessen, a bibliographer has since demonstrated that Melville did not write the word "soiled." The two authorized editions say "coiled fish of the sea" referring perhaps to a seahorse or similar creature. The word "soiled" was introduced by a typesetter in a twentieth-century edition long after Melville's death.[7]

Though parallel stories have been told of German books, including Goethe's, my point is that American textual scholars can cite so many instances that we have come to believe that misprints and inadvertent texts are the norm, that the discrepancies between artifact and aesthetic object are real, palpable, and emendable. Every book is likely to have a buried landmine typo ready to go off like a soiled bomb if one is not careful. The reason for this, it has been alleged, is that English and

---

[6] F. O. Matthiessen, *American Renaissance* (New York: Oxford University Press, 1941), p. 392.

[7] Only the first American and first English editions have any authority. The substitution of "soiled" for "coiled" was introduced by the Constable edition of 1922. Matthiessen's error was first pointed out by John W. Nichol, "Melville's 'Soiled' Fish of the Sea,'" *American Literature* 21 (November 1949), 338–9. A good account of this critical error and its exposure is in Gordon N. Ray's "The Importance of Original Editions," *Nineteenth Century English Books* (Urbana: University of Illinois Press, 1952). The issue is resurrected and rehearsed from a different point of view by James Thorpe in "The Aesthetics of Textual Criticism" (*PMLA* 80 1965; rptd. in Thorpe, *Principles of Textual Criticism*, pp. 3–49).

American printers are notoriously careless craftsmen. The records of the Stationers Register in London, the guild of printers, which was maintained from the sixteenth through the nineteenth centuries, is littered with advice against, and fines for, drunkenness in the composing room and pressroom.[8]

Whether there is truth and justice in the charge of drunkenness I do not know, but the record of angry and disgusted authors railing against printers is even more entertaining and horrific. Mark Twain wrote a letter to his friend William Dean Howells complaining that he had just been reading proofs for a story and had discovered that the printer had made extensive adjustments to the punctuation. Twain remarked to his friend that he knew more about punctuation in his little finger than the printer knew in his whole body. Furthermore, he claimed, he had sent an angry telegraph message to have the printer shot without being given time to pray.[9] The preface to the poet A. E. Housman's *A Shropshire Lad* (1891) notes that he had expended great care proofreading the book to ensure its utmost accuracy, but the last word of this explanation is the sad expression: "Alas."

Non-scholarly traditions of editing in England and America may also have contributed to the general sense that new editions need to be changed textually as a normal aspect of preparation; for from Caxton's editions of Chaucer's *Tales* and *Le Morte Darthur* onward, printers, publishers, and editors have actively sought ways to grant added value to their new texts, improving them, adapting them to new or younger or more sophisticated audiences. It seems that if a new edition can be advertised as containing new materials or to be based on previously unknown manuscripts or to be more readable by young people, readers will flock to the bookstores. Families of recently dead authors are famous for editing the works of their illustrious ancestors, carefully manipulating the texts to put the best face on what the author did, either to protect a reputation or extend a copyright or both. Scholarly editors have then extended the sense of a need for change by pointing out these manipulations and restoring original "authorial" forms; for they frequently

[8] A brief search for comparable warnings or conditions in continental European print houses has not yet yielded results – perhaps because northern European print houses were better regulated than English ones. The stereotyped notion of German orderliness may point to the existence of conditioned behavior among both authors and printers such that a mixture of authorities in a single document was rare, thus removing much of the appeal of eclectic editing from German editorial projects.

[9] These and a good many more examples are found in "The Treatment of Accidentals" in James Thorpe, *Principles of Textual Criticism* (San Marino: Huntington Library, 1972), pp. 141–51.

argue that the process of manipulation started when the author first submitted a manuscript to a publisher.

An example of what we have come to expect as normal practice for American books can be seen in William Faulkner's *Go Down, Moses*.[10] In a passage describing incessant abundant rains, we find in all editions the phrase: " . . . the valley rose, bled a river . . ." (p. 45). Readers have been struck, no doubt, by this "Faulknerian locution," but in the typescript, which we know Faulkner typed at his own typewriter, we find the following: " . . . the valley rese,bled a river." We can imagine the process by which "rese,bled" – which is clearly an error for "resembled" (for what Faulkner "intended" to type was that the "valley resembled a river") – we can imagine the process by which "rese,bled" became "rose, bled." The typesetter set: "rese, bled a river" with a space after the comma; someone corrected this to "rose, bled"; and that is what every reader has thought Faulkner wrote.

It is not what Faulkner wrote. That is a fact. And it is not what Faulkner meant to write. That is a well-informed conjecture. No textual artifact from Faulkner's lifetime has what Faulkner intended to write. And that is so frequently the case in the textual histories of Anglo-American works, that scholarly editors have developed an attitude toward surviving documents that influences what they believe to be their purpose. The first edition of *Go Down, Moses* also contains "stride" for "strike," "ditching the dyking machines" for "ditching and dyking machines," "mawin" for "mawnin," "later" for "lather," "boiling" for "moiling," "land" for "landing," "his" for "him," "Joe Baker" for "Jobaker," "straw" for "stray," "him" for "them," "that" for "than," "one" for "ones," and the utterly incomprehensible passage:

> Well, I wouldn't say that Roth Edmonds
> can hunt one doe every day and night for two weeks and
> was a poor hunter or a unlucky one neither. A man that
> still have the same doe left to hunt on again next year –

This problem has a simple solution: just reverse the order of the second and third lines:

> Well, I wouldn't say that Roth Edmonds
> was a poor hunter or a unlucky one neither. A man that

---

[10] The following examples come from an especially marked-up copy prepared by James B. Meriwether and his students in 1968, by comparing the typescript for the short story, the typescript for the book, and the Modern Library (1942) edition.

can hunt one doe every day and night for two weeks and
still have the same doe left to hunt on again next year –

The documents are flawed. All of them. The manuscripts are inade-
quately punctuated and poorly spelled, the typescripts are littered with
typos, the galley proofs offer some corrections and introduce new errors,
the first editions are the products of compositors' intentions as much as
they are of authorial intention. And the compositors' actions frequently
reveal intentions that are muddled, conventional, or ignorant and in any
case undesirable by comparison with those of the author.

"Well," I anticipate historical-critical editors will say, "that is not a
problem. Each text is important as a text. Choose the authorial document, if you like, instead of the compositorial document as the main text
in your edition and show the variants in the apparatus." No doubt many
editors believe that there is enough freedom granted to the editor in
making a choice amongst documents. What follows is an attempt to
explain why such a solution does not seem viable, at least to this Anglo-
American editor.[11]

In chapter two, above, I described briefly the differences between
W. M. Thackeray's rhetorical punctuation, followed in his manuscripts,
and his publisher's syntactical punctuation – a difference of practice with
significant effect on reading experiences. But the problem, in truth, is
more complicated because Thackeray's manuscripts are radically under-
punctuated even by the loose standards of rhetorical principles. Although,
as Thackeray's editor, I have produced accurate transcripts of the
manuscripts, I imagine only another textual scholar would have the
patience to read them in that form. The original compositors, of course,
read them – and misread them, too. Thus, the compositors were both
beneficial and hurtful to the accuracy and polish of the work. The greatest
benefit bestowed by the compositors on Thackeray's manuscript texts was
a consistency of conventional punctuation, particularly in the use of
quotation marks in dialogue. Although Thackeray was not careful about
much of the routine punctuation like quotation marks, he was clearly
following rhetorical principles in the punctuation he did use. As mentioned in chapter two, rhetorical punctuation indicates the length of
pauses required for expressive reading, while syntactical punctuation

---

[11] Two lines of argument could follow from this point. The one I have chosen examines the material
texts to find reasons in their composition and material existence for finding each in some serious
way unacceptable. A different approach would be to examine the reasoning by which the "rules for
authorization" have developed.

indicates grammatical units. The result is that Thackeray's expressive punctuation is wedded, in the manuscript, to a textual artifact that lacks much of the routine punctuation that readers of books normally expect. The first edition – the alternative textual artifact – has the required conventional punctuation but has overridden and obscured Thackeray's expressive punctuation. It would be ludicrous to expect a reader of either the manuscript or the first edition to supply from an apparatus the necessary changes that would allow the construction of an aesthetic object resembling Thackeray's intended text: one with his expressive punctuation intact combined with conventional pointing in routine matters. No one would do it, because, as a typical example, in *The History of Henry Esmond,* the printed text of which is about 500 pages long, there are over 18,000 variants between the manuscript and the first edition alone.[12] So the Anglo-American scholarly editor provides readers with a new textual artifact, a text that more closely represents the aesthetic object of authorial intention, and provides the record of surviving historical textual artifacts in the apparatus.[13]

Upon hearing this explanation, one German editor said to me, "Well, I can see what you are talking about, but we do not do it that way in Europe." The question is: Why is it done that way in America? American textual scholars have thought long and hard and rationally about textual matters. Fifty years of intense scholarly editorial activity stretching forward from W. W. Greg's "The Rationale of Copy-Text" (1950) cannot be dismissed as thoughtless. Instead, our differences may result from what is perceived to be the normal conditions of American and English material texts. If the documents were just flawed, we could correct their errors and remain content, as our Continental counterparts seem to do. But the documents are not just flawed, they are mixed.

I have often heard Continental European editors allege that by mixing readings eclectically from several documents American editors produce texts of mixed authority. What I do not hear often expressed is the observation that each existing historical document already represents a mixture of authorities. Very few documents represent unmixed authority. One caveat to that conclusion is, of course, that it depends on what one means by "authority." If authority resides in the document, then each

---

[12] I would not have had the patience to record all 18,000 variants had it not been for CASE computer collation programs to speed the detection and recording processes.

[13] The manuscript is in the Trinity College Library, Cambridge, England. The collations were done using CASE (a computer collation program) that recorded all 18,000 variants. The scholarly edition, edited by Edgar Harden was published in New York by Garland Publishers, 1989.

document is a single authority for whatever it represents. But if authority is conferred upon documents by "the agents of textual change" (i.e., the author or other persons whose work is inscribed on, and preserved by, the document), then any document can hold the record of work by more than one authorized agent of textual change or include the record of unauthorized persons invading the process of textual inscription on the document. In that sense, each document is already a patchwork of mixed authorities.

When this chapter was presented in a conference, a German voice from the audience exclaimed "No!" to the idea that a document could represent "mixed authority." The reaction probably pinpoints an issue of misunderstanding or disagreement amongst us relating to the definition of "authority" or of "authorization." This subject is worthy of full separate treatment,[14] but for now, I suggest that, since W. W. Greg's exposure of the "tyranny of copy-text" (the idea that if a document contained any KNOWN authorial revisions, the editor was bound to accept ALL of the readings from that document as potentially authorial[15]), Anglo-American editors have elected to think of *authority* as extending only to those readings in a document that are known to be authorial or can be shown to have originated from a specifically authorized agent. Greg's solution was to separate the authority for "accidentals" (forms such as spelling, punctuation, fonts, formats) from the authority for "substantives" (words and word order) and to advocate for editorial adjudication in the case of "indifferent variants" (those for which the evidence of authority or origin was ambiguous).[16] Anglo-American editors tend to say that a document that has some general authorization may contain authorial readings, which will be used only if it can be shown that the author made the changes or directed explicitly that they be made. They feel compelled in some cases to hazard educated guesses about which changes are authorial and which are not. European editors, I believe, tend to say that all the readings in an authorized document are authorized readings unless they can be shown to be errors. Thus, to a

---

[14] My own attempt is in "Authority and Authorization in American Editing," *Autor – Autorisation – Authentizität*, ed. Thomas Bein, Rüdiger Nutt-Kofoth, and Bodo Plachta. Special issue of *editio* (Tübingen: Max Niemeyer Verlag, 2004), 73–81.

[15] W. W. Greg, "Rationale of Copy-Text," *Studies in Bibliography* 3 (1950–1), 19–36.

[16] Among Anglo-American editors there has been some dispute about how to apply this distinction. Greg was not distinguishing between important and unimportant variants; he was distinguishing between those parts of the text that compositors respected and left, for the most part, unchanged (substantives) and those parts over which compositors routinely took command and changed to suit their understanding (accidentals).

German, it is probably strange to think of a document as containing "mixed authorities"; but to an Anglo-American it is normal. The burden of proof for authority is shifted.

Many of the examples I have given above are of the sort that German editors, as well as Anglo-Americans, would correct because they are errors and because the correct form exists in a previous or subsequent authoritative document. In this, there is no difference between Anglo-Americans (eclectic) and Europeans (historical-critical) editors. However, it can be argued that if an editor is willing to make a correction of an error, the web of signifiers that make up the text of a document has already been violated. Already, that is, the document's general authority has been questioned and adjusted to the editor's construct of the aesthetic object. Many European editors are, furthermore, already willing to go one step further. In the case of "rese,bled / rese, bled / rose, bled" there is no document (there never was a document) containing the correct "resembled"; moreover, there is no documentary evidence to indicate that the author ever noticed or objected to "rose, bled." An editor correcting this reading is exercising individual judgment in the face of incomplete, albeit very convincing, evidence. An editor who is willing to take this step has replaced a viable (though strange) reading with one that is conceived by inference to be authorial. The level of speculation is small, but if an editor is willing to make that change, then the door is open to other changes that respond critically to the implications of extant evidence. Already the blanket authorization of whole documents is destroyed.

Unafraid of this open door, Anglo-American editors conclude that the only way to produce a text of unmixed authority is to proceed eclectically, selecting the readings that represent one authority (one authorizing agent) rather than accepting the mixed results of the hasty commercial demands that produced the now extant historical documents. But that way of putting it may very well reveal what is fundamentally different between European and Anglo-American modes of editorial behavior. One should, however, be careful to note that the "critical edition" or "eclectic text" thus produced is not seen by very many Anglo-American editors (myself included) as superseding historical documents. That may have been the goal at one time, but now, in the age of multiple intentions and growing attention to the history of the book, we all acknowledge the solidity and importance of historical documents. The critical edition, produced eclectically to restore a lost or create an unachieved text, becomes simply another (previously unavailable) iteration of the text, taking its place in the array of historical texts of that work.

It is true that German and Dutch documents are all flawed, also. But perhaps the question is, how flawed are they? Or, what is the nature of their flaws? I bring this up because one of the most influential of current American editors, Jerome McGann, seems to be leading American editorial theory and practice closer to the German ideal. McGann is famous for having edited the works of George Gordon, Lord Byron in the eclectic method pursuing authorial final intentions; but, having completed the work, he has changed his mind about how editing should be done and declares that he would not have edited Byron now as he in fact did. Byron's manuscripts are not perfectly executed; he was careless of many formal details. Printers cleaned up his punctuation, his spelling, and sometimes his grammar. McGann's current thinking seems to follow two arguments: the first is that the originally printed texts have a bibliographical significance and a historical impact that is to be respected and not edited away; and the second is that Byron's writings needed to be cleaned up as the original printers did. So, for two reasons at least, McGann now rejects the Anglo-American normative editorial practice as developed by W. W. Greg, Fredson Bowers, and G. Thomas Tanselle of choosing an early document for copy-text and emending it to incorporate later authorial forms, thus eliminating much of the production intervention while retaining the author's formal textures. In fact, McGann now seems to believe that Byron's own texture of forms was careless and not worth bringing into the foreground of textual attention.[17]

Having completed the Byron edition, McGann then embarked on an important electronic archive of the works of the poet and painter Dante Gabriel Rossetti, a man whose practice seems just the opposite of Byron's. Because Rossetti was a very fastidious and careful proofreader and kept very close control of his printed texts, it turns out that McGann believes that Rossetti was well served by his printers, even though their work on Rossetti's texts was quite different from their work on Byron's.[18] Once again, McGann's rejection of eclectic intentionalist editorial principles seems to be based primarily on a special case that runs counter to the prevailing Anglo-American author's experience. McGann is dealing with

---

[17] Jerome McGann, "Literary Pragmatics and the Editorial Horizon," in *Devils and Angels: Textual Editing and Literary Theory*, ed. Philip Cohen (Charlottesville : University Press of Virginia, 1991) pp. 1–21. McGann also has a programmatic explanation, developed first in *A Critique of Modern Textual Criticism* (Chicago: University of Chicago Press, 1983), in which the "shared authority" of author and production processes unseats the notion of a unitary, authorial authority.

[18] Jerome McGann, "Rossetti's Iconic Page," in *The Iconic Page*, ed. George Bornstein and Theresa Tinkle (Ann Arbor: University of Michigan Press, 1998), pp. 123–40; and "The Rossetti Hypermedia Archive: An Introduction," *Journal of Pre-Raphaelite Studies* 8 (Spring 1997), 5–21.

two authors who, in his opinion, were well served by their publishers (one by being changed and one by not being changed), and so the attraction to an eclectic procedure is reduced or eliminated.

I begin to think that perhaps the Dutch and Germans have reasons similar to McGann's for shaking their heads in disbelief at the tradition of Anglo-American editing. It may be that European printers were seldom if ever drunk. It may be their authors normally produced carefully prepared manuscripts. It may be that their printers had a greater respect for the manuscripts from which they copied. Or it may be that if their authors did not do a careful job they also needed the benevolent and wise care bestowed on their works by the compositors and printers. If so, that which Europeans find common and ordinary appears to be uncommon and extra-ordinary in English and American publishing.

Another American textual scholar who has argued on behalf of arti-factual editing is James Thorpe, who argued that works of literary art did not "become works" until they were published.[19] He comments at length on the case of Herman Melville's *White Jacket* and concludes that, although "soiled fish of the sea" is not Melville's own phrase, the word "soiled" nevertheless has a respectable place in the work's textual and critical history and, furthermore, has an aesthetic appeal that raises it above the level of a merely authorial or authorized reading.[20] This line of reasoning would very likely be criticized by European editors even though some might agree with the editorial option he was trying to defend. Thorpe also provides a list of contrastive illustrations showing many cases in which authors have declared themselves well served by their printers and publishers.[21] He, and perhaps McGann, tend to believe that in "normal practice" authors are well served by their printers and that editorial practice should begin with the assumption that the textual artifact – the document, not the aesthetic object – is "the thing" on which editorial scholarship needs to focus.

But I believe Thorpe and McGann have had unusual rather than normal textual problems to address. Many other American and British editors have experience with manuscripts and published texts revealing that authors have been poorly served by their printers. Anglo-American editors by and large will always, I think, cling to the view that although

---

[19] *The Principles of Textual Criticism* (San Marino: Huntington Library, 1972).

[20] James Thorpe, "The Aesthetics of Textual Criticism," *PMLA* 80 (1965), reprinted Thorpe, in *Principles of Textual Criticism*, pp. 3–49.

[21] Thorpe, "The Treatment of Accidentals," in Thorpe, *Principals of Textual Criticism*, pp. 141–51, *passim*.

textual artifacts are the foundational evidence for works, they are normally confused and flawed and are frequently inadequate representations of works of art. In most cases the manuscript forms of works are incomplete or never reached a carefully prepared "fair copy." Perhaps a logical consequence of this is that production personnel felt free or even compelled to fix the problems. There is nothing in the manuals of training for Anglo-American printers to tell them where their responsibility for fixing the text stops. In fact, one of the most famous compositor's manuals laments that authors even bother to try to punctuate their manuscripts. Would it not be better, the manual writer suggests, for authors to turn in manuscripts with no punctuation, leaving this important aspect up to compositors who know the business much better?[22]

So, for many American editors, the nature of the textual problems they have worked on has conditioned their responses to the editorial enterprise and led them to provide readers with texts representative of authorial intentions because extant textual artifacts are incapable of providing readers with close approximations. Such approaches are admittedly tricky business. But rejection of such approaches is equally tricky, as is suggested by a poem by Malcolm Lowry:

> I wrote: in the dark cavern of our birth.
> The printer had it tavern, which seems better:
> But herein lies the subject of our mirth,
> Since on the next page death appears as dearth.
> So it may be that God's word was distraction,
> Which to our strange type appears destruction,
> Which is bitter.

In addition to the obvious binary confusions between cavern/tavern, death/dearth and distraction/destruction, there is another confusion in the text. The last line, echoing the second line, is "Which is bitter" in *Selected Poems* (edited by Earle Birney), but it reads: "Which is better" in the scholar's edition, *The Collected Poetry of Malcolm Lowry* (edited by Kathleen Scherf). Unfortunately, the Scherf edition does not give enough information to resolve the issue. Scherf notes that there are three versions in the Lowry manuscript archives; the first says "bitter", the third "better", but Scherf does not report what the second says, nor does she report whether the second or third versions are in Lowry's own hand or in a typescript made by his wife or what. We are left, in this case, with a

---

[22] C. H. Timperley, *The Printers' Manual* (London: H. Johnson, 1838), p. 4.

temptation to make an aesthetic judgment in the absence of published evidence, though perhaps sufficient evidence exists in the archive. The original reading, "bitter" seems a more accurate indication of our reaction to "destruction" and bitter also is our realization that in textual matters we are at the mercy of printers and of editors.

Such questions will be addressed by future scholars, no doubt, and in print, the results will be available in those libraries that purchase the journals or books with the answers. They will also be available by interlibrary loan to readers in other locations, who can get knowledge of new developments from the annual bibliographies of new scholarship. Or, the information could be added to an electronic knowledge site of the sort described in chapter four, where questions could be posted and answered as if all the scholars interested in and working in the field of a knowledge site could work together or in concert and all the readers wanting to come up to speed in a topic would have full access to the world of scholarship, as if they lived within the range of a great research library – a brave new world imagined, begun, and brought to earth again in the next chapter.

CHAPTER 10

Ignorance in literary studies

Ignorance in other men may be censured as idleness, in an academick
it must be abhorred as treachery.
> Samuel Johnson, "On the Character and Duty of an Academic"
> (ms first published in 1995)

The truth is that all forms and states of knowledge, including factual
and documentary knowledge, are mediated in precise and determinate ways ... Scholarship is interpretation, whether it is carried
out as a bibliocritical discourse or a literary exegesis.
> Jerome McGann, *The Textual Condition* (1991)

[I]t's clear that what I know is two parts of bugger-all. All that I don't
know, on the other hand, is truly impressive & the library of Alexandria
would be too small to contain the details of all my ignorance.
> Richard Flanagan, *Gould's Book of Fish* (2001)

The title of this chapter was first suggested in jest. How it survived the
initial level of levity I am not sure. I recall, however, the circumstances that
caused me to suggest it. The first was the conference, already referred to in
chapter one, where a technology expert responded to my question about
how accuracy would be preserved when putting on a hard disk the contents
of all the libraries of the world by saying simply: We all have to learn to put
up with noise. Although as scholarly editor I objected, my concerns
may have been unrealistic. The future has arrived and is noisy. The texts I
imagined with the word "not" left out, the texts in which the word
"celibate" was inadvertently substituted for the word "celebrate" , "death"
given as "dearth" and "cavern" as "tavern" have appeared. Of course, they
appeared long ago in print before they reappeared in electronic form. Error,
even if called noise, is the concern of any and everyone using electronic
texts – or any text for that matter. Upon reflection, I admit that the
invention of huge hard-disk storage capacity did not invent or introduce
the problem of erroneous texts. A second circumstance contributing to the

topic of ignorance was that I have sat through conference presentations and read articles in professional journals that seemed unfortunately marred by ignorance of one kind or another: some erring on the side of making sweeping generalizations on the basis of insufficient or irrelevant evidence, others failing to see the significance of detailed information tediously and unrelentingly conveyed, and some based on what Thomas Jefferson is reported to have called "false facts" – facetiously, I would think. There are more important long-standing philosophical reasons to be interested in ignorance, but these were the immediate spur for this chapter.

One could add that ignorance might explain how economics and insouciance combine to allow academics to commit blunders in writing about books because they simply do not have the facts about the texts readily or compellingly available to them. Even for those who want to, there is often insufficient time to verify everything. We are, many of us, teachers in a practical world with deadlines for preparing lectures and with classroom insights to be shared fresh before verification can intervene. Even in scholarly publications fuzziness might be forgivable, if it were caused by the destruction and unavailability of evidence or by ambiguities in the evidence. Moreover, I am ready to argue that, so far as textual criticism and the production of scholarly editions go, the forbidding arrangement of the information commonly employed in scholarly editions does very little to invite examination from literary critics and cultural historians who in any case may believe that textual criticism is an esoteric pursuit that should predate and support but not interfere with their own intellectual concerns. In some cases, however, failure to engage with the facts is too often caused by failure to take advantage of the evidence that is on offer.

But there are serious justifications for a meditation on the role of ignorance, particularly with regard to textual studies. It is important to see both how inability to dispel all ignorance affects our work and how the way our findings are reported make them easily ignored by others. Contemplation of these issues might lead to a plan to re-organize the relationship between textual scholarship and its means of dissemination. One scholar, perhaps in a spirit of badinage or because he had a more serious sense of the potential of the topic, said he actually liked it because "it drags the theoretic back into relationship with the empirical, the abstract back to the material, literary theory back to bibliography."[1] In fact it could do those things, even merely by focusing attention on how to deal

---

[1] Email, November 2002, from Paul Eggert, who has been a support in many ways to the writing of this book.

with what is not or even cannot be known – something that would correct and not just dampen the optimism of unchallenged intellectual spinning. However, just so could this topic easily drag bibliography back to literary theory and the material back to the abstract and the empirical back into relationship with the theoretic. Or to put it in terms more congenial, this topic might put the fact and the generalization – the material and the abstract – into more productive and less polemical and less exclusive relationships. A case for that can be made. The jest in the title was now serious.

I begin with a list of some things most of us probably already agree are important to literary study, to which I suggest that ignorance and its role should be added as a fully acknowledged family member.

Facts – the things we know or think we know about texts, persons, and histories. Facts can be "gotten right" or "gotten wrong," or they can have disappeared and be no longer available. Their disappearance might in some cases be ascertained as a fact.

Contexts – that which we take to be relevant background for our foreground:

(1) In so far as facts are involved in recognizing contexts, they can be right or wrong or missing; and
(2) In identifying contexts, judgment and selection are matters of taste and of insight, which are involved in sorting the relevant from the irrelevant.

Structures – the familiar and new ways we put facts together and construct or identify what we think we know. Contexts, for example, can be structured as narratives, arguments, descriptions, categories, hierarchies. Or they can be structured by points of view or places to stand and look: Occidental, Oriental, Capitalist, Socialist, Religionist or A-religionist, Central or Marginal.

Assumptions – what we do not acknowledge perhaps because we believe it goes without saying. These perhaps reveal the ideologies, the largely unspoken values or hierarchies, by which we tend to filter facts, sorting the important from the unimportant, or tend to structure facts, identifying the links that show cause and effect.

Methodologies – the types of analyses and the range of questions posed.

Theories – of knowledge or epistemology, of communication, of gender, of identity, of situatedness, of what we take to be the rules of evidence and of hermeneutics.

To these add the role of **Ignorance**.

One hesitates to suggest that ignorance is actually a tool in the academic's arsenal, rather than the name of the enemy, because we are trained to assault ignorance and to push back the darkness with which it is associated by bringing to bear what is called the light of inquiry. Furthermore, it is difficult to assert the importance of ignorance when one recalls Dr. Samuel Johnson's admonitions. He wrote: "An academic is a man [or woman, we might add] supported at the public cost, and dignified with public honours that he may attain and impart wisdom ... Ignorance in other men may be censured as idleness, in an academick it must be abhorred as treachery."[2]

And yet, the subject is worth further examination, at least in part because ignorance can be divided into two parts: that which we are able to do something about and that which we cannot do anything about. One can disagree with that division as do some dictionaries that define ignorance only as those things one does not know but could know – thus, somehow exempting us from responsibility for not knowing what we are incapable of knowing. It seems, however, that though there are things we cannot know, we still suffer the consequences of not knowing them. But certainly "not knowing" whether it is called ignorance or not, consists both of those things you can do something about and those you cannot. The consequences of ignorance about which we can do nothing is not always bad. Umberto Eco in *Serendipity* speaks of the Force of Truth, which we are familiar with in phrases like "The truth will out"; but he offers the counter force: The Force of the False, which he points out has been responsible for a great many history-changing events and conditions. Eco very interestingly points out that Columbus, for example, is often mistakenly thought to have been opposed in his enterprise to reach China by sailing west – opposed by flat earthers convinced that he would fall off the edge. In fact, this theory of a flat earth was, according to Eco, only very narrowly subscribed in the middle ages. The idea that the theory was central to medieval thinking really began at the end of the nineteenth century, the result of a poorly researched but influential book published in 1897.[3] Columbus was impelled, according to Eco, by a different, but still serious, mistake: his belief that the world was smaller than it actually was. Opposition to his scheme came, says Eco, from the wise men who

---

[2] Samuel Johnson, "On the Character and Duty of an Academic," first published in "J. D. Fleeman: A Memoir" by David Fairer, *Studies in Bibliography* 48 (1995), 1–24, see 24.

[3] Eco cites E. J. Dijksterhuis, *Mechanization of the World Picture* (Oxford: Clarendon, 1961).

knew that the way west to China was far too long to prove a feasible alternative to the known route. But Eco's point is: "Though they were right, the sages of Salamanca were wrong; and Columbus, while he was wrong, pursued faithfully his error and proved to be right – thanks to serendipity."[4] While pursuing some less happy ideas relative to ignorance, we should keep two defenses of ignorance in the background, to which I will return: first, that ignorance, as a kind of noise, is inescapably always with us; and, second, that pursuits based on error have led and can lead to important new discoveries.

Another way to dissect ignorance is to note that it comes in two major forms with infinite, it seems, sub-variations: The first consists of absence of knowledge. It is the condition felt when one is confronted with a question the answer to which is "I do not know." The second form is far more pernicious because it frequently goes undetected. It is the condition that arises when we are confronted with a question for which we have an answer we believe to be applicable but that in fact is not applicable or is flawed by undetected misinformation. "The greatest obstacle to discovery is not ignorance – it is the illusion of knowledge."[5] But the illusion of knowledge IS ignorance, too.

A brief anatomy of type one – absence of knowledge – might include the following:

Accidental or inadvertent ignorance resulting from the bad luck of having searched for and failed to find all the relevant knowledge or having failed to imagine the question that would have led to discovery.

Insouciant ignorance resulting from a short attention span, lack of energy, or some other form of laziness in the search for the relevant. Its mottoes are "Enough already" and "I hope this will do."

Willful or deliberate ignorance resulting from a desire to protect an idea, conclusion, bias, or tradition from too close a scrutiny and too intense a barrage of testing information. On this subject Francis Bacon's discourse on the Four Idols that oppose clear thinking is an excellent text.

Non-fatal or trivial ignorance consisting of information that even if known would not make a difference. Such information when present and known might be thought of as noise, even when the information is

---

[4] Umberto Eco, *Serendipities: Language and Lunacy* (New York: Harcourt Brace, 1998), p. 7.
[5] Attributed to Daniel Boorstin, without a source, by Wisdom Quotes (http://www.wisdomquotes. com/001426.html), and in the following form, also without a source, by Brainy Quotes: "The greatest obstacle to discovering the shape of the earth, the continents, and the oceans was not ignorance but the illusion of knowledge." (http://www.brainyquote.com/quotes/authors/d/ daniel_j_boorstin.html)

accurate, such as the scratches on a vinyl record or audience coughs in a live recording, which we tend to edit out, though they have a factual presence.

Fatal ignorance consisting of a failure to know that which would cause us to abandon our position altogether or which causes decisions leading to disastrous, disappointing, or dead-end investigations.

It is the second form of Ignorance, however, consisting of unexposed misinformation or error, that is the most pernicious and dangerous; for it leads to misunderstanding, and misunderstanding – until detected as such – goes by the name of understanding. It too can be anatomized:

Bogus information, false positives, and "false facts" may possibly be innocent in that holding this type of intellectual currency may qualify the holder as a victim rather than the perpetrator of deceit. It could be that every effort had been made to eliminate error and the effort has fallen short. Innocence in this case does not, however, exempt the victim from the consequences of error. Error tends to persist, though frequently it persists because it is perpetuated by writers who fail to test the validity of their evidence.

Fraud, scientific malfeasance, fakes, and forgeries are anything but innocent; the perpetrators deserve our scorn and abhorrence.

Forgetting is very much like ignorance in that one sometimes knows that one has forgotten and can take steps to retrieve that which memory will not serve up voluntarily. But memory sometimes pretends that it has not forgotten, and we are frequently the victims of false memories. To aid memory, pens, paper, and computers were invented, and to prevent false memories, verification and double checking are required. Milan Kundera's novel titled *Ignorance* is an excellent text on the problems of memory.

Although this has been a rehearsal of the obvious and well known, it is worth saying that reminders of the dangers of ignorance do not help us identify an enemy that can be overcome by hard work, deeper digging, more comprehensive reading, more precise thinking, or better research techniques. However much we may fail as individuals, as scholars we are committed to doing all that can be done to overcome ignorance. But like noise and poverty, ignorance will never be suppressed because it cannot be attacked in all its forms. Let us look at the consequences of the irrepressibility of error and of not knowing. Let us contemplate the role of ignorance IN literary studies and not focus for now on what can or should be done to ban ignorance FROM literary studies. If ignorance cannot be banned from literary or any other kind of study, we must confront that notion and learn to live with it as a basic condition.

Put that a different way: If we believe that scholarship is devoted to discovering truth and to beating back the dark veil of ignorance, we must also believe that truth can be ascertained and established. If that were so, those who possess the certainty of truth would be right to impose their views on those who have failed to possess the truth. In that view of things, ignorance is a deplorable but temporary condition. Put starkly, a world in which truth could be established requires the separation of that which is right from that which is wrong, that which is verified from that which does not pass the test of verification, that which can be relied upon from that which is proven unreliable. In its extreme form, this view of the scholar's task demands absolute standards: answers to questions would then either be absolute or unsatisfactory.

Support for this view transcends academia, for it carries political strength and provides, for some, religious comfort. We see it in claims that a single truth is necessary to the orderly continuance of society as we know it, and that to tolerate the notion of competing truths is to introduce chaos and uncertainty into socio-political conditions leading to unnecessary contentiousness at best and anarchy at worst. It is some form of this idea of certainty that makes Empire possible, be it military, political, cultural, or commercial. The notion that we are right easily transforms into the notion that we have the right. This position makes what most thinking persons will already have recognized as a confusion. Let me try to be clear about this: It is possible that there is a right and a wrong in matters about which men and women dispute. It is not necessarily the case that there are multiple right views. But the role of ignorance IN scholarship and, indeed, in life itself is to undermine the certainty that anyone's view of a subject actually corresponds with that true one. The question of whether there is or is not a single correct way to view things is quite different from the question of whether any one person, group, or government has with certainty hit upon that correct view. Tolerance for multiple points of view does not introduce uncertainty. Uncertainty already inheres in the whole inquisitive and communicative enterprise because, even if there were no other reasons, ignorance is inescapable. There will always be some things one cannot know and some things one thinks one knows that are not so. This is not an enemy of intelligence and of illumination; it is a condition of the medium in which we exist. The consequences of this condition are that postures of certainty, familiar to us both in politics and academia, are not intellectually sustainable.

The way in which ignorance is a tool of literary study is that it prevents arrogance, intellectual tyranny and absolutism, and encourages humility, alertness, tentativeness, and tolerance for alternative explanations. It also promotes a spirit of inquiry and testing that prevents the acceptance of dicta handed down by authorities in the field. Every proposition remains always open for question and revision.

One does not, because of the prevalence of ignorance or uncertainty, give up the pursuit of facts or the attempt to analyze them and draw conclusions. No more does a farmer, upon discovering that his field is rocky, with rocks under every rock he removes, cease to cultivate or plant. Upon establishing the ground conditions of his existence, he determines which crops do well in that soil and proceeds accordingly. Recognizing the inevitable conditions of ignorance, noise, terror, evil, and poverty, we must determine what can be done and proceed accordingly. My first point, then, is that recognizing the inevitability of ignorance leads to an acceptance of uncertainty. And it follows that certainty, dogma, arrogance, and the forceful imposition of one's views upon others cannot be intelligently sustained. What other course do we have? What discipline is left open to us?

Let us reject without discussion the option of closing one's eyes, clamping the bit in one's teeth, and proceeding as if we had not noticed anything was amiss. Let us also reject radical relativism: the conclusion that if uncertainty dogs every position, then any position is as good as any other. Just as the Force of Truth and its supporters may at times confuse the possibility that there is a single truth with the notion that their understanding of it is the correct one; so, too, the Force of Relativity and its supporters may at times confuse the possibility that there are multiple successful explanations for relations and the possibility that inconstant conditions may render previously successful explanations inapplicable or that the prevalence of error makes all explanations unsatisfactory – I say, relativists may confuse those possibilities with the notion that every explanation is of equal value and that every view is to be respected as a viable view. That option lacks discipline and reminds one of John Dewey's famous distinction between freedom and whimsy. A person whose notion of freedom consists of having the right to follow any whimsy, Dewey remarked, is not free but a prisoner of chance; Dewey preferred freedom based on disciplined and thoughtful choice. Perhaps I should also remark that radical relativists seem to be committed to the notion that there is no possibility of error or that if error is possible it does not matter. Falsifiability does seem to me to be possible, and I prefer the freedom of a disciplined approach to subjects over uncritical acceptance of every theory on offer.

Not all relativism is radical. Since the early modern period, at least, relativity theory has asserted itself in a variety of fields with a force of truth of its own. That is to say, reasoned and disciplined examinations have been made of the effects upon understanding resulting from noting the relations between things rather than from attempts to fathom the essence of things. Resistance to this development seems almost always associated with a received dogma and with the notion that the new idea threatens the single truth as already conceived and held dear by those in power, perhaps because it helps them to remain in power. The steady and complicated history of the struggle between the certainty of dogma and the uncertainty of relativists was accentuated by the Copernican over-throw of Ptolemaic astronomy, by the theory of evolutionary origins and development in biology, and by Einstein's formulation of the theory of relativity in physics. In each case the new insight challenged the received opinion by stressing the relations between things rather than the essential constituency or existence or constancy of the thing itself. In each case it was the proponents of a dogma that led the opposition until it became clear that their opposition was itself the proponent of error and ignorance.

It seems fairly clear now, furthermore, that the search for viable and pragmatic alternative explanations for physical phenomena, for astro-nomical observations, for how life forms develop, for how language works, for how societies are structured, and so on, have been very pro-ductive when looking at how things relate to one another rather than just at what things essentially consist of. At some level of understanding, we have become used to the idea that size and weight might depend on elevation or speed; that red and blue might be a function of direction and speed rather than being constant or essential; that words, rather than meaning what a dictionary appears to prescribe for them, mean what they mean in relation to the words that surround them and to the words that could be substituted for them in a given context and by who it is that is speaking or writing; or that familial and political hierarchies can be structured productively in a number of different ways. Though in practice we speak as if the sun RISES in the east and SETS in the west, none of us actually believes that is true; although we drive on the right-hand side of the road under some conditions, we readily drive on the left in others, without worrying about the absolute truths of road sharing; so, too, we use the metric system regardless of what the really correct way to measure things might be; and we no longer ask with moral earnestness if it should be lawful for a man to marry his deceased wife's sister. For many reasons, we accept pragmatic and relative options for doing and explaining very important matters.

The points so far, then, are that we have two compelling reasons to believe that our pursuit of truth remains tentative and that our attempt to dispel or eradicate ignorance is doomed: there will always be gaps and noises in what we know, and the relationship between the facts we know may change or may depend on where we stand to look at them. These two conditions give us ample reason to want to listen to alternative explanations. Yet it is important to note that a turn to relativity as a response to the prevalence of ignorance and ineradicability of error is not a surrender. That is to say, radical relativism and bull-headedness are not the only alternatives when one abandons absolutism and essentialism. Nor is acknowledgment of ignorance a reason to give up. I remember with some sadness my own first response to the idea that uncertainty would always affect my work: "If you can't know for sure," I said, "What's the point? Why bother at all?" That attitude I now see was based on a misconception of the grounds of our intellectual existence. Certainty is not and never was an option, though it was offered by the religionists and other optimists of my youth. Despair is not inherent in the discovery of uncertainty. The discipline of verification is compatible with acknowledgment of fallibility.

A third point can be made: that although we now occupy the very privileged position of the present, and although the dead cannot array themselves against us in self-defense, and we can therefore pretend that our version of the truth is the correct one, there is, nevertheless, another truth that precedes our privileged and self-indulgent truths based upon our power to assert ourselves and our views. We sometimes forget that Descartes' famous foundation for refuting radical scepticism, "Cogito, ergo sum," began actually with "Dubito." I doubt, therefore I think; and I think, therefore I am. The pursuit of truth is best when it is tempered by doubt that arises most clearly from the fact that we do not know it all – that we do not know enough – that what we know may be undetected error. That should keep us from trying to impose our views and wills upon others, just as it should keep us from accepting as equally viable any view on offer. The abstraction is brought to book by the material evidence, bibliography finds its rationale in theory, theory gains its significance from the empirical. And ignorance and doubt attend it all, demanding endless curiosity about alternatives, about more evidence, about more theories.

It is recorded in Matthew 15:14: "If the blind lead the blind, both shall fall into the ditch." It seems to me that in academia, as in politics, belief in the correctness of one's own views constitutes a kind of blindness and leads to indefensible acts of aggression, arrogance, and to ditches not worth dying in.

Bibliography

Altick, Richard. *The English Common Reader*. Chicago: University of Chicago Press, 1957.

Austin, J. L. *How to Do Things with Words*. Oxford: Clarendon, 1962.

Beowulf. See Kiernan, Beowulf project.

Bickerton, Derek. *Roots of Language*. Ann Arbor: Karoma Publishers, 1981.

Binder, Henry., ed. *Red Badge of Courage*. New York: W. W. Norton, 1979.

Blake. See Viscomi, Blake Archive.

Bornstein, George. *Material Modernism*. Cambridge: Cambridge University Press, 2001.

Bowers, Fredson. *Bibliography and Textual Criticism*. Oxford: Clarendon, 1964.
   Essays in Bibliography, Text, and Editing. Charlottesville: University Press of Virginia, 1975.
   Textual preface and "Textual Introduction" to *The Scarlet Letter* and *The House of Seven Gables* in *The Centenary Edition of the Works of Nathaniel Hawthorne*. Columbus: Ohio State University Press, 1962, 1964.
   "Textual Criticism," in *The Aims and Methods of Scholarship in Modern Languages and Literatures*, ed. James Thorpe. New York: Modern Language Association, 1970, pp. 23–42.

Braun-Rau, Alexandra. *King Lear* project. www.textkritik.uni-muenchen.de/ abraun-rau/lear/King_Lear/startseite.html (accessed 15 November 2004).

Bryant, John. *The Fluid Text: A Theory of Revision and Editing for Book and Screen*. Ann Arbor: University of Michigan Press, 2002.

Burton, Anthony. "Thackeray's Collaborations with Cruikshank, Doyle, and Walker." *Costerus* n.s.2 (1974), 141–84.

CSE Guidelines for Scholarly Editions. www.jefferson.village.virginia.edu/~jmu2m/ cse/CSEguidelines.html; and www.sunsite.berkeley.edu/MLA/intro.html.

Caldwell, T. Price. "Molecular Sememics: A Progress Report." *Meisei Review* 4 (1989), 65–86.
   "Whorf, Orwell, and Mentalese." *Meisei Review* 19 (2004), 91–106.

Calvin, William H. *Conversations With Neil's Brain: The Neural Nature of Thought and Language*. Reading, Mass.: Addison-Wesley, 1994.

Cambridge, Ada. *A Woman's Friendship*. Ed. Elizabeth Morrison. Kensington, NSW: University of New South Wales Press, 1989.

Chaucer. See Robinson, Chaucer.

Chesnutt, David, Susan Hockey, and Michael Sperberg-McQueen. Model Editions Project. www.adh.sc.edu.

Cohen, Morton, and Anita Gondolfo, eds. *Lewis Carroll and the House of Macmillan*. Cambridge: Cambridge University Press, 1987.

Colby, R. A. and J. Sutherland. "Thackeray's Manuscripts: A Preliminary Census of Library Locations." *Costerus* n.s.2 (1974); and Lange, T. V. "Appendix: The Robert H. Taylor Collection." *Costerus* n.s. 2 (1974).

Cross, Nigel. *The Common Writer*. Cambridge: Cambridge University Press, 1985.

Dedner, Burghard. "Editing Fragments as Fragments." *TEXT* 16 (2004), 97–111.

Deppman, Jed, Daniel Ferrer, and Michael Groden, eds. *Genetic Criticism: Texts and Avant-Textes*. Philadelphia: University of Pennsylvania Press, 2004.

De Smedt, Marcel, and Edward Vanhoutte. *Stijn Streuvels, De Teleurgang van den Waterhoek. Elektronisch-kritische editie/electronic-critical edition*. Amsterdam: Amsterdam University Press/KANTL, 2000(CD-Rom).

Dickinson. See Smith. Dickinson.

Dijksterhuis, E. J. *Mechanization of the World Picture*. Oxford: Clarendon, 1961.

D'Iorio, Paolo, et al. HyperNietzsche Project http://www.hypernietzsche.org accessed 28 October 2004.

"Draft Guidelines for Electronic Scholarly Editions." Committee on Scholarly Editions http://www.iath.virginia.edu/~jmu2m/cse/Editors.rpt.htm.

Duggan, Hoyt, et al. *Piers Plowman Archive*. www.iath.virginia.edu/piers/archive.goals.html.

Eco, Umberto. *The Limits of Interpretation*. Bloomington: Indiana University Press, 1990.

   The Open Work. Cambridge, Mass.: Harvard University Press, 1989 (first published as *Opera aperta* in 1962).

   Serendipities: Language and Lunacy. New York: Harcourt Brace, 1998.

   "After Secret Knowledge." *TLS* (22 June 1990), 666.

Eggert, Paul. "Document or Process as the Site of Authority: Establishing Chronology of Revisions in Competing Typescripts of Lawrence's *The Boy in the Bush*." *Studies in Bibliography* 44 (1991), 364–76.

   "The Golden Stain of Time." *Books and Bibliography: Essays in Commemoration of Don McKenzie*, ed. John Thomson. Wellington: Victoria University Press, 2002, pp. 116–28.

   "Textual Product or Textual Process: Procedures and Assumptions of Critical Editing" in *Editing in Australia*. Sydney: University of New South Wales Press, 1990, pp. 19–40; rept. in Phil Cohen, ed. *Devils and Angels*. Charlottesville: University Press of Virginia, 1991, pp. 124–33.

Eggert, Paul, Phill Berrie, Graham Barwell, and Chris Tiffin. JITM (Just In Time Markup). www.unsw.adfa.edu.au/ASEC/PWB_REPORT/JITM/.pdf; and www3.iath.virginia.edu/sds/Eggert-Berry.html.

Eliot, Simon. *Some Patterns and Trends in British Publishing, 1800–1919.* Occasional Papers of the Bibliographical Society, No. 8, 1994, sections A and C.

Faulkner, William. *Go Down, Moses.* New York: Random House, 1942.

Feltes, N. N. *Literary Capital and the Late Victorian Novel.* Madison: University of Wisconsin Press, 1993.

 Modes of Production of Victorian Novels. Chicago: University of Chicago Press, 1986. [See my review in *JEGP* 87 (1988), 262–5.]

Fiormonte, Domenico, and Cinzia Pusceddu. "The Text as a Product and as a Process. History, Genesis, Experiments." *Verslagen en Mededelingen van de KANTL* (forthcoming, 2006).

 Digital Variants. http://www.selc.ed.ac.uk/italian/digitalvariants/.

Flanagan, Richard. *Gould's Book of Fish: A Novel in Twelve Fish.* London: Atlantic Books, 2001.

Flanders, Julia, et al. Women Writers Project. www.wwp.brown.edu.

Frankel, Nicholas. *Oscar Wilde's Decorated Books.* Ann Arbor: University of Michigan Press, 2000.

Gabler, Hans Walter, George Bornstein, and Gillian Borland Pierce, eds. *Contemporary German Editorial Theory.* Ann Arbor: University of Michigan Press, 1995.

Gaskell, Philip. *A New Introduction to Bibliography.* Oxford: Clarendon, 1972.

Gatrell, Simon. *Hardy the Creator: A Textual Biography.* Oxford: Clarendon, 1988.

Geisel, Theodore Seuss (Dr. Seuss). *The 500 Hats of Bartholomew Cubbins.* New York: Vangard, 1938.

Goethe, Wolfgang. "Venetian Epigrams". MSS at the Goethe Archive. Weimar, Germany.

Google. www.google.com.

Greetham, David C. *Theories of the Text.* London: Oxford University Press, 1999.

Greg, W. W. "The Rationale of Copy-Text." *Studies in Bibliography* 3 (1950–1), 19–36.

"Guidelines for Scholarly Editions." Committee on Scholarly Editions. http://sunsite.berkeley.edu/MLA/guidelines.html and http://jefferson.village.virginia.edu/~jmu2m/cse/CSEguidelines.html.

Hagen, June Steffensen. *Tennyson and his Publishers.* London: Macmillan, 1979.

Haight, Gordon, ed. George Eliot, *The Mill on the Floss.* Oxford: Clarendon, 1980.

Harden, Edgar. *A Checklist of Contributions by William Makepeace Thackeray to Newspapers, Periodicals, Books, and Serial Part Issues, 1828–1864.* No. 68 ELS Monograph Series. Victoria, B.C.: English Literary Studies, University of Victoria, 1996.

Harris, Margaret. *A Checklist of the "Three-Decker" Collection in the Fisher Library, University of Sydney.* Department of English, University of Sydney, 1980.

Harvey, J. R. *Victorian Novelists and their Illustrators*. New York: New York University Press, 1971.

Hernadi, Paul. "Literary Theory," in *Introduction to Scholarship in Modern Languages and Literatures*, ed. Joseph Gibaldi. New York: Modern Language Association, 1981, pp. 98–115.

Hill, W. Speed. [Review of Dave Oliphant and Robin Bradford's *New Directions in Textual Studies* (1990).] *TEXT* 6 (1994), 370–81.

Hirsch, E. D. *Cultural Literacy*. Boston: Houghton Mifflin, 1987.

Validity in Interpretation. New Haven: Yale University Press, 1967.

Holdeman, David. "The Editor as Artist." Presented at the Society for Textual Scholarship, New York, April 2001; revised, Annual Faculty Lecture, English Department, University of North Texas, November 2001.

Housman, A. E. "The Application of Thought to Textual Criticism." *Proceedings of the Classical Association* 18 (1922), 67–84; rpt. in *Selected Prose*, ed. John Carter. Cambridge: Cambridge University Press, 1961, pp. 131–50.

Institute for Advanced Technology in the Humanities. www.iath.virginia.edu/.

Jackendoff, Ray. *Patterns in the Mind: Language and Human Nature*. New York: Harvester / Wheatsheaf, 1993.

Johnson, Samuel. "On the Character and Duty of an Academic," first published in "J. D. Fleeman: A Memoir," David Fairer. *Studies in Bibliography* 48 (1995), 1–24.

Jonson, Ben. *The Cambridge Edition of the Works of Ben Jonson*. http://uk.cambridge.org/literature/features/cwbj/project/ accessed 15 November 2004.

Joyce, James. *Ulysses*, ed. Hans Walter Gabler. New York: Random House, 1987.

Kamuf, Peggy. "Preface," *A Derrida Reader: Between the Blinds*. New York: Columbia University Press, 1991.

Karlsson, Lina, and Linda Malm. "Revolution or Remediation?: A Study of Electronic Scholarly Editions on the Web." *HumanIT* 7.1 (2004), 1–46.

Katz, Joseph, ed. [Reviews of paperback editions.] *Proof* 2–4, 1970–72.

Keane, Robert. *Dante Gabriel Rossetti: The Poet as Craftsman*. New York: Peter Lang, 2002.

Kiernan, Kevin. Beowulf. www.uky.edu/~kiernan/eBeowulf/guide.htm accessed 15 November 2004.

[Probable location for] Boethius project. www.uky.edu/~kiernan/eBoethius/pubs.htm accessed 15 November 2004.

Landow, George. See Victorian Web.

Law, Graham. *Serializing Fiction in the Victorian Press*. London: Palgrave, 2000.

Lawrence, T. E. *The Mint*. London: Jonathan Cape and Garden City, New York: Doubleday, 1955. (Limited edition unexpurgated; trade editions expurgated until 1973.)

Lochard, Eric-Olivier, and Dominique Taurisson. "'The World According to Arcane.' An Operating Instrumental Paradigm for Scholarly Editions" in *Perspectives of Scholarly Editing / Perspektiven der Textedition*, ed. Bodo Plachta and H. T. M. van Vliet (Berlin: Weidler Buchverlag, 2002), pp. 151–62.

Lougy, Robert E. "The Structure of *Vanity Fair*." *PMLA* 90 (1975), 256–69.

Lowry, Malcolm. *The Collected Poetry of Malcolm Lowry*. Ed. Kathleen Scherf. Vancouver: University of British Columbia Press, 1995.

    Selected Poems. Ed. Earle Birney, with assistance. from Margerie Lowry. San Francisco: City Lights Books, 1962.

Luke, Hugh J. "The Publishing of Byron's Don Juan." *PMLA*, 80 (June 1965), 199–209.

Mailloux, Steven. *Interpretive Conventions: The Reader in the Study of American Fiction*. Cornell University Press, 1982.

Martens, Gunter. "(De)Constructing the Text by Editing: Reflections on the Receptional Significance of Textual Apparatuses," in *Contemporary German Editorial Theory*, ed. Hans Walter Gabler, George Bornstein, and Gillian Borland Pierce. Ann Arbor: University of Michigan Press, 1995, pp. 125–52.

    "What Is a Text? Attempts at Defining a Central Concept in Editorial Theory," in *Contemporary German Editorial Theory*, ed. Hans Walter Gabler, George Bornstein, and Gillian Borland Pierce. Ann Arbor: University of Michigan Press, 1995, pp. 209–231.

Marx, Karl. *Communist Manifesto*. Translated by Helen MacFarland in volume with George Julian Harney, *Red Republican*. London, 1850.

Marx, Karl, and Frederick Engels. *Manifesto of the Communist Party* www. anu.edu.au/polsci/marx/classics/manifesto.html accessed 19 November 2004.

Matthiessen, F. O. *American Renaissance*. New York: Oxford University Press, 1941.

McGann, Jerome J.. *Black Riders*. Princeton: Princeton University Press, 1993.

    A Critique of Modern Textual Criticism. Chicago: University of Chicago Press, 1983.

    Radiant Textuality: Literature After the World Wide Web. New York: Palgrave, 2001.

    The Textual Condition. Princeton: Princeton University Press, 1991.

    "The Gutenberg Variations." *TEXT* 14 (2002), 1–13.

    "Imagining What You Don't Know," in *Voice, Text, and HyperText*, ed. Raimonda Modiano, Leroy Searle, and Peter Shillingsburg. Seattle: University of Washington Press, 2003, pp. 378–97.

    "Literary Pragmatics and the Editorial Horizon," in *Devils and Angels: Textual Editing and Literary Theory*. ed., Philip Cohen. Charlottesville: University Press of Virginia, 1991, pp. 1–21.

    The Rossetti Archive. www.iath.virginia.edu/rossetti/fullarch.html.

    "The Rossetti Hypermedia Archive: An Introduction." *Journal of Pre-Raphaelite Studies* 8 (Spring 1997), 5–21.

    "Rossetti's Iconic Page," in *The Iconic Page*, ed. Theresa Tinkle and George Bornstein. Ann Arbor: University of Michigan Press, 1998, pp. 123–40.

    "Theories of the Text." *London Review of Books*. (18 February 1988), 20–1.

McKenzie, D. F. *The Sociology of Bibliography* (Panizzi Lectures, 1985). London: British Library, 1986.

McKerrow, R. B. "The Treatment of Shakespeare's Text by His Earlier Editors, 1709–1768." *Proceedings of the British Academy* 19 (1933), 89–122.

McLaverty, James. *Pope, Print, and Meaning*. London: Oxford University Press, 2001.

Mehl, Dieter. "Editorial Theory and Practice in English Studies in Germany." *Problems of Editing* biehefte zu *editio*, ed. Christa Jansohn (1999).

Modiano, Raimonda, Leroy Searle, and Peter Shillingsburg, eds. *Voice, Text, and HyperText*. Seattle: University of Washington Press, 2003.

Myers, Gary. "For Now and Always." *New Yorker* (28 October 1985).

Nichol, John W. "Melville's '"Soiled" Fish of the Sea.'" *American Literature* 21 (November 1949), 338–9.

Nietzsche. See D'Iorio.

Nowell-Smith, Simon. *International Copyright Law and the Publisher in the Reign of Queen Victoria*. London: Oxford University Press, 1968.

Parker, Hershel. *Flawed Texts and Verbal Icons*. Evansville: Northwestern University Press, 1984.

Patten, Robert. *Charles Dickens and his Publishers*. Oxford: Clarendon, 1978.

Pickwoad, Nicholas. "Commentary on Illustrations," in *Vanity Fair*, ed. Peter Shillingsburg. New York: Garland, 1989 and in *The History of Pendennis*, ed. Peter Shillingsburg. New York: Garland, 1991.

Pizer, Donald. [Review of the Pennsylvania *Sister Carrie*,] *American Literature* 53 (January 1982), 731–7.

Plachta, Bodo. "In Between the 'Royal Way' of Philology and 'Occult Science': Some Remarks About German Discussion on Text Constitution in the Last Ten Years." *TEXT* 12 (1999), 31–47.

"Teaching Editing–Learning Editing." *Problems of Editing* biehefte zu *editio*, ed. Christa Jansohn (1999).

Plato. "Ion," Translated by. Trevor J. Saunders. in *Plato: Early Socratic Dialogues*. London: Penguin, 1987.

Phaedras. Translated by R. Hackforth. Cambridge: Cambridge University Press, 1952.

Republic. Translated by Robin Waterfield. Oxford: Oxford University Press, 1993.

Postal, Paul M. *Skeptical Linguistic Essays*. www.nyu.edu/gsas/dept/lingu/people/faculty/postal/papers/skeptical.pdf (downloaded 4 July 2003).

Purdy, R. L. *Thomas Hardy: A Bibliographical Study*. London: Oxford University Press, 1954.

Ray, Gordon N. *Bibliographical Resources for the Study of Nineteenth Century Fiction*. Los Angeles: Clark Library, 1964.

ed. *The Letters and Private Papers of William Makepeace Thackeray*. 4 vols. Cambridge, Mass.: Harvard University Press, 1946.

"The Importance of Original Editions." *Nineteenth Century English Books*. Urbana: University of Illinois Press, 1952.

Reiman, Donald. *The Study of Modern Manuscripts: Public, Confidential, and Private*. Baltimore: Johns Hopkins University Press, 1993.

"'Versioning': The Presentation of Multiple Texts." *Romantic Texts and Contexts*. Columbia: University of Missouri Press, 1987, pp. 167–80.

Renear, Alan. "Literal Transcription – Can the Text Ontologist Help?" in *New Media and the Humanities: Research and Applications*, ed. Domenico Fiormonte and Jonathan Usher. Oxford: Humanities Computing Unit, on behalf of Instituto Italiano di cultura per la Scozia e l'Irlanda del Nord, 2001, pp. 23–30.

Robinson, Peter. 'Collation, Textual Criticism, Publication and the Computer.' TEXT 7 (1995), 77–94.

Chaucer: *The Wife of Bath's Prologue on CD-ROM*. Cambridge: Cambridge University Press, 1996. [*Canterbury Tales* project, demonstration] http://www.cta.dmu.ac.uk/projects/ctp/desc2.html (accessed 19 December 2003). See also Robinson's work in Elizabeth Solopova, ed., *The General Prologue on CD-ROM*. Cambridge: Cambridge University Press, 2000 [CD-ROM].

Scholarly Digital Editions. www.sd-editions.com/.

"Where We Are With Electronic Scholarly Editions, and Where We Want To Be." *Jahrbuchs für Computerphilogie* 5 (2003), 126–46; also at http://computerphilologie. uni-muenchen.de/jg03/robinson.html (accessed 26 June 2004).

Roethke, Theodore. *Collected Poems of Theodore Roethke*. New York: Doubleday [1966].

Rossetti. See McGann, Rossetti Archive.

Sacks, Oliver. *The Man Who Mistook His Wife for a Hat*. London: Picador, 1985.

Scheibe, Siegfried. "Theoretical Problems of Authorization and Constitutions of Texts" 1990–1; translated in Hans Walter Gabler, George Bornstein, and Gillian Borland Peirce, eds. *Contemporary German Editorial Theory*. Ann Arbor: University of Michigan Press, 1995, pp. 171–91.

Schulze, Robin, ed. *Becoming Marianne Moore: The Early Poems, 1907–1924*. Berkeley: UCLA Press, 2002.

Searle, John R. *Expression and Meaning*. Cambridge: Cambridge University Press, 1979.

Seuss, Dr. See Geisel, Theodore Seuss.

Shillingsburg, Miriam. "Computer Assistance to Scholarly Editing." *Bulletin of Research in the Humanities* 81 (Winter 1978), 448–63.

Shillingsburg, Peter. *Pegasus in Harness: Victorian Publishing and W. M. Thackeray*. Charlottesville: University Press of Virginia, 1992.

Resisting Texts: Authority and Submission in Constructions of Meaning. Ann Arbor: University of Michigan Press, 1997.

Scholarly Editing in the Computer Age, 3rd edn. Ann Arbor: University of Michigan Press, 1996.

"A Resistance to German Editorial Theory." *editio* 12 (1998), 138–50.

"Anglo-amerikanische Editionwissenschaft: Ein knapper Überblick," in Rüdiger Nutt-Kofoth, Bodo Plachta, H. T. M. van Vliet, and Hermann

Zwerchina, eds. *Text und Edition: Positionen und Perspektiven*. Berlin: Erich Schmidt, 2000.

"Authority and Authorization in American Editing," *Autor–Authorisation–Authentizität*, ed. Thomas Bein, Rüdiger Nuttkofoth and Bodo Plachta. Special issue of *editio*. Tübingen: Max Niemeyer Verlag 2004, pp. 73–81.

"The Computer as Research Assistant in Scholarly Editing." *Literary Research Newsletter* 5 (1980), 31–45.

"Editing Thackeray: A History." *Studies in the Novel* 27 (Fall 1995), 363–74; reprinted in *Textual Criticism and the Common Reader*, ed. Alexander Pettit. Athens: University of Georgia Press, 1999.

"The Faces of Victorian Fiction," in *The Iconic Page*, ed. George Bornstein and Theresa Tinkle (Ann Arbor: University of Michigan Press, 1998), 141–56.

"Orientations to Texts." *editio* 15 (2001), 1–16.

"Principles for Electronic Archives, Scholarly Editions, and Tutorials," in *The Literary Text in the Digital Age*, ed., Richard J. Finneran. Ann Arbor: University of Michigan Press, 1996, pp. 23–35.

"Thackeray Bibliography." *Cambridge Bibliography of English Literature*, 3rd edn. Cambridge: Cambridge University Press, 2001.

Skinner, Quentin. "Conventions and the Understanding of Speech Acts." *Philosophical Quarterly* 20 (1970), 118–38.

Smith, Barry. "Towards a History of Speech Act Theory," in A. Burkhardt, ed., *Speech Acts, Meanings and Intentions: Critical Approaches to the Philosophy of John R. Searle*. Berlin/New York: De Gruyter, 1990, pp. 29–61. Posted at URL http://ontology.buffalo.edu/smith//articles/speechact.html (accessed 8 November 2004).

Smith, Martha Nell. Emily Dickinson, http://www.iath.virginia.edu/dickinson/about_the_site.html.

Sperberg-McQueen, Michael. "New TA Software: Some Characteristics, and a Proposed Architecture." http://pigeon.cch.kcl.ac.uk/ta-dev/notes/design.htm (accessed 26 June 2004).

"Textual Criticism and TEI." http://xml.coverpages.org/sperb-mla94.html.

'Trip Report' on the 'Text Analysis Software Planning Meeting' held at Princeton, 17–19 May 1996, at http://tigger.uic.edu/~cmsmcq/trips/ceth9505.html (accessed 19 December 2003).

Stillinger, Jack. *Multiple Authorship and the Myth of Solitary Genius*. New York and Oxford: Oxford University Press, 1991.

Stoker, Bram. *Dracula*. London: Constable, 1897.

Stubbs, Estelle and Peter Robinson. The Hengwrt Chaucer Digital Facsimile CD Leicester: Scholarly Digital Editions (www.sd-editions.com), 2000.

Sutherland, John. *The Stanford Companion to Victorian Fiction*. Stanford: Stanford University Press, 1989.

"Victorian Novelists: Who Were They?" *Victorian Writers, Publishers, Readers*. New York: St. Martin's, 1995.

Sweeney, Patricia Runk. "Thackeray's Best Illustrator." *Costerus* n.s.2 (1974), 84–111.

Tanselle, G. Thomas. *Literature and Artifacts*. Charlottesville: Bibliographical Society of the University of Virginia, 1998.

The Rationale of Textual Criticism. Philadelphia: University of Pennsylvania Press, 1989.

Thackeray, W. M. *Letters* (see Ray, Gordon).

Pendennis. Leipzig: Tauchnitz, 1849–50.

Vanity Fair. London: Bradbury and Evans, 1847. (Peter Shillingsburg's edition. New York: Garland, 1989.)

[*Scholarly Editions of*] *Henry Esmond*, ed. Edgar Harden (1989), *Pendennis*, ed. Peter Shillingsburg (1991), *Yellowplush and Gahagan*, ed. Peter Shillingsburg (1991), *Newcomes*, ed. Peter Shillingsburg (1996), *Barry Lyndon*, ed. Edgar Harden (1998), *Catherine*, ed. Sheldon Goldfarb (1998) – the first four published by Garland; the latter three by University of Michigan Press.

Thorpe, James. *Principles of Textual Criticism*. San Marino: Huntington Library, 1972.

"The Aesthetics of Textual Criticism." *PMLA* 80 (1965),: 465–82. Reprinted in Thorpe, *Principles of Textual Criticism*, pp. 3–49.

"The Treatment of Accidentals," in *James Thorpe, Principles of Textual Criticism*, San Marino: Huntingdon Library, 1972, pp. 141–51.

Timperley, C. H. *The Printers' Manual*. London: H. Johnson, 1838.

Todd, William, and Ann Bowden. *The Tauchnitz International Editions in English 1841–1955: A Bibliographical History*. New York: Bibliographical Society of America, 1988.

Tuchman, Gaye, and Nina Fortin. *Edging Women Out: Victorian Novelists, Publishers, and Social Change*. London: Routledge, 1989.

Unsworth, John. "Reconsidering and Revising the MLA Committee on Scholarly Editions' Guidelines for Scholarly Editions." http://www.iath. virginia.edu/~jmu2m/sts2001.html (accessed 7 September 2004).

Vanhoutte, Edward. "A Linkemic Approach to Textual Variation: Theory and Practice of the Electronic-Critical Editions of Stijn Streuvels' De teleurgang van den Waterhoek." *Human IT* 1 (2000), www.hb.se/bhs/ith/1-00/ev.htm (accessed 3 December 2004).

Victorian Web. www.victorianweb.org (accessed 3 December 2004).

Viscomi, Joseph, et al. Blake Archive. www.blakearchive.org/main.html.

Warren, Michael, and Gary Taylor. *The Divisions of the Kingdom*. London: Oxford University Press, 1983.

Wimsatt, W. K., and Monroe Beardsley. "The Intentional Fallacy." *Sewanee Review* (1946), 468–88. Reprinted in Wimsatt, W. K., *The Verbal Icon*. Lexington: University of Kentucky Press, 1954.

Zeller, Hans. "A New Approach to the Critical Constitution of Literary Texts." *Studies in Bibliography* 28 (1975), 231–64.

"Structure and Genesis in Editing: On German and Anglo-American Textual Criticism," in *Contemporary German Editorial Theory*, ed. Hans Walter Gabler, George Bornstein, and Gillian Borland Pierce. Ann Arbor: University of Michigan Press, 1995, pp. 95–123.

Index